T0289436

THE SOUTHERN PRESS

Medill School of Journalism
VISIONS *of the* AMERICAN PRESS

GENERAL EDITOR
David Abrahamson

Selected titles in this series

MAURINE H. BEASLY
First Ladies and the Press: The Unfinished Partnership of the Media Age

PATRICIA BRADLEY
Women and the Press: The Struggle for Equality

DAVID A. COPELAND
The Idea of a Free Press: The Enlightenment and Its Unruly Legacy

MICHAEL SWEENY
The Military and the Press: An Uneasy Truce

PATRICK S. WASHBURN
The African American Newspaper: Voice of Freedom

DAVID R. SPENCER
The Yellow Journalism: The Press and America's Emergence as World Power

KARLA GOWER
Public Relations and the Press: The Troubled Embrace

TOM GOLDSTEIN
Journalism and Truth: Strange Bedfellows

NORMAN SIMS
True Stories: A Century of Literary Journalism

THE SOUTHERN PRESS

LITERARY LEGACIES
AND THE CHALLENGE
OF MODERNITY

Doug Cumming

Foreword by Hodding Carter III

MEDILL SCHOOL OF JOURNALISM

Northwestern University Press
Evanston, Illinois

Northwestern University Press
www.nupress.northwestern.edu

Printed in the United States of America

10   9   8   7   6   5   4   3   2   1

Library of Congress Cataloging-in-Publication Data

Cumming, Douglas O.

The Southern press : literary legacies and the challenge of modernity / Doug
Cumming ; foreword by Hodding Carter III.

p. cm. — (Medill School of Journalism Visions of the American press)

Includes bibliographical references and index.

ISBN 978-0-8101-2394-6 (pbk. : alk. paper)

1. Journalism—Southern States—History—19th century. 2. Journalism—Southern
States—History—20th century. 3. American newspapers—Southern States—History—
19th century. 4. American newspapers—Southern States—History—20th century.
5. Racism in the press—Southern States. I. Medill School of Journalism. II. Title.
III. Series: Visions of the American Press.

PN4893.C78 2009

071.5—dc22

2009005900

♾ The paper used in this publication meets the minimum requirements of the American National Standard for Information Sciences—Permanence of Paper for Printed
Library Materials, ANSI z39.48–1992.

For my ladies, Libby and Sarah

CONTENTS

FOREWORD

Hodding Carter III

Much of what most Americans know about the history and role of the nation's newspapers, like much of what they know about their nation's history, is badly skewed. Much of what we who were or are print journalists believe about our craft's past is also so infused with myth and golden-age nostalgia as to be almost worthless as an accurate account of the who, what, when, where, why, and how of American newspapering. If that is true of the press writ large, it is even more painfully true of our knowledge and understanding of the southern press specifically. Legend abounds; truth is hard to come by. Compared to the rest of the United States, the South remained a frontier in all but name for most of its history. Underpopulated, undereducated, poverty ridden, and enthralled to unashamed and unchecked racism, it was not an ideal testing ground for the assumptions and implicit demands of the First Amendment.

That said, the South has historically turned out ferociously engaged editors, tenacious reporters, and elegant writers by the wagonload, more than any other region in America. Mississippi, it was often remarked, had far more writers than readers, and there was ample evidence for both propositions (thus speaks an objective southerner). At the same time, however, decent newspapers—that is, organizations reporting the news fully and fairly—were few and far between, fewer than anywhere else. This was true during the long stretch of U.S. history when virtually all American newspapers were hand-me-downs of bought opinion, stale news, and public notices. It was barely less true during the twentieth century, when the nation's news business began to pay more than lip service to accuracy and editorial independence. The regional economy gradually but surely caught up. Southern newspapers were a lagging indicator of change. Even when, at last, they prospered toward the end of the past century, they were combining and cloning themselves out of independent existence. Most offered blandly similar faces to a public increasingly too bored to notice or care.

Now, in the twenty-first century's first decade of existential angst for print journalism, southern newspapers are as one with those of the nation in their corporatized embrace of frontal lobotomy as the solution for their troubles. Without discernible anchor or compass, they debase their most valuable asset—hard-digging, fact-based journalism. They do so in the name of arbitrary profit margins, convergence, and new media, but behind the phrases are remarkably similar results: fewer reporters, smaller news holes, a dramatically circumscribed view of their coverage responsibilities.

This is written by one who was born into a newspaper family in the Mississippi Delta, as Deep South as there is; who spent seventeen years on the family newspaper; and who continues to love journalism with near-irrational enthusiasm. I was the son of a man who did not make small enemies, whether their names were Huey Long, Theodore Bilbo, Jim Eastland, or a host of lesser lights. During his thirty-nine years as the founder-owner of dailies in Louisiana and Mississippi, my father practiced the old-time southern religion of personal journalism with scathing enthusiasm. But he also committed his papers to professional standards that routinely won prizes for news and editorial excellence. He won a Pulitzer Prize for editorials on racial tolerance in 1946, wrote twenty-two books (including one on the southern press), and loved the South as much as he despaired of its intransigence.

Most important, in the time and places in which he owned his papers, he regularly broke from the orthodoxies, racial and political, of most of his white readers. And it was in this, rather than in the thunder of his editorial rhetoric or the quality of his paper's reporting, that he most distinguished himself from all but a handful of his regional contemporaries and from the shameful failures of southern journalism.

When it came to the unavoidable issue that had always bedeviled the region, most of the southern press in his time was spineless at best and malevolently ardent in its strident defense of the status quo at worst. There were the cynical opportunists such as J. J. Kilpatrick, the fake southerner who led one last charge against the Constitution while safely stashed away behind the editorial redoubts of his racist owner in Richmond. And there were the nasty, true-believing haters in their editorial legions from Charleston, South Carolina, to Shreveport, Louisiana; from Memphis, Tennessee, to Jackson, Mississippi, to New Orleans to Birmingham, Alabama, and the lands between. Such it had always been, a press no less in cultural captivity than the southern church, whose immoral acquiescence to the fact of slavery and then Jim Crow was an affront to Christ's teachings.

The exceptions, such as Dad, proved the rule. No more than a handful in any southern state, they were vilified with the special vituperation historically reserved for nest foulers and scallawags. If virtually none was a liberal by East Coast standards, or claimed to be, all were too far outside the pale for the white majority. The national acclaim that some of them won was proof positive to their enemies that they were traitors to the South. And yet they persevered, some carrying guns, and others ever mindful of the threats of murder and mayhem that marked their days. They stood out against the bleak background of their contemporaries' lockstep devotion to "our way of life." Halting gradualists sometimes, lurching embracers of change sometimes, and often uncertain about how far they could go and stay in business, their all-important distinction was that they repeatedly brought the message of change to their readers.

Of course, guts were never in short supply in the southern press. It was not for want of physical courage that southern editors were so overwhelmingly inclined to salute each time the doctrine of white supremacy marched by. Throughout the nineteenth century their ranks abounded with brawlers and duelists begging for a fight—some nothing more than hot-tempered frontiersmen, and others masquerading behind the mask of a gentleman's honor. They knew their prejudices and convictions, which they regularly shared with their readers (so long as they stayed within the white creed's magic circle). But although they often knew more than their readers about the realities of the wider world, they rarely thought it useful or wise to circulate uncomfortable facts or dissenting opinions. They knew what their culture embraced, and that was good enough.

The Lord knows that many of them loved to luxuriate in the English language, to massage each sentence and paragraph, to offer up the rolling cadences of their convictions like so many artillery barrages. Some are remembered even now for their satiric wit and poetic fancy. Others are remembered, if at all, as pale copies of Shakespeare's Polonius, emoting fustian platitudes and discount philosophy. But when the moment came to decide whether to help move the South beyond white supremacy, they usually flinched.

That is part of the reason, low pay being the other, that so many of the South's finest journalists had to flee "north toward home" to find newspapers and magazines willing to publish their voices. The list is long. Suffice it to say that at one time or another over the past one hundred years they ran virtually every great paper, magazine, and news organization; covered with rare distinction all the major stories of their time; and offered new narrative techniques to package their reportage and opinions. But not all left. Amazingly good, as well as courageous, newspapers emerged to hold the imagination and idealism of young southerners, most notably in North Carolina. There were always at least two southern papers on the top-ten lists so beloved of journalism. There is hardly a newsroom in the South without its ardent disciples of professional standards. Sadly enough, the ranks are shrinking.

All these are clearly the reflections of my father's son. Temperate, balanced, or forgiving I am not and cannot pretend to be. The costs inflicted on the South, black and white, by foaming racist editors, however artful their language, and by newspapers that provided everything but fair coverage of the social revolution in their midst, are still too fresh in mind. Aging bitter-enders are today given license to rewrite their pasts in late-life bids, à la George Wallace, for a dispensation from the god of history. Too many of the formerly silent now preen before the credulous as heralds of the winds of change.

Read on for a thoughtful, thoroughly researched account of the southern press over time. Professor Doug Cumming, son of another fine southern journalist, is eminently fair, but underlying his work is a clear understanding of the mixed record of an institution that never quite measured up to its responsibilities. Would that more of those he so ably chronicles had been moved to do better.

PREFACE

April in Atlanta is spellbinding enough in itself with its azaleas and dogwoods in bloom. In 1989, for me, it carried the additional intoxication of welcoming me back home, back to the South after fourteen years in New England. I showed up with suitcase in hand at a satiny-modern office on Peachtree Street, the first hire at a new monthly magazine. The editor was a friend of mine from high school days, John Huey. We had both worked hard in journalism since then. I had struggled, too long perhaps, to learn reporting and writing at newspapers in Raleigh, North Carolina, and Providence, Rhode Island, and I had eventually become editor of the Sunday magazine at the *Providence Journal-Bulletin.* Huey had done much, much better. He had run the Atlanta bureau of the *Wall Street Journal,* had established that newspaper's European operation, and now had the backing of Time Warner and its subsidiary Southern Progress for his dream magazine—"the first magazine of the nineties," he called it. Across his new desk in that quiet office, he told me he wanted to start this magazine because he didn't want to end up in New York, "at least ... not yet." He said that he liked the South, and what the hell, he was a southerner. And so was I, he said. "More than anybody, even though you've been away." Or maybe it was because I'd been away that I felt as "southern" now as anybody, at least in Atlanta in April.

The magazine we started, *Southpoint,* wasn't so lucky. Southern Progress killed it a year later. But I've been lucky enough to stay in the South since then, and to find myself now in the sweetest spot in the South—Washington and Lee University. I also had the great good fortune of having David Abrahamson, the editor of this series, ask me to write this book. Officially, my area of southern scholarship was limited to the southern press and school desegregation in the 1950s, the subject of my 2002 dissertation. Abrahamson, aside from being a most gentle and patient editor, must be gifted with uncanny clairvoyance. For as I worked on this book over the past two and a half years, I found that the existing scholarship was surprisingly familiar to me, and the connections I was able to make between literature, history, and journalism came from a part of me that was just under the surface. It was as if the historical facts as far back as the nineteenth century somehow glimmered with something inside of me I had forgotten.

Those connections, I suppose, were tucked away in my experience growing up in the house of my father, Joe Cumming, who happened to be the southern bureau chief for *Newsweek* during the heady years from 1962 to 1979. He was also, and is today, a devotee of history (his major at Sewanee: The University of the South) and of literature. Journalism in the South, in those years, was history in the flesh and was a kind of literature, in the daily front-page columns of Ralph McGill in the *Atlanta Constitution* and in the mass-meeting dramas of the civil rights movement. My father brought this history and literature home in the form of stories from the front. Often, he also brought home fellow journalists and other writers. They were the most wonderful talkers, laughing and drinking and "confabulating on various screened porches over the Southeast," as Marshall Frady himself said in his letter recommending me for a Nieman Fellowship at Harvard many years later. (I got that fellowship, which just proved to me the dark magic of Frady's words.)

Personal echoes aside, many of the ideas that helped see me through the argument in this book came from the writings of four clear-eyed scholars of southern culture, all connected with the University of North Carolina at Chapel Hill. They are the English professors Fred Hobson and Louis Rubin, the historian Joel Williamson, and the sociologist John Shelton Reed. I am even more indebted to the late Margaret Blanchard of that same university, who was my dissertation adviser and the great teacher of a generation of media historians. Washington and Lee University has been more than generous to me in this project, not only in providing a John M. Glenn grant and the summer assistance of student Elliott Walker on a Robert E. Lee Research Program grant but also in accommodating the difficulties our family faced. In the same two and a half years during which this book was being put together, my daughter Sarah's bone cancer was the unexpected life focus for my wife and me. Thanks to the support and good faith of so many people, neither the book nor our daughter's treatment has felt like an ordeal; rather, they have been blessings that now, I believe, are both coming to happy conclusions.

DOUG CUMMING

THE SOUTHERN PRESS

ONE

INTRODUCTION

The American South has had a talent for long good-byes. The Civil War's appalling funeral train provided a four-year drumroll for farewells. But even before the war, southerners indulged a weakness for backward glances. The antebellum planter and yeoman farmer were far more likely than the industrializing Yankee to romanticize a past in England, Ireland, or Scotland. The broadsword clans of Scotland were a particular favorite, to judge by the complete forty-eight-volume sets of Sir Walter Scott's Waverly novels handed down through southern families' libraries. Robert E. Lee courted his future wife by reading the latest Waverly novel aloud to her.[1]

In the 1880s, high-toned newspaper editors in Atlanta, Charleston, and Louisville proclaimed a New South of industry and national reconciliation, but their columns and orations also bid an elaborate adieu to the old. The Atlanta editor Henry Grady, addressing a New York audience in his famous "New South" speech, invoked an image of the returning footsore, tearstained Confederate soldier. "He finds his house in ruins, his farm devastated, his slaves free, his stock killed, his barns empty, his trade destroyed, his money worthless, his social system, feudal in its magnificence, swept away; his people without law or legal status; his comrades slain, and the burdens of others heavy on his shoulders."[2] The two other leading editor-orators of that era, Francis W. "Captain" Dawson of the *Charleston News and Courier* in South Carolina and "Marse" Henry Watterson of the *Louisville Courier-Journal* in Kentucky, supplied reminiscences of their service in the Confederate army as part of a New South sales pitch for northern capital and sympathy.[3]

This weakness for valediction may have been a symptom of the South's experience of historical time. As many writers have noted, southerners did not enjoy the same forward-moving series of triumphs that provided the rest of the nation with at least the illusion of innocence and manifest destiny.[4] History happened to the South in a hard way, and that made a difference. A consciousness of time and loss, with its echoes of guilt, suffering, and inscrutable Providence, seems to be tied to other southern quirks as well. Politics, for example, was a distinctively oratorical art, with a flair for invoking past resentments and metaphors of redemption.[5] Storytelling, another folkway that has been imputed to the South, thrives on a sense of time and place.[6]

Harry Ashmore was executive editor of the *Arkansas Gazette* in Little Rock in 1957 when history, once again, was about to happen to the South. An independent, voluble journalist steeped in southern manners and southern history, Ashmore was the right person at the right time to cover the school desegregation crisis in Little Rock. It was a tense moment, when a self-made country politician, Governor Orval Faubus, called out the Arkansas National Guard to block nine black students from entering the whites-only Central High. The showdown had been building since May 17, 1954, when the U.S. Supreme Court unanimously ruled in *Brown v. Board of Education* that whites-only public schools as they existed by law in seventeen southern states were unconstitutional.

The question of compliance had trembled across the land as if a second Civil War might break out. White resistance was organized and spreading. Violent skirmishes erupted in Clinton, Tennessee; Mansfield, Texas; and Tuscaloosa, Alabama. Deep South states such as Georgia, South Carolina, and Mississippi spoke defiance, and their school boards kept ranks.[7] Arkansas, as a border state, was less committed, but the previously indifferent Faubus saw political advantage in suddenly sabotaging the token desegregation plan of the city's school board. It looked as if the epic American themes of race, states' rights, and civil rights were about to play out around the September opening of a high school year in bland Little Rock. The issue was no longer merely segregation versus integration, Ashmore wrote in a front-page editorial the day after the National Guard surrounded the school. "The question has now become the supremacy of the government of the United States in all matters of law. And clearly the federal government cannot let this issue remain unresolved no matter what the cost to this community."[8]

For the next few weeks, Little Rock tested the character of the American press as it is rarely tested. The *New York Times* had dispatched a number of reporters, including John Popham, whose Virginia-gentleman's style of covering the South by car and conversation since 1947 was legendary.[9] After the National Guard pulled out, and before President Dwight Eisenhower sent in the 101st Airborne Infantry, all hell broke loose. The shouting rabble savagely attacked three black reporters and a black photojournalist.[10]

The *Arkansas Gazette,* the oldest newspaper west of the Mississippi, took flak from the mob, the white Citizens' Council, and the governor. These attacks were aimed randomly at the newspaper's overworked reporters but mostly at Ashmore. A combined writer–editor role like Ashmore's was still widespread in the South. He guided news coverage, controlled the editorial page, and wrote editorials. This made him the primary target of death threats by mail and telephone. A call by the white Citizens' Council for a boycott of the *Gazette* cut circulation by about 10 percent while its lesser rival, the *Arkansas Democrat,* gained proportionately by maintaining neutrality. The segregationists tried to pressure advertisers as well but failed. Still, the drop in circulation and the struggle with its competitor almost put the *Gazette* out of business.[11] In 1958, it won two Pulitzer Prizes, one in public service for calming a community in uproar and the other for Ashmore's "forcefulness, dispassionate analysis."[12]

In the 1950s, the issue of race was beginning to trouble the nation as the press began to pay attention to events stirring up the South. Defiance of the *Brown* decision, the Emmett Till murder trial in Mississippi, the Montgomery bus boycott, violent resistance at the University of Alabama, the crisis in Little Rock—these national headlines drew an increasing number of reporters and camera crews to the South. Southern newspapers were confronted with hard facts and breaking news behind the veil of the long-accepted southern "way of life." *Time* magazine in 1956 called desegregation the South's biggest running story since the end of slavery and said that most southern newspapers were doing a "patchy, pussyfooting job" covering it.[13] This was true. Southern papers typically downplayed the civil rights story when it was close to home, and played up wire copy on racial turmoil outside the South. In opinion columns, segregationist editors in Jackson, Mississippi, and Charleston, South Carolina, blew hot steam over what they called the social engineering of the Supreme Court and the "mongrelization" they foresaw with "race-mixing." Press critics began noticing the demeaning way blacks were covered, or ignored, in most southern newspapers.[14]

Professional journalism standards still meant something in the South. Aside from race, the southern press had caught up to the American pattern. The values of impartiality, independence, civic uplift, and cold war patriotism seemed to be the same in newsrooms everywhere. True, you could count on one hand the number of black reporters working for metropolitan dailies in the South, but the same was true north of the Mason-Dixon Line.

History complicated race relations in every way. "In the South, the past continues; it is now," wrote James McBride Dabbs, a liberal writer-activist whose nonfiction brought into exquisite tension the traditions of remembrance and shame.[15] For the southern press, race could not be faced or understood without first engaging that past and its complicated psychological heritage. Editors like Ashmore became great explainers of these things to a national audience, in magazine articles and books, developing a style of literary journalism that was a specialty of the South. In 1958, Ashmore published a richly mannered book titled *Epitaph for Dixie*— on one level a biting criticism of the South's many failures but underneath this an elegiac farewell. The following year he left the *Gazette* and the South to work under the former University of Chicago president Robert Maynard Hutchins at a think tank in Santa Barbara, California. From there, he wrote five more books, including a biography of Hutchins, and continued writing and giving speeches until his death in 1998.[16]

Epitaph fit a literary genre that had emerged decades earlier and lasted to the end of the twentieth century—the critical but affectionate book on the South by liberal southern journalists.

Jonathan Daniels, who inherited the editorship of the *News and Observer* in Raleigh from his father, wrote *A Southerner Discovers the South* about his motor tour of the region in the slough of the Great Depression.[17] Virginius Dabney, the *Richmond (Virginia) Times-Dispatch* editor whose first book in 1932 argued for a tradition of "liberalism in the South," published the more personal *Below the Potomac* in 1942 and a memoir, *Across the Years,* in 1978. Hodding Carter Jr., the plucky editor of the *Greenville (Mississippi) Delta Democrat-Times* in the heart of the Mississippi Delta, wrote a first-person apologia for his cussed, colorful South in his 1950 *Southern Legacy.* Towering over all of these was W. J. Cash's 1941 masterpiece, *The Mind of the South,* which was not technically autobiographical but in its way contained something of the writer's passion on every page. Cash's rolling sentences had some of the hypnotic, sonorous quality of Thomas Wolfe's novels—Cash was born the same year as Wolfe and only a hundred miles away—with the added quality of mordant wit he learned from his mentor, H. L. Mencken.[18]

In this book, I follow a genealogy of southern journalism that runs in the twentieth century from Mencken to Cash to editors of the civil rights era like Ashmore. As it happened, Ashmore took Cash's editorial-page seat in 1945 at the *Charlotte (North Carolina) News,* left vacant during the war years. Ashmore, in many ways the gregarious and lucky inversion of the solitary and tragic figure of Cash, was as perceptive as anyone about what Cash was up to. In a 1982 memoir, Ashmore wrote:

> Cash's was essentially a literary view, reflecting aesthetic outrage more consistently than social concern. A loner by temperament, rebelling early against his family's solid, middle-class Baptist respectability, he created a bohemian world of his own in the forbid-

ding environs of Charlotte, where he fed his iconoclastic bent with prodigious reading. After graduation from Wake Forest University, he apprenticed on the *News,* returning as book page editor after a starveling period of world travel and free-lance writing. He never found a real home in the bustling, commercial-minded city he once described in the *American Mercury* as a "Calvinist Lhasa," hopelessly isolated from high culture by its impenetrable bigotry and obscurantism, a natural haven for the poisonous Babbittry he saw as the predominant characteristic that set the New South apart from the Old.[19]

Notice the prose style. Ashmore's galloping phrases, his thickets of adjectives and fresh abstractions, sound almost like an echo of Cash forty years earlier. When *Epitaph for Dixie* came out in 1958, the kinship with Cash's *Mind of the South* seemed even more apparent to fellow southern journalists. They said the two editors were spiritual blood brothers. Yet the differences between them were also striking. Cash was a brooding pessimist who felt the weight of the past. Ashmore was more of a laughing pessimist who saw change as inevitable because of modernization and a continuing black exodus, not because of moral effort. If Cash was weak on social concern, Ashmore was not exactly a fighter for desegregation either. In 1956, he worked to keep the white South in the national Democratic camp by advising presidential candidate Adlai Stevenson not to push the North's "abolitionist" agenda.[20] Ashmore's writing, in contrast to Cash's, was brisk and sardonic.[21] Whatever their differences in literary style or temperament, they had similar stories to tell about the South. Their themes were of a land where the fog of romance covered reality and where social order was imposed on chaos at a terrible cost. Modernity would eventually win the day, at least in Ashmore's telling. But in the improvement, something of the human touch and spiritual warmth of the old South would be lost. Books like these by southern journalists became vehicles not only for self-examination but also for long farewells to those tender qualities.

* * *

Three of the best examples of this literature of the southern press since World War II map out themes that recur throughout this book. The works are Ashmore's insightful *Epitaph for Dixie* (1958); Lillian Smith's psychoanalysis of her native region, *Killers of the Dream* (1949); and the memoir of Atlanta's embattled liberal editor Ralph McGill, *The South and the Southerner* (1963). The method, throughout this book, is to approach history through biography and literary text.

This was the method of the critic Edmund Wilson in his distinctive study of Civil War literature, *Patriotic Gore.* Dismissing traditional interpretations of war aims, Wilson focused on the eccentric personalities of a handful of diarists, polemicists, writing generals, and forgotten novelists. This opened up fresh ways to understand the Civil War and American culture. In the introduction, Wilson claims that he tries to avoid generalizations and "to allow the career and the character to suggest its own moral." And yet he is quick to insert broad moral lessons, as when he describes how a strident antislavery (yet antiblack) writer from North Carolina named Hinton Rowan Helper (1829–1909) eventually went insane and killed himself in a cheap rooming house in Washington. "To such mental and moral confusion," Wilson says of Helper, "were the thinkers of the South reduced by their efforts to deal rationally with the presence among them of four million kidnapped and enslaved Africans of a different color of skin and on a different cultural level from their own."[22]

Epitaph for Dixie is a slender book of 189 pages. Ashmore was under contract for it in 1955 with a deadline the following June, but he delayed the project to join the Stevenson campaign.[23] As he was working on the book, the Little Rock crisis blew up, so he had to write it during a time when, as a *New York Times* book reviewer said, "it would have been difficult to find anybody in the United States busier."[24] Ashmore had a gift for fast, polished writing.[25] With neither footnotes nor index, he rendered vast readings of history into sharp little summaries that historians might dispute but not outwrite, such as this picture of the Reconstruction:

> The horrors of Reconstruction, like everything else Southern, have been exaggerated; but they were nevertheless real. The mere sight of black men, drunk with new-found power and carpetbag whisky, careering through the streets and clumsily pawing the machinery of government, fed the white South's ancient fear. The resort, inevitably, was to force; the old Confederates pulled on red shirts and pillow cases and took to horse to put the Negro in his place—not his old place in the slave pen, but a new place beyond the pale of white society. And, typically, they sealed the new order with a political deal; in 1876 the Confederates traded off the votes required to steal the presidency from Mr. Tilden, and in return the Republicans went along with withdrawal of the Federal occupation forces.[26]

Ashmore's verbal nimbleness seems almost a genetic vestige of the tradition of oratory that he mocks. Indeed, his southern style authorizes him to present one of the last great stump speakers, Ellison "Cotton Ed" Smith, as a bombastic fool. Ashmore was a young reporter with the *Greenville (South Carolina) Piedmont* in 1938 when he covered Smith's campaign for a fifth term in the U.S. Senate.

Smith was a stubborn opponent of Franklin Roosevelt's New Deal, so he needed to hoodwink his poor white constituents, who tended to view Roosevelt and the New Deal as friends. Smith entertained them on the hustings with his Philadelphia story, or why he had walked out of the Democratic convention two years earlier. In Ashmore's rendering of this stump yarn, Smith told of finding the South Carolina delegation as a "spot of white" in an integrated checkerboard of race mixing. Smith continued:

> I had no sooner than taken my seat when a newspaperman came down the aisle and squatted down by me and said, "Senator, did you know a nigger is going to come out up yonder in a minute and offer the invocation?" I told him, I said, "Now don't be joking me, I'm upset enough the way it is." But then, bless God, out on that platform walked a slew-footed, blue-gummed, kinky-headed Senegambian! And he started praying and I started walking. And as I pushed through those great doors, and walked across that vast rotunda, it seemed to me that old John Calhoun leaned down from his mansion in the sky and whispered in my ear, "You did right, Ed . . ."[27]

The susceptibility of white rustics to this kind of nonsense was a function of what Ashmore calls "the Southerner's remarkable capacity for unreality." This irrational element is also noted by Cash and the others, but Ashmore comes up with a broader category that he calls the white southern mystique, of which unreality is only one ingredient. In addition, this mystique consisted of racism, pride, a degraded form of the aristocratic tradition, and the "lost cause," a doctrine that retroactively idealized the Confederacy as a last crusade for old-fashioned virtues. The fear of racial amalgamation was the formless heart of the mystique, rooted in the unspoken sexual contradictions of the white southerner's claims of supremacy. "The Southern *mystique* itself—whether one regards it with pride, wonder, or loathing—demonstrates that the barriers of the mind have never needed to be sustained by the barriers of law. Indeed, the final irony is that in the South's own terms there could be no greater insult than the contention that physical separation of the races is necessary to prevent the blue-eyed daughters of Dixie from winding up in the arms of colored lovers."[28]

By the time Ashmore wrote *Epitaph,* the idea of the South had long since proved its value as a salable commodity in the American book market. The old joke about the South having more writers than readers touches on two abiding truths—that illiteracy rates have always been higher in the South than in the North and that readers nationwide have from time to time been eager to consume the romantic, mythic, and sometimes-accurate stories southerners send off to northern publishers. Beginning with the popularity of plantation novels in Victorian America, these southern stories form a kind of kaleidoscope of clashing interpretations and genres. The historian Jack Temple Kirby identifies at least eight major genres in his diligent analysis of popular-culture best sellers about the South, *Media-Made Dixie: The South in the American Imagination.* Historically, the popularity of these genres ebbs and flows. Kirby notes that between 1916 and 1929, no book on a southern subject hit the best-seller list. Then, during the Great Depression, a new genre sympathizing with poor whites and describing their grotesque and gothic lives with social realism captured a share of the popular book market. Among the writers who rode this wave were Caroline Miller, with her Pulitzer Prize–winning novel *Lamb in His Bosom* (1934), and Erskine Caldwell, with *Tobacco Road* (1932) and *God's Little Acre* (1933).[29] In 1935, when the editor in

chief of Macmillan stepped off the train in Atlanta before discovering Margaret Mitchell's manuscript that would revive the
old plantation novel genre in the popular imagination, he had
already been to Richmond, Charlotte, and Charleston searching
for another Caldwell or Miller.[30] The southern journalists who
wrote books about the South starting in the 1930s were writing
not for the same popular market, but for a relatively small, elite
audience. Still, they were explaining the South—explaining, justifying, or celebrating it—largely for outsiders, through publishers in New York and Boston if not through regional university
presses. Alfred Knopf himself had coddled Cash through the long
writing of his book.[31] New York's virtual monopoly on publishing had long been an inescapable fact for southern writers. New
York was where Ashmore found his publisher, W. W. Norton,
and where he went for the liveliest journalism conferences and
cocktail parties.[32]

New York City was also a symbol of what the agrarian and
sentimental South never was. And so, near the end of *Epitaph,*
Ashmore says his good-bye to Dixie by telling a New York lady
friend that he had made his peace with her city. She was surprised
that a regional writer had to make peace with New York, as if the
provinces were still hostile territory for the arts. No, Ashmore explained, he was not talking about the old Sinclair Lewis problem of
artists being cast out by a narrow-minded Main Street. Rather, it
was that New York, as a symbol of power, had expanded to everywhere. It was no longer contained within borders. New York was
anywhere that telephones, television, radio, and airplanes could
reach. "So, I told her, I was at peace with New York not because I
had conquered it, or tried to, but because I had surrendered; like
my grandfathers I had turned in my sword because the invasion
was complete and I had nothing left to defend."[33]

• • •

Lillian Smith (1897–1966) wrote about the ritual dance of the southern tradition, the precise steps dictated by the signs indicating WHITE and COLORED, the silent taboos of places you go and places you don't go. A few tiny graces glimmer across the South she conjures up in *Killers of the Dream*. A certain kind of friendship across the color line, lasting from childhood to death, enriched the individuals involved and sometimes restrained mob violence. She recalls the "flashes of sanity" taught in southern homes like hers, instructions from a father to honor the humanity in every individual, to shun hatred, and to pay back the earth in labor with pleasure. But the pathology she finds in the South's religion, sexual repression, and racial anxiety overwhelm such small virtues. Even the best friendships between white and black were "lopsided" and "belittled." Against this, three powerful black "ghosts" haunt the white imagination with guilt and loathing: the possessed slave, the secret mulatto offspring, and the black mammy. The problem, to Smith, runs deeper than "that old treadmill route that the tortured Southern liberal knows so well." She probes inward and downward, into the physical body and the childhood of white southerners. Using a poetic, literary version of Freudian analysis, she diagnoses segregation as a symptom of a fatal fracture in the psyche, working its way "from the conscious mind down deep into muscles and glands and on into that region where mature ideals rarely find entrance." This sickness was taught by "the unfinished sentence method" of mothers, enforced by an occasional lynching, and preserved by the carefully developed silence of newspapers on such matters.[34]

"Miss Lillian" emerged in the 1940s at the forefront of the southern debate on segregation, where she was at least a decade ahead of other white liberals and stood virtually alone in calling for an immediate end to segregation's laws and practices. She had come to this debate through a lesser-known journalism of the South, so-called little magazines. In 1935, she and her companion Paula Snelling had started a literary magazine called *Pseudopodia* in the small town of Clayton, Georgia. With little money, an obscure title that meant "fake feet" in Greek, and no experience, the two women seemed to be courting failure. But it was an exciting time for a couple of aspiring writers in the rustic mountains of North Georgia. The literary movement known as the southern renascence was flowering, inspired by William Faulkner in Mississippi, the conservative poetry-oriented Fugitive-Agrarians around Vanderbilt University, and the liberal sociology-oriented regionalists at the University of North Carolina.[35] Smith and Snelling reviewed and ran works by black writers, which gave them greater access to black intellectuals than almost any other white southern journalist had at the time.[36] Smith moved increasingly toward reporting and editorial comment, interviewing labor organizers and other reformers.[37] Meanwhile, she was developing her fiction writing. She made a splash nationally in 1944 with her first published novel, *Strange Fruit,* about a secret interracial affair and offspring in a small town in Georgia. The book sold well but was controversial and banned in Boston for its implicit sex.[38]

Smith was sensitive, to a painful degree, to the inner life of others and her own. She refined this sensitivity as a teacher of young girls at two mountain schools, as director of music at a Methodist missionary school in China, and from 1925 until 1948 as director of Laurel Falls Camp outside Clayton. The camp, started by her father near the family's second home in the mountains, became her laboratory for teaching the daughters of genteel southern families new ideas through creative dramatics, modern psychology, sex education, and other progressive classes. Smith herself was raised to be a genteel southern lady, and she never lost some of the courtesies and outward appearances that she learned. Her father had been a prosperous businessman in Jasper, Florida, until his turpentine mills failed in 1915 and the large family moved to their vacation home in the Georgia mountains. Hers was a sweet, privileged childhood but for her sensitivity to "the old guilt I had felt as a child."[39]

Her intense brief against segregation put her at odds with the gradualists, those southern liberal editors like McGill and Ashmore who at the time sought to improve race relations and extend voting and other rights to blacks without upending segregation. McGill, who was then editor of the *Atlanta Constitution* and writing daily columns, conceded that *Killers of the Dream* was honest and eloquent, but he dismissed the writer as too soaked in emotions and Freudian psychology.[40] The year before, the *New York Times* had run a long letter from Smith blasting southern liberals for not taking a stand against segregation and charging that Georgia's newspapers refused to run her letters or quote her. She suggested that this timidity was a mark of the South's own form of totalitarianism, which she said had a lot in common with that of the Soviet Union.[41] Ten years later, she refused to review another "journalistic piece of writing of ephemeral worth" such as Ashmore's *Epitaph for Dixie,* as she wrote to an editor at the *New Republic* who asked if she would review the book. Editors like Ashmore and McGill "are not writing important books about the white people's attitude toward darkness and Negroes, etc. They are defending their public positions."[42]

Killers of the Dream is arguably a more interesting and original work than her better-known novel *Strange Fruit,* which sold more than three million copies in her lifetime and became a Broadway play.[43] The dream is the idea "flung across the stars" of man's individual sanctity and freedom. The killers are fear, taboo, white supremacy, male domination, lynching, and civilized silence, all doing their most effective work when the dream is most vulnerable—in the mind of a child. "The white man's burden is his own childhood. Every southerner knows this."[44] Smith mixes forms. She uses confession, parable, narrative, and polemic tumbling one after another, in pursuit of a running urgency that no rhetorical choice can quite catch up with. Even the polemic is often worth quoting. "There have been excellent books written on southern waste of soil and manpower and forest and minerals, but the wasting away of the nature of man has been the South's greatest loss."[45] Something about a segregated white college "reminds me too much of a mental hospital, for the people inside are shut away from communication with the rest of America's people— not because they are ill, but because the culture outside has lost its health." And the zest of the new regionalists for measuring social conditions in the South? It was "a poor substitute for fantasy, this new diet of facts, but gradually we accepted it, though for a long time the word 'sociology,' said with a southern accent, made a hissing sound of scorn in our ears."[46]

Smith's emotional antennas hurt her but gave her an extraordinary literary power. They also gave her a special clairvoyance about the youth-led civil rights movement that was coming but seemed to catch the other white liberals by surprise. In a letter of 1957 to the editor of a black scholarly magazine that W. E. B. DuBois had started, Smith expressed her desire for a new kind of movement to shake up the old black guard and old white liberals. "Something younger, more vital, more risky, full of fun and ardor. We need to get the youngsters involved; they haven't got sense enough to know there is danger, so they'll go ahead and do what even you and I would gulp over. But we've got to let them try."[47] When the black student protest started in 1960, Smith was delighted, calling it "the first movement in the South that I have ever had a sense of excitement about."[48]

Ralph Emerson McGill (1898–1969), editor then publisher of the *Atlanta Constitution,* was also stirred by the civil-disobedience movement of the 1960s. "As the Freedom Riders and the sit-ins made sociological and political history," McGill wrote in *The South and the Southerner,* "one fact became clear to all but the most hopelessly obtuse. It was that the South could not win. It was again on the wrong side of another morally discredited 'peculiar institution.'"[49] But he arrived at this conviction late, by way of a different path and through a different South. Although he was Lillian Smith's contemporary, McGill's roots were in the hard-scrabble farmland of East Tennessee, where loyalties were divided between the Union and the Confederacy, between Republican and Democrat. No plantations were there to leave ruined columns or romantic myths, nor was there much of a black population. McGill's encounters with blacks were rare and seem to be innocent of the paternalism encoded in Lillian Smith's childhood. In an article in the *Atlantic* in 1959, he recalled a summer job he had in 1919 working as the only white person on a roofing crew supervised by a humpbacked black man who became like a father that summer. "I was never taught any prejudice . . . since that was not according to Scripture," McGill wrote.[50] But McGill was marked with a sense of guilt somehow more mysterious than the guilt Smith associated with the South's racial legacy. All his life, he wrote in *The South and the Southerner,* he was plagued by moods of sadness growing out of an "inexplicable personal loneliness."[51]

An old-fashioned, Tennessee-style journalism also affected his outlook, giving him a lusty taste for violent politics. When he was ten years old, he drove elderly and lame voters to the polls on election day in a horse-drawn surrey for the GOP ward boss, and he absorbed politics through his pores like the heavy smoke from the cigars passed out by candidates in the firehouse where voting took place.[52] After the polls closed, he loved taking the trolley with his father to the *Chattanooga Times* building to watch the results displayed on a large screen outside.[53]

McGill also acquired a prose style that was both tough and romantic. At Vanderbilt just when the Fugitive-Agrarian literary movement was emerging there—poet Allen Tate was his classmate—McGill was stirred by "the new ideas, the new poets and novelists."[54] But failing at poetry, he turned to the student newspaper and to part-time police reporting for the *Nashville Banner*. When McGill worked for the *Banner* in the 1920s, most of the staffers kept handguns in their desks, and the editor, Major Edward B. Stahlman, stamped his personality and convictions even on the news pages.[55]

At the height of his career in Atlanta, McGill would annoy his allies by flip-flopping on political positions, such as giving support and protection to the rabid segregationist Governor Herman Talmadge after waging years of mortal combat with his father Gene Talmadge's political machine.[56] His inconsistency was not from an upwelling of objectivity but from a "curse" of being able to see things from all sides and to see "all around a person." He attacked big business in the 1930s but pulled back from full support of labor organizing in the South, seeing negatives on both sides. "I cannot be a good crusader," he said.[57]

So McGill's growing reputation as "the Conscience of the South" was complicated. (He uses that phrase as a chapter title in

The South and the Southerner but to refer to a collective moral unease.) The Georgia novelist Carson McCullers spoke of the conscience of the South as early as 1940 when she and McGill were chatting about the region ("Southerners enjoy talking shop," he writes) just after she published *The Heart Is a Lonely Hunter.* The phrase to McCullers meant more than the moral debt over slavery and segregation. McCullers told McGill it was a consciousness of guilt "not fully knowable, or communicable," a sense "of loneliness and solitude."[58] The obscure depths of such guilt allowed some wiggle room on the question of Jim Crow, which McGill took. He also felt a responsibility, unlike McCullers and Lillian Smith, to keep from getting too far ahead of his white readers on the race issue.[59] Moreover, he was under pressure from his bosses at the newspaper not to be the "liberal" that the *Atlantic Monthly* praised him for being, a label he never embraced for himself.[60] Boosterism was the spirit of Atlanta, and McGill found that spirit more congenial. The kingpin of Coca-Cola, Bob Woodruff, paid McGill lavishly for freelance pieces he wrote for the company magazine.[61] Woodruff sent McGill to his ranch in Wyoming to recover from "exhaustion" and promised him a job at Coke as a safety net. McGill fretted more than once about being fired or muzzled, especially after the *Atlanta Journal* owner Governor James M. Cox of Ohio took over the *Constitution* in 1950.[62] Although conscience did not make a coward of McGill, it helped make him an ambivalent moderate.

McGill was a man of compulsions, given to excesses of food, drink, remorse, ambition, and a kind of Scottish-terrier stubbornness.[63] Writing was one of his compulsions, which provided the *Constitution* with more than ten thousand columns between 1938 and his death in 1969.[64] But the compulsive nature of his writing, driven as much by his job duties as by his personality, handicapped

McGill's literary output. He succeeded in getting magazine editors in Boston and New York interested in having him write about the South, but the articles he cranked out, often while traveling and pulling all-nighters at his office, were always sent back for revision. The books he published in the 1950s—*Israel Revisited* (1950), *The Fleas Come with the Dog* (1954), and *A Church, a School* (1959)—were mere collections of his newspaper writing, mostly columns.

The South and the Southerner, his first narrative book, was proposed by the *Atlantic Monthly* editor Edward Weeks in 1959 after McGill won a Pulitzer Prize for his columns. The *Atlantic* had published several articles by McGill and wanted him to expand these for its publishing arm—Little, Brown—into "a sort of reminiscence, experience book," McGill said in a letter seeking Harry Ashmore's advice. McGill worried the project would flop, like some of his other efforts. But *Atlantic* editors felt they were birthing something important, and Weeks was not disappointed, calling it "the most telling and noble book I have read about the South in my time."[65]

The South and the Southerner packs a variety of literary voices into its 297 pages. A sometime orator himself, McGill describes the rhetorical power of legendary demagogues who shaped the deformed tree of southern hatred "as the twig is bent." After Reconstruction, populism was born out of the farmers' anguish from worn-out soil and economic oppression. "Its yeasty ferment caused men long inarticulate to have the gift of tongues," McGill writes.[66] Against the twentieth-century Ku Klux Klan, he uses a comic mockery, depicting its leaders as low-rent shysters and costumed bullies. For their followers, he has only pity. McGill voices a deeper loathing for the small-town rich man, the type Ashmore merely mocks as a Flem Snopes and a striver. McGill questions what it means to love the South—its "rivers and pines, its red rural roads, its hills and fields, its people"—if one must also embrace the types who constituted the industry-seeking committees of the 1920s and 1930s.

The power of McGill's memoir is in its detailed invocation of physical experience—the smells, noises, and textures of a pre-industrial South that connected with a lasting humane tradition. There are the keen sensations of the paddle-wheel steamboat he took from Chattanooga upriver to his grandparents' farm for summer work. And the memory of the gristmill where he would be sent by an aunt or grandmother with a sack of shelled corn flung across a plow horse's withers. "There was mystery in holding one's hand under the meal falling from the grinding stones, feeling it warm to the touch, and smelling the released nutty smell one somehow never imagines was locked in the grains."[67] When McGill recalls the sensations of election day—the cigar smoke in the firehouse where ballots were cast—one senses an almost religious dedication to grassroots democracy. But he is just as tender about what he remembers seeing beyond the ballot box in that firehouse. "The huge, wonderful horses would be there in their stall, their heavy harness suspended above them ready to drop at the clang of a bell. . . . Even a small boy could pat the horses on the neck and twine himself about the pole, imagining the swift descent amid the clamor of bells."[68]

What is the purpose of these rich invocations except to point to a wholeness that was lost when segregation cleaved it to the core? "Segregation is estrangement," McGill writes. "It is a withdrawal from humanity that is close at hand, that passes in the streets, that lives just over the way."[69] *The South and the Southerner* was one of the two books Martin Luther King Jr. read while he sat in the Birmingham jail in April 1963 (the other being W. E. B. DuBois's *The Souls of Black Folk*).[70] Claude Sitton of the *New York Times*'s southern bureau called McGill's book the most significant contribution yet made to an understanding of the region.[71]

. . .

The witness of social change, as written by southern journalists such as Ashmore, Smith, and McGill, is constructed out of personal stories that connect with the past—with childhood or with history. Such storytelling continued to be a natural form for southern journalists long after the great social revolution ended. Around the time McGill's book was published in 1963, Rick Bragg was just a boy of three taking in his first memory, which seems in its later telling more literary than probable: he is riding the sack his mama dragged along rows of cotton in a life of draining poverty in northern Alabama.[72] Bragg has a southerner's flair for resonating turns of phrase and a hypersensitivity to class and regional injustices, all of which distinguished him quickly as a young reporter at the *Anniston (Alabama) Star,* the *St. Petersburg (Florida) Times,* and then the *New York Times.* He covered the South for the *Times* with a word magic that won a Pulitzer Prize for feature writing in 1996. The next year, at age thirty-seven, he published a best-selling memoir, *All Over but the Shoutin'.* For all the changes that had transformed the region in his lifetime—the gargantuan downtowns and exurban office parks, the in-migration of wealthy sophisticates, the entirely new codes of ethnic and gender disposition—Bragg sets his memoir "in a time when blacks and whites found reason to hate each other and a whole lot of people could not stand themselves."[73] The setting is a craftsman's choice. Bragg's South is like the South of McGill's book in other ways as well. He is a storyteller, and he maintains that this is a legacy of listening to front-porch talkers, "aunts and cousins and grandmas and a girlfriend or two." Bragg attributes the power of his news writing to this southern inheritance:

> I owe those storytellers, all of them, because without them I would have no skills, no foundation, no accent, no voice. Their blood had trickled down to Alabama from a lot of places, from Ireland and Germany and France, mixing along the way with that of the Cherokee and Creek, finally pooling here. A drop from that pool is in every story I have ever written for wages, and I believe that if there is anything good in the stories I have done for newspapers, even those for the *New York Times,* it can be traced back to Sunday afternoons under willow trees, to the words and sweat that mixed over hard, pick-and-shovel work, to the music of the mountains.[74]

The storytelling tradition, for journalists of the South, was not just an oral tradition but also a literary one. It required publication and a paying readership, which put the southern journalist in a complicated relationship with the publishing centers of New York and Boston and with markets that were national more than regional. The roots of this tradition go back not only to Scots-Irish porch-sitters but also to antebellum men of letters who identified more with European publishing than with the new forms of journalism emerging in northern cities in the nineteenth century. There is one southerner who towers over all others in this literary journalism but who is generally not considered a southerner or a journalist—Edgar Allan Poe. This history begins with him.

TWO

POE AND THE EUROPEAN POSE

The finest minds of Europe are beginning to lend their spirits to magazines.
　　—Edgar Allan Poe, letter to Fitz-Greene Halleck, June 24,
　　1841, *The Letters of Edgar Allan Poe*

Edgar Allan Poe always wanted his own magazine. This might seem a modest goal for a writer and poet who would eventually be immortalized as the first great modernist: the mad-genius inventor of the detective story, modern science fiction, the gothic tale of horror, and such familiar poems as "The Raven" and "Annabel Lee." But what he angled for his whole career was to be proprietor and editor of a successful magazine. He sketched out his first magazine prospectus in Baltimore while doing little more than hackwork for newspapers.[1] Later, he designed a Philadelphia magazine called *Penn* that never came into being, briefly owned and ran the *Broadway Journal* in New York City until it failed, and was seeking one thousand subscribers around the South for an expensive magazine called *Stylus* when he died in the streets of Baltimore in 1849. Eking out a living in New York in 1844, and still dreaming of his own periodical, he told an acquaintance on the faculty at Columbia that this had always been his "ultimate purpose" in everything he wrote and read. "Thus I have written no books and have been so far essentially a Magazinist."[2]

The problem was that Poe was a southerner, regardless of where his poverty or ambition led him. In those days, as they would be later, the publishing and magazine industries were largely huddled in the cities of the North. In relation to these literary enclaves, Poe was not only a solitary outsider but also a caustic and unpredictable one. The proprietor of a Philadelphia magazine where Poe once worked scolded him for the severity of his criticism of such idolized literati as James Fenimore Cooper, in whose works Poe said even the public suspects "a radical taint in the intellect, an absolute and irreparable mental leprosy."[3]

Moreover, his home ground, the antebellum South, was an uncongenial setting for quality magazines. The first magazine in the South for women, for example, was called *Toilet*. That is *Toilet* with a French accent, as in, "My bright and joyous room-mate, bustling about o'mornings, making his *toilet* after his exhilarating bath, often sang snatches of Parisian operas, or repeated long passages from Shakespeare, Byron, and Walter Scott, for he was full of romance."[4] This, from a southern aristocrat's memoir, is a fair reflection of the class of southerner whom Poe thought of as the niche readers of his hoped-for magazine. Southerners who occupied plantations or professions of the upper rank were generally "full of romance" and fancied European magazines along the line of *Edinburgh Review* and *Blackwood's Edinburgh Magazine*. These titles represented a new breed of variety periodicals, laced with moral lessons, politics, personal essays, and verse. Such magazines

were starting to come out of the South's most cultivated antebellum city, Charleston. But they did not last, earning the city the
title "Graveyard of Magazines." *Toilet: A Weekly Collection of Literary
Pieces Principally Designed for the Amusement of the Ladies,* edited by
an anonymous Charlestonian, closed after two months in 1801.[5]
Southern Review, edited by and filled with the erudite reviews of
politician-scholar Hugh Swinton Legaré, survived four years, from
1828 to 1832.[6] William Gilmore Simms, an influential antebellum
novelist with a town house in Charleston, edited five newspapers
and seven magazines, including such short-lived titles as *Album,
Southern Literary Gazette, Cosmopolitan, Magnolia, Orion, Southern
and Western Monthly,* and *Southern Quarterly Review.* Poe, however,
burned with ideas that set him apart from aristocratic men of letters like Legaré and Simms.[7]

Poe's idea of himself as a professional magazinist was a concept
he borrowed from the flourishing British periodicals of the 1820s
and 1830s. The identifying characteristics of magazines in general—their convenience, currency, variety, and readability—suggested to Poe that they would replace books as the next new form
of serious literature in the industrial age. "The whole tendency of
the age is magazineward," Poe wrote in a review of *Graham's.* Such
magazines, as opposed to the older literary quarterly, met the rush
of modern life by favoring "the condensed, the pointed, the readily
diffused" without falling into the ephemeral "pop-gunnery" that
Poe saw in the newspapers of the penny press.[8] The English periodical writer Thomas De Quincey (1785–1859), whose magazine
debut was the anonymous "Confessions of an English Opium-
Eater," and the poet Samuel Coleridge (1772–1834), whom the
public assumed had written the sensational "Confessions," both
saw the same potential in the contemporary British magazines.
But no one saw that promise in the states as keenly as Poe. A

literary artist to the core, Poe believed magazines would become "the *most* influential of all the departments of Letters."[9] His viewpoint was aristocratic. He had the typical southern writer's scorn for the popular mass-circulation magazines that were emerging in Victorian America, such as *Godey's Lady's Book* and *Graham's Magazine.* But Poe's relationship to the masses was ambiguous. He was popular, and he used this for what little power it gave him in the literary marketplace. Poe wrote for most of the early mass-market publications in northern cities, and he even edited *Graham's.* But he always dreamed of a more refined reader.

Optimistic editors and publishers believed the South harbored such readers on its farms and plantations. This hope of intellectually engaged planters on their galleries reading vellum-bound volumes of Cicero and Voltaire in the original, and sending their sons to Princeton and on grand tours of Europe, is not so far-fetched. The historian Michael O'Brien, in his two-volume *Conjectures of Order,* traces the contours of an extraordinarily rich intellectual life in the antebellum South. One scion of this lifestyle, a Virginian and South Carolinian named William Campbell Preston, traveled from 1817 to 1819, with letters of introduction from men such as Thomas Jefferson and James Monroe, to Dublin, Liverpool, Edinburgh, Naples, Rome, Paris, and back to Edinburgh. He visited, met, or traveled with the likes of the novelist Washington Irving, the Charleston essayist Legaré, the Boston publisher George Ticknor, *Blackwood's* celebrated critic John Wilson, and the Scotsman novelist and poet Sir Walter Scott.[10] Such literary enthusiasts as William Preston were viewed not only as ideal readers for a high-quality southern magazine but also as potential writers. "The South is full of talent," the New York novelist James Fenimore Cooper wrote in the first issue of the *Southern Literary Messenger* of 1834. "If sons, whom I could name, were to arouse from their lethargy, you would not be driven to apply to any one on this side the Potomac for assistance."[11]

Standing against this aristocratic view of belles lettres was what might be called the Jeffersonian tradition in the South. This is not to be confused with Thomas Jefferson himself, a prolific and graceful writer who was as fond of European literary fashions as any Virginia nouveau aristocrat. But in the history of the southern press, Jeffersonian ideals animated liberal and populist editors well into the twentieth century. In the 1830s in Virginia, democratic Jeffersonian principles stood in opposition to literary journalism as Poe envisioned it.[12]

There are several reasons for this. First, the Jeffersonian ideal was agrarian while magazines are essentially a metropolitan life-form. Jefferson maintained that the yeoman farmer, the small-scale freeholder who cultivated fifty acres of diverse food crops, was the true inheritor of ancient Anglo-Saxon independence and the best hope of American republicanism. He was for thrift and self-sufficiency, not the system that produced a wealthy aristocracy—cash crops like tobacco and cotton worked by slaves with no skills on vast plantations inherited through the law of primogenitor.[13] Second, Jefferson embodied the hopeful rationalism of the Enlightenment, not the deadweight of a gothic or romantic past that Poe so masterfully exploited for its dark effects.[14] Third, the Jeffersonian notion of a free press was almost entirely political. It was a check on those in power, which for Jefferson and James Madison meant installing poet Philip Freneau as editor of the anti-Federalist *National Gazette* in Philadelphia. Jefferson appreciated good newspapers—Thomas Ritchie's *Richmond Enquirer* in Virginia was his favorite—and helped journalists in distress, such as the renegade *Richmond Examiner* writer and pamphleteer James

Callender. But he also developed an intense loathing for the lies and attacks of the partisan press, which was particularly vicious in the case of Callender turning on Jefferson with a publicity campaign accusing him of having fathered several children with his slave "Black Sally."[15]

However, neither Jefferson's commitment to a free press nor his hatred of a lying press was relevant to anything like Poe's aesthetics of a literary press. For all his writing, Jefferson refused to contribute his own work to the press. "My greatest wish is to go on in a strict but silent performance of my duty," he wrote in 1789, "to avoid attracting notice and to keep my name out of the newspaper, because I find that the pain of a little censure, even when it is unfounded, is more acute than the pleasure of much praise."[16] The sons of wealth who flocked to the university he created in Charlottesville frustrated Jefferson's trust in human nature. He designed the neoclassical buildings and grounds, hired the faculty, and served as its first rector. With few rules, rather than learn self-control, the students drank to excess, gambled wildly, and raised a ruckus, hurling bottles at professors and getting arrested for disturbing the local peace. Poe happened to be one of those students and was at the university when Jefferson died a few miles away in Monticello on July 4, 1826.[17]

The difference between Poe and most of his fellow belletrists in the South was that he considered magazine work a full-time occupation. The proper attitude of the southern gentry was that writing was a dalliance, which required a measure of modesty and anonymity, if not embarrassment. It was not a trade or a career. *Russell's Magazine,* a southern literary monthly based in Charleston, complained as late as 1858 that "professional writers in our regions are indeed *rarae aves,* and in the infancy of our literary achievements, or rather efforts, we have to depend on amateur authors."[18] To Poe, magazine writing was a wage-earning endeavor, and he wagered his all in the field.

If the South could distill its spirit of romance and resentment into a human legend, it would look something like the childhood of Edgar Allan Poe. His parents were itinerant actors in the cities of America's early republic. His father, David, reputedly a third-rate actor and first-class drunk, was the son of a somewhat-celebrated Revolutionary War general from Baltimore. His mother, Eliza, an English-born child actress and singer, was also born to actors and was orphaned in childhood. She and David Poe Jr., who met in Richmond, were performing on Boston stages over a three-year period when her second child, Edgar, was born on January 19, 1809. Less than three years later, she was back in Richmond, abandoned by her husband, performing Shakespeare, and singing ballads for wages that barely sustained her and her three children. Although she was popular in cities around the South, she was growing pale with grief and perhaps some fatal fever. On November 29, 1811, a notice appeared in the *Richmond Enquirer* "To the Humane Heart." It read: "On this night, Mrs. Poe, lingering on the bed of disease and surrounded by her children, asks your assistance, and asks it for perhaps the last time." She died December 8, at age twenty-four. Among the socially prominent theatergoers willing to help were John and Frances Allan. Childless, they agreed to raise young Edgar and provide him with a gentleman's education.[19]

John Allan was a handsome, demanding Scottish émigré, also orphaned in childhood. With his business partner Charles Ellis, he had expanded a general store in Richmond into an international trading concern that moved shiploads of tobacco and flour to such distant ports as Liverpool, Rotterdam, and the Azores. He aspired to the refinement and liberal education he had been denied. But being from the rising business class, he was given only conditional entry into Virginia's planter society. His wife, Frances Valentine Allan, was a delicate, cultivated woman who pampered young Edgar when she was not indisposed by health problems. Allan's business had its ups and downs, but he enjoyed financial support from a Scottish-born uncle reported to be the richest man in Virginia, William Galt. When Galt died a childless bachelor in 1825, he owned a business, plantations, sawmills, gristmills, several hundred slaves, and urban real estate all over the commonwealth. Allan, who had been a ward and business apprentice to Galt from the age of sixteen, came into an inheritance worth hundreds of thousands of dollars.[20]

Edgar Allan Poe, as he was renamed upon entering the lavish new world of the Allan household, did indeed receive an outstanding education, at first. Beginning at age five, he was sent to a teacher at the Allans' church, then to a Richmond schoolmaster. He memorized and recited classical lines of English poetry. He was clothed in tailored suits, declared charming and intelligent, and exhibited among dinner guests like a miniature toastmaster. He also received his grand tour of Europe at a precocious age. In 1815, to establish a branch of Allan and Ellis in London after the War of 1812, the Allans sailed with six-year-old Edgar to England. That would be his home for the next five years, at the height of the romantic era and corresponding to Charles Dickens's childhood. The family stayed a few weeks in Scotland, then rented a fine house in Russell Square, near the British Museum. Poe attended a boarding school in Chelsea for two years, then another boarding school about four miles north of London in Stoke Newington. Stoke Newington had long been a community of intellectual dissenters. Its nonconformist academy was the school of Daniel Defoe, who invented modern magazines with his *Review* in 1704 and inspired Poe as much as any other writer did.[21] Poe's school in Stoke Newington was the manor house of the Reverend John Bransby, a Cambridge-educated Anglican priest given to quoting Shakespeare and Latin poets. Poe excelled in history, literature, French, and scansion of Latin poetry. But he felt alone, the beginning of a lifelong alienation that some biographers have attributed to his having a father vanish, a mother die, a substitute father alternately praise and correct him, and a foster mother love him within the limits of her illness.[22]

The poverty of Poe's earliest years, followed by the uncertain luxury of new money, can be viewed as underlying the writer's exaggerated aristocratic pose. He came to expect John Allan's largesse. At times, his guardian spoiled him with money and finery.[23] But later, especially after Poe turned seventeen and enrolled at the relatively expensive University of Virginia in Charlottesville, Allan withheld all but the thinnest support. They quarreled frequently, Allan taking the position that earning one's own way builds character and self-control. This enraged Poe, who by now had great expectations of a gentleman's inheritance. The University of Virginia drew the most indolent offspring of the state's planter class. The students gambled at cards and cockfights, fought violently, dressed well, required servants, and drank heavily. Poe was too poor and too well behaved, at first, to fit in. One classmate described him as "pretty wild" with his displays of athletic agility, while another called him "sober, quiet and orderly." It is possible that his lifelong problems with drinking and gambling began at the university. Eventually the gambling debt he ran up out of desperation for money drove him to leave school after only eight months.[24] Four years later, Poe entered West Point, but conflicts with Allan again kept him from finishing. Frances Allan was dead by then, and Allan had married a much younger woman, expecting heirs. Poe, sensing final disinheritance, wrote a long, bitter letter to Allan threatening to have himself expelled. Receiving no reply, he succeeded in being court-martialed and thrown out of West Point.[25]

His sense of disinheritance ran deep, a template of the southern aristocracy's injured pride. "If I have erred at all," he said in a letter professing sacred love to one of his platonic muses, "it has been on the side of what the world would call a Quixotic sense of the honorable—of the chivalrous. The indulgence of this sense has been the true voluptuousness of my life. It was for this species of luxury that, in early youth, I deliberately threw away a large fortune, rather than endure a trivial wrong."[26] Some critics suggest that Poe's outlook reflected tensions between the southern planter society and the mercantile class.[27] In any case, he often conveyed himself as a southern aristocrat—conservative, confident in his superior intellect, and disdainful of the moral preachments of abolitionists and other reformers.[28] Poe could be fanatically anti-democratic, in just the era when Jacksonian democracy and the penny press were blossoming.[29] One of Poe's most bitter swipes at democratic mobocracy is in the futuristic short story "Mellonta Tauta," written around 1848: "Every man 'voted,' as they called it—that is to say, meddled with public affairs—until, at length, it was discovered that what is everybody's business is nobody's, and that the 'Republic' (so the absurd thing was called) was without a government at all. . . . [D]emocracy is a very admirable form of government—for dogs."[30]

But his class identity was complicated. In several of his satires, Poe burlesques the aristocracy in settings of exaggerated continental decadence.[31] The public of Jacksonian America despised inherited privilege, yet loved to read in magazines about royalty and upper-class society. "For all his fear of 'mob' and for all his Southern-aristocratic pretensions," wrote critics Levine and

Levine, "Poe at times revealed the same healthy democratic bias against the prerogatives of aristocrats."[32]

The prose style in antebellum America at this time, to the modern reader, seems insufferably windy, moralistic, full of classical references, and clotted with modifying phrases. The difference between this antique style of English prose and our own is so vast that it is difficult from this distance to separate southern from nonsouthern literary lineages. Antebellum "southern" writing was certainly romantic and florid, but so was the writing from New York and New England. "Northern" literary output was full of the Calvinistic self-reflection of the sermon and diary forms, but the same preachy style is found in southern writing. Around the time of the Civil War, this languid, wordy pattern began to tighten up into a modern idiom. As Edmund Wilson puts it in *Patriotic Gore,* "The plethora of words is reduced; the pace becomes firmer and quicker; the language becomes more what was later called 'efficient,' more what was still later called 'functional.'"[33] The brutal contingencies of the war had produced what Wilson called a "chastening" of American prose style, dramatically illustrated in the Gettysburg Address and later in the memoirs of General Ulysses S. Grant and General William Tecumseh Sherman, both far more popular in the North, of course.[34] Newspaper writing had developed a leaner style much earlier, with the penny press that began in New York in the 1830s. "The spirit, pith, and philosophy of commercial affairs . . . is what we aim at, combined with accuracy, brevity, and spirit," wrote editor James Gordon Bennett in his *New York Herald* in 1838.[35] But this style, like mass-circulation newspapers in general, came slowly to the South. Mark Twain would later say that the older prose style held sway in the South well after the Civil War because the region remained for decades longer under the romantic spell of Sir Walter Scott's novels.

Southerners were drawn, especially, to Scott's romantic picture of a chivalric past. The late-nineteenth-century Georgia poet Sidney Lanier had four uncles named for characters out of Scott's Waverly novels, and Frederick Douglass replaced his original name, from his slave master, with a name out of a Scott novel. But Scott's influence on the South was a disaster, according to Twain. He blamed Scott for causing the Civil War by "setting the world in love with dreams and phantoms, . . . sham chivalries of a brainless and worthless long-vanquished society." And he asserted that, if not for "the Sir Walter disease," the South would be wholly modern rather than a mix of modern and medieval.[36]

This is an exaggeration, of course. But the prose style of the Waverly novels did infect southern writing for at least a generation after the Civil War. Poe's fiction owes something to Scott: its gothic elements, self-consciously archaic language, and the use of a twilight past. But where they differ is in tempo. Scott, like most novelists who followed in his footsteps, moved through a narrative and its prose at what Wilson calls a "phlegmatic pace," as if writer and reader both had all the time in the world. Poe tightens up the pace considerably, for two reasons. One is that he was a craftsman with perfectionist jitters. Every sentence was constructed to build toward an ultimate effect, and every word had to count. The other reason is that Poe recognized that modern magazine readers were becoming addicted to a faster cascade of sensations. "The brief, the terse, and the easily circulated will take the place of the diffuse, the ponderous, and the inaccessible," Poe wrote in 1841.[37] The magazine form was behind Poe's innovations in prose style. He was not interested in the chastened style that Wilson associates with modern realism, which led to Hemingway. Instead, Poe sought a wild variety of styles to pack magazines with sensation. The short story was the perfect form for a magazine because it delivered its effect in one sitting, giving the writer psychological control. This was the point Poe famously made in his review praising Hawthorne's *Twice-Told Tales:* "During the hour of perusal the soul of the reader is at the writer's control. . . . In the whole composition there should be no word written, of which the tendency, direct or indirect, is not to the one pre-established design."[38]

The gentlemen writers of the nineteenth-century South were romantic, more or less—but Poe was far more so. He took as his models the most extreme figures of English romanticism. Foremost among these was Lord Byron, the aristocratic rebel whose clubfooted romps around the Continent blended the real person with the dark, ironic sensualist of his verse epic, Don Juan. Raised without a father in Aberdeen, Scotland, Byron inherited an English title at age ten. He used the privileges of peerage not to ingratiate himself with British society but to pursue a lonely and emotional path as a classically educated outsider. Legaré complained in the *Southern Review* that Byron's life and work showed signs of a diseased and intemperate imagination. Simms, too, recoiled from Byron's "morbid misanthropy." But to the youthful Poe, who had published three books of poems by 1831, the Byronic life was ideal. Poe's stepfather was not pleased with such aspirations, so the young Poe was forced to renounce the dissolute pose to secure continued funding from his parents.[39] Nevertheless, Poe for the rest of his life costumed himself in black, gave himself over to macabre moods, concocted brainy hoaxes, and tried in countless other ways to play the role of Byronic genius.[40]

Poe also imitated another romantic British figure of some controversy named Sir Edward George Earle Lytton Bulwer, or Bulwer-Lytton, a prodigious novelist and editor, briefly, of the *New Monthly Magazine* in London. Bulwer was given to extreme passions and behaviors considered immoral by early Victorian standards. His literary legacy has since been spotty; indeed, today he is popularly known as the namesake of a wretched-writing contest based on the opening line of his 1830 novel *Paul Clifford:* "It was a dark and stormy night." In his day, Bulwer was highly regarded by his literary contemporaries. But like Byron, he was a bit too much for the moral magistrates of the American South. The *Southern Literary Messenger* in Richmond had been hostile to Bulwer's fiction in its first year, beginning in August 1834, under an editor named James E. Heath. But then the magazine's cautious publisher, Thomas W. White, hired Poe, who admired Bulwer. Poe identified with Bulwer's obsession with the immortal soul as an occult and mystical force, a bulwark against the growing forces of vulgarity and rationality. "There *may* be men now living who possess the power of Bulwer," Poe wrote in a review, "but it is quite evident that very few have made that power so palpably manifest." Poe followed Bulwer's example in devising elaborate theories on the mechanics of literary effect and in using magazine reviews to belittle other writers.[41]

This dagger, or tomahawk, style of reviewing set Poe apart from his peers, southerners and northerners alike. He wrote of one novel under review that it should be read "by all who have nothing better to do." Another "should have been printed among the quack advertisements."[42] It was the style of the most successful new periodicals of Edinburgh and London at the time. During the twelve fruitful months that Poe edited *Southern Literary Messenger,* beginning in December 1835, he produced ninety-four reviews. The heavy labor Poe took upon himself made *Southern Literary Messenger* one of the most interesting monthlies in the country. According to the *Richmond (Virginia) Whig, Southern Literary Messenger* attracted more attention in the press and was "more uniformly admired and praised upon the appearance of its successive numbers, than all the Literary Periodicals in the United States put together."[43] Poe's reading, as editor, filled him with snatches of every type of journalism then in circulation. Stacks of review copies of books piled up on his desk, to be ransacked, and then sold to make ends meet. He devoured books and magazines with a speed-reading technique all his own. Poe sharpened his daggers with a steady intake of the British reviewers, specifically Francis Jeffrey of *Edinburgh Review,* William Gifford of *London Quarterly,* and John Wilson of *Blackwood's,* who used the pseudonym Christopher North and wrote the regular feature "Noctes Ambrosianae." These British journalists—being even more vituperative than Bulwer—were Poe's models for magazine reviewing.[44]

A key point Poe learned from the popular new British magazines was that snobbishness sells. *Blackwood's* set the standard for the snooty put-down of other writers. If the attacked writer counterattacked in a competing periodical, this was even better, for it stirred public interest.[45] These so-called controversies, called "personalities," were a deliberate marketing trick, as Michael Allen argues in *Poe and the British Magazine Tradition.* The high-minded literary judgment appealed to the refinement of the aristocratic few, while the sport of a literary skirmish appealed to the status anxiety of the many. One way Poe made these personalities more interesting to the public was by conflating the writer with the protagonist of that writer's fiction. Thus, the literary gossip could be extended to the characters in the novels under review, or in the serialized chapters and short stories that ran in the magazines. Moreover, Bulwer and Poe projected themselves into their own fiction, harking back to the Byronic mode of identifying with one's fictional creations. Poe also appeared, disguised, in others' fiction. A short story in the *Messenger* called "The Doom" alluded to Poe's legendary six-mile swim in the James River, and Poe responded with a letter to the editor boasting that the comparison with Byron's swim across the Hellespont grossly undervalued Poe's feat.[46] Poe's youthful courtship of Sarah Elmira Royster, thwarted by her father, was mythologized by his writer friend Lambert A. Wilmer into a poetic drama titled *Merlin*.[47] So the literary duels put on various disguises and slipped in and out of the pages of magazines and books, fiction, and criticism.[48] Poe boasted that his controversies increased circulation sevenfold at the *Southern Literary Messenger* and, after he became editor of *Graham's Magazine* in Philadelphia in 1841, increased circulation there sevenfold again.[49]

The rancor of Poe's criticism can be explained as something other than the cynical adoption of the British magazine pattern to boost readership. Edmund Wilson, in a work of literary criticism from 1943, called it simply neurotic, "as all of Poe's work is neurotic."[50] Robert D. Jacobs, whose 1969 biography emphasized Poe's identity as a southerner and a journalist, honors the vehemence of Poe's reviews as a brave fight to raise the standards of American literature. "Poe's distinction lay in the fact that while others were talking of higher standards he was doing his best as critic to enforce them, subject, of course, to the limitations of his temperament and taste," Jacobs writes.[51] Sidney P. Moss, also insisting on Poe's context being the business of journalism, argued in *Poe's Literary Battles* that if his critical project seemed mean-spirited, it was because he was single-handedly trying to create conditions in the American publishing industry favorable to the emergence of genuine talent in America's future.[52] At the same time, he was scornful of the movement, centered in Ralph Waldo Emerson's New England, that sought to celebrate a unique American literature apart from universal, that is, European, literary standards. "In a word," Poe concluded, "so far from being ashamed of the many disgraceful literary failures to which our own inordinate vanities and misapplied patriotism have lately given birth, and so far from deeply lamenting that these daily puerilities are of home manufacture, we adhere pertinaciously to our original blindly conceived idea, and thus often find ourselves involved in the gross paradox of liking a stupid book the better, because, sure enough, its stupidity is American."[53] Whatever the source, the poison in Poe's critical pen gave his publisher, Thomas White, fits.

Thomas Willis White, a stout, entrepreneurial, poorly educated son of a tailor, had been a printer in Richmond but was otherwise ill suited to run a showcase of southern literary journalism. He was forty-six years old when he launched the *Southern Literary Messenger* in 1834, in offices over a shoe shop on a corner in downtown Richmond. By starting the *Southern Literary Messenger,* White hoped to stir the South's pride in its culture and find works of literary genius, preferably as unpaid contributions.[54] He called on acquaintances of more refinement, gentlemen who sought to hold Virginia to a conservative, idealized version of its Jeffersonian past. James Heath, the journal's unpaid editor, was a state auditor, secretary of the Virginia Historical and Philosophical Society, and writer of a novel that romanticized plantation life. Nathaniel Beverley Tucker, a distinguished law professor who would later write fiery novels and essays fueling southern nationalism, advised White and contributed a defense of slavery dryly titled "Note to Blackstone's Commentaries, Vol. I, Page 423." A third adviser and contributor was Lucian Minor, an attorney for the Virginia commonwealth whose "Letters from New England" in the *Messenger* would be reprinted in the *Atlantic Monthly* in 1870.[55]

Heath grew tired of working without pay, and he quit. Minor declined to take the editor's post. Poe was then recommended to White by John Pendleton Kennedy, a southern novelist who had become a patron for Poe in Baltimore. Kennedy was moved by Poe's desperate poverty but also impressed by his scholarly touch and luminous imagination. White published a gothic tale by Poe, "Berenice," in March 1835, and offered him a job that summer reading proofs, writing reviews, and helping with the mechanics of putting out the magazine. But White was troubled by Poe, and so he declined to name him editor. White, a teetotaler of conventional middle-class habits, was particularly bothered by Poe's dark moods and alcoholic episodes. With a physical intolerance for alcohol, Poe would nevertheless drink socially in the manner of the southern gentry and, in bad times, drink alone before breakfast. These vices took over during an emotional crisis when Poe feared he would lose the close relationship he had with his aunt Maria "Muddy" Clemm and her daughter Virginia (Poe's thirteen-year-old cousin and soon afterward his wife). White fired Poe, who then returned penniless and despairing to Baltimore, where the Clemms were living. White sought to bring Poe back, if he would only live with the Whites or some other family that abjured liquor. By December, by strange good fortune, Poe had returned to Richmond, had finally become editor of the *Southern Literary Messenger,* and was taking financial responsibility for the Clemms in Richmond. Poe, finally, had "a fair prospect of future success," as he wrote to Kennedy.[56]

White had an untrained instinct for good writing, but his judgment was fretted by caution. Poe's lifestyle was hard enough for White to abide. But Poe's writing seemed to threaten White on a deeper level. "Berenice," for example, was too full of horror for White.[57] The gothic tale, an early example of Poe's aesthetic obsession with the death of a beautiful woman, features a madman extracting the teeth of his beloved after his grotesque discovery of her premature burial. Poe, in a letter to White, explained that the exaggerated shock value was a deliberate technique found to be wildly successful with magazine readers in Britain. His additional explanation, suggesting that Poe was playing White for a fool, was that this technique was "the ludicrous . . . heightened into the grotesque: the fearful coloured into the horrible: the witty exaggerated into the burlesque: the singular wrought out into the strange and mystical."[58] White was bothered even more by Poe's literary criticism.[59] But his writings were obviously popular with readers of all sorts. When Poe was given more authority upon his return, starting with the December 1835 issue, White boasted to readers, "Every side has rung with praises of his uniquely original vein of imagination, and of humorous, delicate satire."[60]

Poe was a strong partisan for the best southern writers, but he was frank in noting the South's backwardness. The glory that was Virginia, he wrote in the magazine, was dying and becoming "in the North, a bye-word for imbecility."[61] In praising Augustus Baldwin Longstreet's *Georgia Scenes,* Poe wrote, "Thanks to the long indulged literary supineness of the South, her presses are not as apt in putting forth a saleable book as her sons are in concocting a wise one."[62] And he defended the travel journal published in 1835 by British actress Fanny Kemble, who had developed a loathing for the slave South during her unhappy marriage to the plantation heir Pierce Butler. Poe, the likely reviewer, approved of the *Edinburgh Review* for defending Kemble and for "very justly" giving the South "a rap over the knuckles for our overweening vanity, self-sufficiency, and testiness of temper."[63] White may have also worried about possible libel suits. "Poe has evidently shown himself *no lawyer*," he wrote to Minor regarding Poe's withering review of a novel titled *Norman Leslie*.[64]

White gave Poe notice in September 1836, but he was persuaded to take him back again "under certain conditions," which Poe apparently again violated.[65] Sobriety and pleasantness may have been among these conditions, but White's private letters suggest he was also frustrated by Poe's snappy, impish style of reviewing books. Lacking the intellectual weight to oppose Poe, White relied on conservative friends such as Minor and Tucker to hear his private complaints against his willful editor. White dismissed Poe for the last time that December, as gently as he could.[66]

Whatever self-destructive behaviors drove Poe in December 1836 away from the *Southern Literary Messenger* and from the South, his sustained battles as an editor were primarily against the mediocrity of the publishing business at large. Those battles were often a literary version of the sectional conflicts between North and South. As Poe saw it, publishing in America was dominated by self-perpetuating coteries of writers in the North. Publishers and magazine owners, mostly in New York and Boston, formed a kind of interlocking directorate that used puffery and copying to promote mostly those in the favored circle of writers. Instead of advertising, publishers at this time marketed their books by having friends and associates puff them in magazine reviews. Furthermore, a weak international copyright law allowed magazine proprietors to reprint for free the British works already market-tested and publicized among British readers. With these advantages, publishers usually forced American writers to assume all financial risks with books they published. Writers often had to pay to be published, and they received no royalties. New writers and outsiders, particularly southerners, received the worst treatment of all.[67]

Poe's hatred of the clique system that controlled the publishing industry, and his conviction that this system blighted the prospects of America's literary future, were vented in 1841 in a review published in *Graham's Magazine*. The work under review was a trivial verse satire on the very system Poe deplored, by his friend Lambert A. Wilmer, called "Quacks of Helicon." Reviewing the work gave Poe an opportunity to bemoan the state of American letters, crying out, "As a literary people, we are one vast perambulating humbug." Poe continued:

> The intercourse between critic and publisher, as it now almost universally stands, is comprised either in the paying and pocketing of black mail, as the price of a simple forbearance, or in a direct system of petty and contemptible bribery, properly so called. . . . [Cases of independent editors giving unbiased critiques] are insufficient to have much effect on the popular mistrust; a mistrust heightened by late exposure of the machinations of *coteries* in New York—*coteries* which, at the bidding of leading booksellers, manufacture, as required from time to time, a pseudo-public opinion by wholesale, for the benefit of any little hanger on of the party, or pettifogging protector of the firm.[68]

Poe believed this stranglehold on publishing worked against genius and, not incidentally, against himself. Also, to the end of his life, he believed that it worked against writers of the South. As Sidney Moss puts it, Poe's opposition to this sectionalism was so strong that it pushed him into a kind of sectionalist fight against it. In 1849, the year of his death, he was back in Richmond writing for the *Southern Literary Messenger,* seeking patrons for his long-cherished southern magazine, and courting the love of his youth, the widowed Sarah Elmira Royster of Richmond. His resentment against the literary cliques of the North burned as hot as ever. He noted that writers like Simms and Tucker failed to get proper attention because they were born too far south. The "cabal of the *North American Review* [in Boston] first write all our [i.e., America's] books and then review them," he wrote. "It is high time that the literary South took its own interests into its own charge."[69]

THREE

OLD TIMES NOT FORGOTTEN

But dem wuz laughin' times, an' it looks like dey ain't never comin' back.

—*Told by Uncle Remus: New Stories of the Old Plantation,* Joel Chandler Harris

The South languished in developing civic institutions, including a public press. At first, in the early years of the republic, primitive conditions hardly distinguished Savannah from Boston. "The dark ages of partisan journalism," as the press historian Frank Luther Mott called the era from 1801 to 1833, were years when newspapers were small in circulation and content but large in influence and insult.[1] Starting slowly in the 1830s, northern cities began to acquire the ingredients—rotary steam presses, salaried reporters, mass-market advertising, and economies of scale—for what would become the profitable modern news business. The South remained satisfied with the traditional ways of colorful editor-essayists, copied news, and citizen "correspondents." The Civil War suddenly gave the South an appetite for fresh, factual news, and even saw the brief life of the Press Association of the Confederate States.[2] But otherwise, the South clung to a more personal, literary, and sometimes-violent style of journalism.

This fit the region's slower-paced agrarian life, which characterized the South even in the age of the telegraph and railroad after the 1840s.[3] Politics was controlled by the planter class, which in turn supported certain newspaper editors. Backcountry editors were more independent but no more in favor of ending slavery or appealing to the unpredictable interests of a mass audience.[4] The southern "masses" were never large anyway. The waves of new immigrants surging into New York for the rest of the century did not go south, except in isolated cases such as for contract work on canals or rail lines.[5] It is not that the common folk of the South avoided democratic politics. Next to religion, politics was the favorite preoccupation. But most voters experienced it as gossip and oratory around the courthouse square, not as reading material. Illiteracy was widespread among the lower ranks and nearly universal among slaves and free blacks, who were denied education by law and indifference.[6]

Virginia looked back to the past wistfully. The Old Dominion, "the mother of states and statesmen," was at its peak in 1800, when it was the most populous state in the nation for the last time. In contrast, the more humble states to the southwest, such as Georgia, Alabama, and Tennessee, were rough frontier.[7] Swamps and forests cut off commerce but also promoted a raw individuality, because wilderness promised freedom or fortune to those clever enough to master it. Towns and villages were small and the distances between them great, like the distances between farms and plantations. "[I]f all the wealth produced in a certain district is concentrated in the hands of a few men living remote from each other," wrote Frederick Law Olmsted in his report on the plantation system published serially in 1853 and 1854 in the young *New-York Times,* "it will not bring thither local newspapers, telegraphs, and so on."[8] Excluding the vibrant port cities of Baltimore and New Orleans at its edges, the South had no cities to compare with New York or Philadelphia.[9]

A satire of the typical Georgia newspaper in the early republic appeared in the magazine *Magnolia* in June 1843 under the title "The Gnatville Gem."[10] The author was Augustus Baldwin Longstreet (1790–1879), a judge, college president, newspaper editor, Methodist church leader, and literary pioneer of the Deep South. The short story, which was the last of twenty-seven "Georgia scenes" Longstreet published in newspapers and magazines starting in 1833, provides a valuable, if ridiculous, picture of small-town partisan journalism in the South for most of the nineteenth century. Longstreet's popular book, *Georgia Scenes,* reflected the antebellum South more fully than did the later plantation romances of William Gilmore Simms or Thomas Nelson Page.[11] Likewise, Longstreet himself was more representative of the region than were Simms or Page. Indeed, John Donald Wade, a member of the literary circle at Vanderbilt University in the 1920s known as the Fugitive-Agrarians, subtitled his 1924 biography of Longstreet "A Study of the Development of Culture in the South."[12]

Longstreet was born September 22, 1790, in Augusta, Georgia, where he received his childhood schooling. His parents had arrived only a few years earlier from New Jersey, both descendants of a long line of colonials "always ready to change their residence on the chance of bettering their condition," as Wade puts it.[13] Georgia was filling up with such migrants, from North Carolina, Virginia, and the Northeast.[14] His father, William, was an inventor who was prosperous enough but whose inventions all fell just short of making history—a steamboat before Robert Fulton's, a cotton gin before Eli Whitney's, and a precursor to the sewing machine.[15] Young Gus experienced the excitement of the city—Augusta was full of governors, generals, admirals, senators, judges, and poets, and such wealth that a boy perhaps could run a mile down Broad Street entirely on cotton bales.[16] He also experienced the country, learning to love hunting and wild wrestling when his family lived on a farm in South Carolina.[17] His best friend was George McDuffie, later a U.S. congressman, senator, and governor of South Carolina, who was taken into the Longstreet home as a boarder. Longstreet followed in the footsteps of McDuffie's mentor, John C. Calhoun, the influential southern statesman who was vice president and a U.S. senator, by completing his education at the Waddel School in Willington, South Carolina, Yale College in New Haven, and then a law school in Litchfield, Connecticut.[18]

It has been said that Longstreet might have achieved more lasting fame, like his literary heirs Mark Twain and William Faulkner, had he focused on one field instead of what Wade calls "things innumerable."[19] But the variety of his achievement typifies the fluid mix of politics, journalism, law, religion, and education that was southern public life in the nineteenth century. Longstreet was accepted to the Georgia bar in 1815 and soon became a traveling judge. He married a wealthy young woman he met in Greensboro, Georgia, where he settled. He was elected state representative, then became a superior court judge. After suffering a deep emotional blow from the death of a son in 1827, he joined the Methodist Church.[20] Longstreet lost his judgeship when a new political faction gained control of the state assembly, so he bought a plantation near Augusta and "commenced planting and lawing with high hopes."[21] His enthusiasm for grafting apple trees and riding horses did not a planter make, so he sold his wife's fifty or so slaves and focused on a lucrative law practice.[22] In the growing political turmoil in the South pitting Unionism against states' rights, the people of Georgia were tilting toward the Union. Never one to bend to popular opinion, Longstreet started a newspaper in Augusta in 1834 to tout the opposite cause, the *State Rights Sentinel,* even though the influential *Augusta Chronicle* was already pushing that side.[23] Longstreet's twice-weekly paper, costing subscribers three dollars a year paid in advance, became relatively successful, benefiting from the loyalty of fellow Methodists and allies of Longstreet's temperance campaign. The paper was full of announcements, such as for new publications or runaway slaves, and advertisements, mostly for wonder drugs to cure everything from scurvy to "venereal taint." It contained local and weeks-old European news, mostly from "exchanges," a practice of cutting and typesetting articles from other papers encouraged by postage-free sharing among newspapers during these years before the telegraph. Into this miscellany, Longstreet inserted nineteen of his Georgia scenes.[24] His editorials turned gradually from politics to more general topics. In 1836, having failed to sway Georgia to the principle of nullification or to turn a profit, he sold his paper to the *Chronicle* but continued writing political essays for the rest of his life.[25] Longstreet's judging gave way to a year of preaching. Then he was called to the presidency of Emory College, a fledgling Methodist school in Oxford, Georgia, which grew almost to the size of the University of Georgia in its eight years under Longstreet's hand. His success at Emory led to his appointment later as president of the University of Mississippi (1849–56) and of South Carolina College (1857–61).[26]

The major reason Emory began drawing so many students was that Longstreet, in addition to his literary fame, became a hero of southern sectionalism through his role in a crisis within the Methodist Church.[27] Representing Georgia at the General

Conference of the Methodist Episcopal Church in New York in 1844, Longstreet was appalled that abolitionist clergy from the North were suddenly in control, calling for the resignation of Georgia's Bishop J. O. Andrews unless he gave up the few slaves he owned. Longstreet read to the conference a manifesto, signed by the delegates of all but one of the slaveholding states, proclaiming that southern Methodists could no longer stay in the national church under such a misunderstanding about their situation. Over the next two years, with Longstreet tugging hard on the southern hem, one of the largest Protestant denominations in America tore in two, not to reunite until well into the twentieth century.[28]

In the *Southern Christian Advocate,* Longstreet published a series of letters to northern churchmen espousing a biblical justification for slavery. "You of the North believe slavery is sinful; we believe it innocent," he wrote. "The only arbiter, therefore, is the Bible. If you will show us that the Bible condemns slavery, the most violent of us will yield readily."[29] These letters, running seventeen thousand words in all, were also published in a pamphlet titled *Letters on the Epistle of Paul to Philemon.* In the North the pamphlet received no reply from those to whom the letters were addressed and little attention from the public. In the South it was read widely, especially by ministers, and praised in the press.[30] Longstreet next raised his sights, and doubled his ammunition, by publishing a thirty-five-thousand-word essay in a Baltimore magazine, *Western Continent.* Again, the South applauded Longstreet's propaganda—it was reproduced in a book so popular that it ran through eight editions by 1849; the *Southern Review* said every southern man should read it—but the North yawned. The *Southern Review* reported that copies of the book sent to a northern bookseller were returned by the next mail.[31]

Although Longstreet was sadly predictable in his proslavery pamphleteering, his *Georgia Scenes* brought forth a new comic mode of great originality. One element of this literary breakthrough was the semifictional voice Longstreet created. Writing under the pen names of "Hall" or "Baldwin," Longstreet invented a type of narrator that would become the persona of Mark Twain and other slightly detached, yarn-spinning journalist-observers. "Some years ago," begins Baldwin in the first published sketch, "I was called by business to one of the frontier counties, but then recently settled."[32] Literary critics identify Longstreet as the father of the genre called old southwestern humor, a line running from *Georgia Scenes* to Davy Crockett stories and the work of such contemporaries as William Tappan Thompson (*Major Jones's Courtship,* 1840), Johnson Jones Hooper (*Some Adventures of Captain Simon Suggs,* 1845), Joseph Glover Baldwin (*Flush Times of Alabama and Mississippi,* 1853), and George Washington Harris (*Sut Lovingood: Yarns Spun by a Nat'ral Born Durn'd Fool,* 1867), up to the master, Twain (*The Adventures of Tom Sawyer,* 1876, and *The Adventures of Huckleberry Finn,* 1884). The style cuts through the miasma of southern romance and sentimentality. In this sense, it is the beginning of literary realism, as Edwin Mims and Vernon Parrington would recognize a century later, despite the exaggerations and hoaxes that characterize the southwestern humorists.[33] Longstreet wrote about social class, frontier violence, and human vanity with a reporter's eye for what was real, as opposed to the romantic ideal. That was part of the humor. It was also the reason Longstreet believed he was writing social history, primarily as documentation and secondarily as entertainment.[34] Entertaining as the stories are, he apologizes in a preface for "the minuteness of detail" and for including things that would not be used in a mere "creation of fancy."[35]

Georgia Scenes was popular throughout the remainder of the nineteenth century, in the North as well as the South. Literary critics recognized it as something new and wonderful. A writer in the Charleston *Southern Literary Journal* declared the sketches irresistibly funny, with scenes worthy of William Hogarth and more original than Dickens's *Pickwick Papers*.[36] The most lavish praise and longest review, among the southern literary journals, came from Edgar Allan Poe in *Southern Literary Messenger*. Poe found the unknown writer gifted with "an exquisitely discriminative and penetrating understanding of *character* in general, and of Southern character in particular."[37] Humor would not become the strong suit of the southern press as it grew proud, defensive, and resentful about its sectional peculiarities over the next century. "The weak point in the literary armor of the South is the lack of satire—the inability to laugh at itself," Edwin Mims wrote in his 1926 book *The Advancing South* about a late-emerging liberalism. "Romantic, interested in the pretty, the South is 'suspicious of a smile and jealous of criticism.'"[38] Longstreet showed that another way was open—a deep, comic sense that the South could occasionally find in its otherness.

"The Gnatville Gem" is about the role that one-party politics played in the social and economic life of frontier southern communities. A mysterious stranger shows up one day in the "handsome, thrifty little village" that the writer disguises as Gnatville, Georgia, and sets this Eden of harmony on edge. Observing the stranger's unexplained rambles through the village and county, the Gnatvillian males conclude that Mr. Asaph Doolittle had come to cheat them out of their lands, somehow. It turns out Doolittle is from Connecticut, where he had learned printing under the famous Croswell for thirteen years, and wishes to provide this village with its first newspaper. As a practical, unprincipled Yankee, he is willing to do anything for broad support before starting. The locals advise Doolittle against a paper of "Arts, Sciences and Polite Literature," in favor of pure Jeffersonian politics. He is shocked—being a Federalist who had always equated Jefferson with Satan—but turns himself into an instant Jeffersonian Democrat. His paper's prospectus sets out its goals: its columns will be open to all parties; its tone, moderate; its key purpose, to elevate public morals; its second to help the farmer, and to serve commerce and factories. Federalist papers attack without delay, which helps boost Doolittle's subscription list, because locals now consider him "a persecuted man, themselves insulted." A long newspaper war ensues "which grew hotter and hotter with every number."[39]

From the heat thus generated, more personal spats break out in Gnatville through the pages of the *Gem*. Lawyer Jeter publishes a thinly disguised witticism against Magistrate Whatcut, after losing a case in his court, that caricatures Whatcut's potbelly and his drinking habits. Whatcut barges into the *Gem* office and finds Doolittle setting type. The encounter is a good example of how Longstreet used dialogue in a modern style to show character and move the action along:

> "Are you the author of a piece signed Justice in yesterday's paper?" said he to Doolittle.
> "No sir."
> "Well, who is?"
> "It's against the rules of the Office."
> "Don't tell me about your rules, sir. Tell me who wrote the piece, or I'll floor you in an instant with this stick," flourishing an awful hickory stick over his head.
> "Stop sir!" said Doolittle, dodging—"Jeter wrote it."
> Away went the Judge, and soon returned with

A RECEIPT FOR MAKING A JACK LEGGED LAWYER.

CATCH A POLE-CAT, STUFF HIM WITH BRASS, AND CALL HIM CHEATER, and he will make an excellent lawyer.[40]

With the *Gem* now serving as a general engine of enmity, new characters introduce a new set of hostilities. A young suitor, rejected by the lady of his heart, pens a ribald poem belittling her for comments she was heard making. It is eventually published in the *Gem,* and the result is a widespread uproar throughout an array of offended citizens. Poor Doolittle finally rides out of town in the dark. The village stops meeting in the streets in friendship. The revolution is complete. This would have been a fit ending, but Longstreet indulged his tendency to moralize at the end of stories. So, after many long years, he writes, a religious revival brought the village back into a brotherhood of love "that neither politics, nor newspapers, nor time, could sever."[41]

A tall tale and a parable, the story also conveys the actual world of the old-time southern newspaper, as Carl R. Osthaus describes it in his *Partisans of the Southern Press.*[42] Larger towns produced at least one newspaper for every competing political party, but the South was sprinkled with Gnatvilles too small for competitive parties or even for one paper.[43] Editors in the South often had migrated from the North, even at such fire-eating southern periodicals as the *Charleston (South Carolina) Mercury.*[44] Most papers in this era were small, with a circulation of only about one thousand.[45] Such papers could barely scrape by on political patronage. Thus, the *Gnatville Gem* depended on its solidly Jeffersonian subscribers and was willing to run ads for cockfights despite its goal of moral uplift. Doolittle, who made locals suspicious at first by checking courthouse records, was actually looking through a year of newspapers that ran the sheriff's sales and other public notices, for this was also the patronage a newspaper needed to survive. The content in southern papers did not come from professional reporters—only huge New York papers by the 1850s could afford reporters to cover modern city life fresh each day, which became the modern meaning of news.[46] Instead, typical southern papers ran a mix of letters, exchanges, quips, poetry, and editorial comment, with names and facts often disguised into a blur of anonymity and fiction. The violent tone in much of the partisan commentary in the press was a mere shadow of the actual physical violence editors risked, or perpetrated. "Editorial clashes engendered an endless list of brawls, canings, and bloody duels, especially in the South," Osthaus writes.[47] Longstreet was not the only writer to find humor in these bloody affairs.

Samuel Clemens, as Mark Twain, lampooned such violence in his short story "Journalism in Tennessee." Twain knew antebellum journalism well. He had been a printer's devil, then an assistant at his brother Orion's weekly journal in Hannibal, Missouri. His skills as a typesetter supported his rambles in the 1850s from St. Louis to New York to Philadelphia. In 1862, after escaping from his brief enlistment in the Confederate army, Twain got his first job as a newspaper journalist on the staff of the Virginia City, Nevada, *Territorial Enterprise*. He sometimes published outlandish hoaxes or personal insults that seemed a rather bizarre form of journalism in the western territories but had precedent in the fictions and feuds of Poe and other southern editors. Later, Twain claimed that he nearly fought a duel with a rival editor in Nevada over one of his more insulting fabrications but was forced to leave the state because of laws against dueling. Or maybe he fled out of fear of getting shot, as one writer suggested in a 1980 literary analysis in *Mississippi Quarterly*. In any case, Twain's writings are full of the theme of dueling and chivalric courage.[48]

His satirical "Journalism in Tennessee," however, depicts not gentlemen following the strict code duello but the unruly violence of the backwoods editor. Although the editor of the story's *Morning Glory and Johnson County War-Whoop* turns news copy into dripping vituperation, the hapless reporter-narrator recalls, "Somebody shot at him through the open window, and marred the symmetry of my ear." The violence escalates by the minute, with a hand grenade exploding in the stove, an armed colonel appearing at the door spewing insults and bullets, and a disgruntled reader wielding cowhide. The reporter is hit in the cross fire each time. "I came South for my health, I will go back on the same errand, and suddenly," the reporter concludes, taking his leave.[49]

Never mind fictional satire. When it comes to the reckless violence of southern journalism, the historical record is entertaining enough. One of the most notorious duels in American history, aside from the Hamilton-Burr rencontre in 1804, was between editors of the South's leading newspapers: Thomas Ritchie Jr. of the *Richmond Enquirer* and John Hampden Pleasants of the *Richmond Whig*. On February 25, 1846, on the banks of the James River, the two met to settle a dispute that began in the pages of their newspapers over politics and degenerated to name-calling. Southern gentlemen, especially those who bought ink by the barrel, had a rich lexicon for personal invective. All their thundering insults ("poltroon," "scoundrel," "prince of hoaxes," "prevaricator") boiled down to two basic concepts—liar and coward. These two disparagements violated gentlemen's honor, a concept that had particular meaning to a certain highborn southern class at this time. Pleasants, nearly fifty years old and unfamiliar with arms or the code of the duel, was called a coward in the *Enquirer,* so he challenged the much younger and duel-ready Ritchie. Accompanied by seconds and a surgeon, they met bristling with weaponry, as described in a 1968 article in *Virginia Cavalcade* magazine:

> Pleasants carried a revolver in his coat pocket, a bowie knife in his vest, a sword cane under his left arm, and a pistol in each hand. Ritchie had two pistols stuck in his belt, a revolver in his coat pocket, a cutlass on his belt, and a pistol in each hand. The two antagonists stood quietly for a few moments, and then Pleasants began to walk towards Ritchie. Silently and steadily Pleasants moved toward his stationary opponent. When the distance between the two duelists narrowed to thirty yards, Ritchie opened fire. Pleasants kept advancing and fired his only fully-loaded pistol harmlessly into the air. Ritchie, aiming to kill, scored hit after hit.

The combatants finally came close enough to slash feebly at one another with swords, until Pleasants collapsed in a bloody heap.[50] He died two days later. We might imagine, looking back on such an affray, that hotheaded anger simply boiled over in this case and that southern gentility must have been aghast at the results. Not at all. The code of honor, which forbade anger, was strictly observed. The dying Pleasants, having received "satisfaction" that he was no coward, praised his killer's courage and cleared him of blame. Thomas Ritchie Sr., the survivor's father and one of the most respected editors in the nation, deeply regretted the death of his old political rival Pleasants but was proud that his son had not disgraced himself. "He stands acquitted in the eyes of reason and right," the elder Ritchie asserted.[51] Three years earlier, the old man was equally proud of another son, William Ritchie, for coming within an hour of dueling with Pleasants without backing down on any "point of honor." The father had boasted that congratulations were pouring in on William, who had become "the

Lion of the City."[52] The father's main concern after the butchering of Pleasants was to "set public opinion right" in his son's favor. Apparently this was done, for a friend told Ritchie Sr. that people "of all classes & *all parties* . . . *ladies* & all" were eager to grant the younger duelist "his honorable acquittal."[53] And indeed, a jury found him not guilty, as southern juries were prone to do whenever a gentleman was brought to trial under antidueling laws.[54]

The code duello, practiced in its purest form among the gentry of old Virginia and the South Carolina low country, became an occupational hazard for many southern editors. A gentleman's honor, after all, was a public matter, and that usually involved publication—of the offending insult, the challenge, the posting, or the vindicating report of a duel "bravely" conducted. Frequently, newspaper editors themselves wrote the offending statements that prompted a challenge. John Moncure Daniel of the *Richmond Examiner,* who spiced his attacks on political enemies with such terms as *jackass, hyena, sleek fat pony,* and *curly-headed poodle,* is credited with fighting nine duels. He bequeathed his dueling pistols to his successor at the *Examiner,* H. Rives Pollard.[55] A column Daniel wrote in 1847 somehow insulted the then-famous Poe, who happened to be back in Richmond and drinking again. When Poe barged into Daniel's office to challenge him to a duel, the *Examiner* editor managed to silence his friend by pointing to a set of large pistols waiting on a table.[56]

The aristocratic notion of honor was like "reputation" in a libel suit, except that damages to honor could never be compensated with money or settled in court.[57] That is why so many cities and town in the South had a dueling ground as well as a courthouse, from the Oaks at the north end of Esplanade Street in New Orleans to Bloody Island in the former North River beside Lexington, Virginia.[58] Duelists could even buy instruction manuals, such as one published in 1838 by a former governor of South Carolina.[59] Keeping in practice was always a good idea, especially for newspaper editors, "who are most of them very good shots," noted a British traveler in the 1830s.[60] Like libel law, the code of the duel was said to be a force of restraint on a boisterous press. If only the North would adopt dueling, the novelist Simms wrote to an editor in Boston in 1841, "it would soon put a stop to the blackguardism of the press, the insolence of petty knaves, and the slanderous personalities of their writings."[61]

The punctilios of the code were less likely to be followed in the up-country scrublands or in the latter decades of the nineteenth century. Still, gunplay and bludgeoning in many forms remained a sideline danger for editors, predictably so in the South. "It is probable that an editor is flogged, in some part of the United States, almost every day in the year," wrote Poe's friend Lambert A. Wilmer, a Baltimore writer who by 1859 had been unhappily trapped in newspaper work for thirty years.[62] Frederick Hudson, whose 1873 history of American journalism indexed twenty-two references to duels, added that "the details of all the duels, assaults, and assassinations in the journalistic world would fill several volumes like this." This mayhem was far more likely in the South, of course. The historian Clement Eaton in 1940 wrote that southern newspaper editors suffered an astonishing rate of mortality over affairs of honor, and John Hope Franklin in 1956 noted that no class of southerner went to the dueling ground more frequently than newspaper editors.[63] Five editors in a row were killed or wounded at the inflammatory Vicksburg *Sentinel* in Mississippi before the Civil War.[64]

Some southern editors took a serious stand against the violence. William Rule, founding editor of the *Knoxville Chronicle* in Tennessee, told a reader who challenged him to a duel in 1873 that nothing would be gained "by either of us losing his life in the manner proposed."[65] This made a strong impression on a young printer's devil at Rule's paper at the time, a local lad named Adolph Ochs. "It is not necessary that an editor and publisher should be a pugilist or a duelist," Ochs told the National Editorial Association in June 1891, when he was running the *Chattanooga Times.* After Ochs bought the *New York Times* in 1896 and moved north, he totally rejected the old brawling style of southern journalism by formulating a creed that set the stage for modern objectivity—to publish straight news facts and unbought opinion "without fear or favor."[66] The *Charleston News and Courier* editor Francis W. Dawson, a Confederate veteran who became a major spokesman for the New South, opposed dueling on moral grounds as a Roman Catholic but also because he knew the practice was bad for South Carolina's business climate. In 1876, he faced the hot-tempered editor Robert Barnwell Rhett Jr. in the streets of Charleston in a bizarre showdown in which Rhett menaced Dawson with his concealed sidearm but knew Dawson was unarmed. After an especially brutal episode known as the Cash-Shannon duel of 1880 in up-country South Carolina, Dawson successfully campaigned in his paper for stronger antidueling laws. Dawson's brother, a Roman Catholic priest in England, brought this crusade to the attention of the Church, which rewarded the editor with knighthood in the Order of Saint Gregory the Great, founded by Pope Gregory XVI. Dawson's end in 1889 was violent. He confronted a married man whom he suspected of having a dalliance with the Dawsons' Swiss governess, and the man shot the editor dead. A jury acquitted the gunman.[67] As late as 1893, the *Richmond Times* editor Joseph Bryan was challenged to a duel by an offended reader. He told his adversary that the "absurd and barbaric practice" no longer prevailed among gentlemen and pressed charges.[68]

Dueling was disappearing, but not the legacy of violence or the kind of nerve that the brassier southern editors would need in the twentieth century. In 1903, the aristocratic Cuban American editor N. G. Gonzales, who had been Dawson's key political reporter in the *News and Courier*'s crusade against violence, was gunned down unarmed in the streets of Columbia, South Carolina. His assailant, Lieutenant Governor James H. Tillman, had been relentlessly attacked by Gonzales's newspaper, the *State,* as "a man without character." Tillman was acquitted of murder charges on claims of self-defense.[69] When Ralph McGill started working at Tennessee's *Nashville Banner* in 1922 under the fiercely opinionated old editor Major Edward Bushrod Stahlman, he found that most reporters kept loaded pistols in their desks, along with bootleg whiskey. McGill's demanding mentor, a corncob-pipe-smoking political reporter named Marmaduke Morton, kept a pair of .32 Smith and Wesson revolvers carefully hidden in his desk, "apparently not knowing that most of the staff was armed."[70] Beginning in the 1930s, editors like McGill who challenged the orthodoxies of the southern way on racial matters faced threats of bodily harm. Hodding Carter Jr., one such editor, was no crusader for racial equality. But he did show a level of respect for blacks in the pages of his *Delta Democrat-Times* that was rare for Mississippi. He was constantly threatened, and with a bantam courage, he threatened back, preferably face-to-face. He kept his office and home well supplied with loaded guns, according to his son Hodding Carter III, who was also armed with a pistol or two when he edited the paper until 1964. The son defined courage, for the southern white man in the first half of the twentieth century, as the impulse to fight rather than run. "For the most part, it was understood to be physical at its core. Those who demonstrated it were respected, if not necessarily loved."[71]

The fighting southern editors of the nineteenth century were often writers of mere political bombast or florid nostalgia. But the best of them longed for literary distinction as proof of the superior culture they claimed for the South, even if being a professional man of letters was considered undignified.[72] Sometimes, a truly gifted writer would emerge among these newspaper editors and magazinists to fulfill the literary ideal. Poe and Longstreet are the earliest examples. In the next generation, a Virginia doctor named George W. Bagby (1828–82) would come to be recognized by his peers as one of the finest writers in the southern press.

Bagby was born into an old Virginia family and married a woman of even higher estate, Lucy Parke Chamberlayne, descended from one of Virginia's dominant colonial families, the Byrds. His schooling was entirely in the North, which seemed to sharpen his affection for Virginia as well as his powers of observation. His literary reputation was as a humorist and a realist, in the vein of Longstreet but with more polish. Bagby had no career models. Drawn to books, writing, and friendship with newspapermen, he dropped his medical practice in Lynchburg to become a full-time writer, whatever that might have meant in the 1840s. At first, it meant starting a newspaper that failed, then writing humorous sketches and light essays, two of which were published in *Harper's Magazine.* He moved to Washington, D.C., to become the Capitol correspondent for the *New Orleans Crescent* daily newspaper from 1857 to 1859. During this period, he began writing comic sketches, in dialect with phonetic misspellings, for the *Southern Literary Messenger.* These "letters" from "Mozis Addums" were a big hit, reprinted countless times in newspapers and making Bagby a popular comic lecturer. But he had more serious literary ambitions, so he moved to Richmond to write while holding several posts as a library administrator. He became editor of the *Southern Literary Messenger* during most of the Civil War years and a war correspondent for newspapers throughout the South with the pen name Hermes. After the war, Bagby helped launch, edit, and fill a weekly paper called *Native Virginian,* a "literary and humorous publication" that lasted until 1870.[73] He continued to lecture and write until his death in 1882, a quiet and genteel artist who was contented with the short, ephemeral forms of the periodical press.

Bagby was perhaps Virginia's highest expression of the tendency in the southern press toward literary journalism. He viewed fellow newspaper drones with amused detachment. "The Virginia Editor is a young, unmarried, intemperate, pugnacious, gambling gentleman," he wrote in a satire of the 1850s. "Between drink and dueling-pistols he is generally escorted to a premature grave." He calls this archetypal editor a "literary ostrich" for rooting around in the courthouse "with swollen red nose and diminished, calfless shanks" to hatch whatever writing he could produce with the support of the party to which he sells out.[74] Bagby also deplored the daily grind. "I am sick unto death of this life of scribbling drudgery," he wrote to a female friend on having to take over the dying *Southern Literary Messenger* in 1860.[75] But as a writer, he never rose above the low-pay, low-status business of working for the daily and periodical press, for there was not much of an alternative, even for an aristocrat.[76]

Another ill-fitting literary aristocrat in the top range of Virginia's rough-and-tumble journalism was Bagby's mentor, John Moncure Daniel, whom Bagby eulogized in a Pickwickian essay titled "John M. Daniel's Latch-Key." Others feared Daniel, who died in 1865, as the brilliant bully of the Richmond press and the harshest critic of the Confederacy's President Jefferson Davis during the war. Forty years later, southern literary reviews would come to recognize that Daniel was underappreciated in his time.

"Like Poe—whom he befriended and defended—[Daniel] was condemned by a moral tribunal when he should have been judged by an aesthetic one," said a writer in the *Sewanee Review* in 1907.[77] "The entrance of John M. Daniel into the editorial ranks was like turning an electric eel into a fish-pond," wrote *South Atlantic Quarterly* in 1905.[78] To Bagby, Daniel was a natural-born editor, a genius who could have succeeded as a diplomat or magazine essayist but for his love of newspaper work.

Still another professional journalist who made original literature out of the vanished preindustrial South was Joel Chandler Harris (1848–1908). Harris, the creator of Uncle Remus and his Brer Rabbit folktales, has been unfairly diminished in his cultural standing today by the classic Disney movie made from these stories, *Song of the South*. Premiered in a segregated Atlanta in 1946, the movie, featuring black and white actors interacting with animated animal characters, was picketed and criticized for its stereotyped portrayal of blacks on a Georgia plantation.[79] The caricatures and carefree sweetness of the thing was "bound to enrage all educated Negroes, and a number of damnyankees," *Time* predicted, and indeed the harshest critics were the National Association for the Advancement of Colored People (NAACP), the National Urban League, *Ebony,* and the *New York Times.* Lost in the controversy was the extraordinary achievement of Harris as previously recognized by leading black intellectuals of the 1920s such as James Weldon Johnson and W. E. B. DuBois—that Harris had respectfully and uniquely translated a vast body of African American folktales.[80] More than that, Harris, a painfully shy and self-effacing white Georgia newspaper editor, had for a thirty-year span produced novels, children's books, poetry, short-story collections, and an *Uncle Remus's Magazine* that, all told, had made him one of the most beloved and celebrated writers in America. Experts in various fields gave him the highest praise for his sympathy for black characters, his delineation of middle-class Georgians, and his inside knowledge of plantation life.[81] He was a genius, President Theodore Roosevelt wrote to Harris's son Julian Harris when the elder writer died in 1908. "He never wrote anything which did not make a man or woman reading it feel a little better."[82] For thirty-eight years, until retiring to his "Wren's Nest" in the West End of Atlanta in 1900, Harris had been a humble worker around the presses and rolltop desks of Georgia newspapers.[83]

Harris was a half orphan, born in 1848 to a day-laborer father who vanished without giving the boy his name and a thirty-five-year-old seamstress, Mary Harris, of whom no picture exists. The town of Eatonton, Georgia, in effect, raised "Joe" Harris between the humble cottage provided to his mother and grandmother and the home of a relatively well-to-do family next door that donated the cottage. Thus, the redheaded boy grew up with an unusual vantage, skittering happily across boundaries of wealth, class, and even race in the democratic spirit of a middle Georgia town in the 1850s.[84] In March 1862, the thirteen-year-old boy eagerly read a new newspaper that arrived in the post office— Eatonton had no paper of its own—called *The Countryman,* which claimed to be the only newspaper in America published on a plantation. He noticed an inconspicuous ad that would open his destiny: "Wanted: An active, intelligent white boy, 14 or 15 years of age to learn the printer's trade." He expressed his interest in a letter to the planter-editor, Joseph Addison Turner, whose Turnwold plantation was nine miles away in the same county. Turner took the boy and his few possessions to live at Turnwold. There, as the Civil War raged closer and closer, Harris would learn typesetting and the traditions of English literature (including the eighteenth-century journalism of Turner's namesake, Joseph

Addison), and he would absorb the magic of African American folk legends in the slave cabins of Putnam County.[85]

But Turner's greatest effect on Harris was to instill a prejudice for southern writers against the judgments of northern critics. In book reviews that Harris began writing for *The Countryman,* he rejected as "vapid nonsense" a New York critic's negative views of a southern poet named Henry Lynden Flash and said it was time for the South to "atone for her former coldness to her sons of song." Harris, though only fifteen, was absorbing the books of Turner's library of more than a thousand volumes and peppering his reviews will references to Poe, Tennyson, and Bulwer.[86]

Over time, Harris developed a far more sophisticated vision of southern literature. He wrote reviews at the *Macon (Georgia) Telegraph,* where he began as a typesetter in 1866.[87] When he discovered a new literary magazine in New Orleans, *Crescent Monthly,* he gushed over it. Here was finally a publication that would "show the world that the Southern mind has more genius than it has ever had credit for." He advised everyone to subscribe, out of loyalty to the region. "To possess a literature peculiar to ourselves," Harris wrote, "we must ignore such periodicals as *Harper* and *Leslie,* and support such periodicals as the one under review." Harris even managed to get himself a job as secretary to the editor of *Crescent Monthly,* and he ventured down to New Orleans for what turned out to be a lonely and disappointing sojourn of eight months. The confusing river city did not suit his imagination as much as the slow agrarian pace of middle Georgia, where he happily spent his next four years at the *Monroe Advertiser,* a county weekly. Harris's humorous writings as a paragrapher eventually won him a job in 1870 as a daily columnist for the *Savannah Morning News,* which the popular southwestern humorist William Tappan Thompson had founded in 1850.[88]

The popularity of his humorous daily column in the Savannah paper, "Affairs in Georgia," led to Harris's recruitment in 1876 as columnist and associate editor of the *Atlanta Constitution*. Thus, at age twenty-seven, he found himself working alongside two other rising editorial stars of the southern press, the editor in chief Evan P. Howell and the associate editor Henry W. Grady, who was hired that same historic year. (The election of President Rutherford B. Hayes signaled the withdrawal of federal troops and the end of Reconstruction.) In his columns in the *Constitution,* Harris worked up a fictional character named Uncle Remus. Harris also reviewed magazines, showing himself far more broad minded than in his Macon days about northern periodicals like *Atlantic Monthly, Galaxy, Scribner's,* and *Lippincott's.* It was an article in *Lippincott's* on southern "Negro" folklore, in fact, that inspired him to begin drawing on the legends and songs he had heard from blacks as a boy.[89] Before these wildly popular columns were collected in a series of books, Harris wrote a column in 1879 laying out his new philosophy of literature in the South.

The editorial is such a subtle and prophetic analysis that Harris's biographer, Paul M. Cousins, runs it in full. Harris sympathizes with southern writers who wish to leave the South for a more cultured climate. But being among fellow artists is not half as important, Harris says, as sloughing off "the thousand and one special hindrances and trammels peculiar to the South and to the spirit of sectionalism that has fastened upon Southern thought." In other words, a literary artist doesn't need friends so much as scope, "an enlarged vision." The enemy of such broad horizons, according to Harris, was sectionalism—the ideology, resentment, and prejudices that were shaping southern politics and culture. As Henry Grady fought this sectionalism on the economic front for the next decade, inviting northern capital to invest in a New South, Harris fought it on the cultural-literary front. Literary standards, he said, must be universal, or at least national: "The stuff we are in the habit of calling Southern literature is not only a burlesque upon true literary art, but a humiliation and a disgrace to the people whose culture it is supposed to represent."[90]

This does not mean that writers should avoid local color and regional peculiarities. Indeed, Harris says, anticipating William Faulkner, localism is the "very spice and flavor of all literature— the very marrow and essence of all literary art." Harris rejected sectionalism but embraced localism. "No literary artist can lack for material in this section," he concluded. "They are here all around him, untouched, undeveloped, and undisturbed; unique and original; as new as the world; as old as life; as beautiful as the dreams of genius."[91]

Atlanta was blessed by a couple of natural disasters—elsewhere. A yellow fever outbreak in Savannah in 1876 led Joel Chandler Harris to evacuate with his wife and two young children to Atlanta, where he accepted work from the *Constitution*. Harris would henceforth live and die in Atlanta, its most famous author until the *Atlanta Journal* writer Margaret Mitchell published her blockbuster novel. The other profitable disaster was in 1886, when the biggest earthquake to hit the South in modern times rattled cities up and down the East Coast. Grady, then managing editor of the *Constitution* but always a high-energy reporter, rushed from his shaken home to the newspaper building, which had swayed ominously, to read the wire dispatches. Every city hit by the quake sent dramatic news—except Charleston, South Carolina, which was silent. Grady, with editor in chief Howell and a few citizens, headed for Charleston, where telegraph lines were down and where forty people had died. Grady's party had to abandon the broken rail line and commandeer a horse-drawn carriage, then a small boat where a dam had collapsed. He wired the head of the South Carolina Rail Road for a special engine to carry the Atlantans from there. He made it, spent three days in Charleston, and telegraphed reams of vivid coverage for the *Constitution* and the *New York World*. Grady's reporting from Charleston, with his byline, made him a news celebrity, eclipsing Charleston's own elegant New South newspaper editor Francis Warrington Dawson.[92] It undoubtedly enhanced Grady's name recognition with the elite New England Society of New York, which invited him to address its annual dinner that December. In the sparkling banquet hall of Delmonico's, after General William T. Sherman had been toasted and the band had played "Marching Through Georgia," Grady delivered his famously riveting and reconciling New South speech, the first Grady ever gave outside of Georgia. "It stirred the whole country from one end to the other, and made Mr. Grady famous," Harris wrote without much exaggeration in his brief biography that followed Grady's untimely death in 1889, at age thirty-nine.[93] Hundreds of newspapers and commentators lauded the speech as if it announced the final cessation of hostilities between North and South, and in the tongue of angels.

Grady's name is given to a hospital and a high school in modern Atlanta, and to the communications school at the University of Georgia; his statue gazes down on the city street that runs in front of the *Atlanta Journal-Constitution* building. He is memorialized as a great editor, visionary, and orator. He orchestrated cotton industry expositions in Atlanta in 1881, 1887, and 1889.[94] In 1882, he declined a local campaign to draft him to run for Congress, and in 1888 he was considered as a possible Democratic candidate for vice president.[95] His gentle "no thanks" to the Atlanta elite who tried to get him to run for Congress signaled perhaps

a historic turning point in the southern press away from partisan journalism: "Journalism is a jealous profession, and demands
the fullest allegiance of those who seek its honors or emolu-
ments," Grady responded to his petitioners. "Least of all things
can it be made the aid of the demagogue, or the handmaid of the
politician."[96]

He never wrote a book, but behind the success of almost everything he tried was an irrepressible literary sensibility. Grady
was a master of the southern traditions of rhetoric, lyricism, and
storytelling. After graduating at age eighteen from the University
of Georgia as a star student-orator, he enrolled in postgraduate
studies at the University of Virginia to hone his rhetorical skills.[97]
He joined a student literary society and nearly won top oratory
honors. Then, in the spring of 1869, he encountered the fiction of
Bret Harte, the California editor who had come to be known as
the "Dickens of America" for his humorous short stories. Grady
decided to become a journalist and began sending witty, Harte-
like dispatches to the *Atlanta Constitution*. This was a newspaper
started the year before with a name suggested by President Andrew
Johnson to indicate its "constitutional" fight against the so-called
radical Reconstruction.[98] Grady's letters, published in the *Constitution* with the pen name King Hans, show a remarkable confidence
and polish for a young man barely nineteen years old. *Arena* magazine noted his literary powers shortly after his death: "The genius
of Henry W. Grady so far arose above the plane of ordinary talent
that it was capable of transmuting into any of the fine arts," wrote
Dr. J. W. Lee in the 1890 article.[99] In a 1927 dissertation analyzing Grady's early writings, Russell Franklin Terrell found that this
overlooked body of work deserved far more attention. Even as a
mere boy, Terrell wrote, Grady was "one of the journalists who
used his literary ability to promote journalism."[100]

In 1876, when the presidential election turned on questions of voter fraud in three southern states, including Florida (as it would again in 2000), Grady's ground-level coverage was more than a little bold. He beat the pack of national reporters to the telegraph office after the Florida board of canvassers ruled in favor of Republican Rutherford B. Hayes. Then he bought the telegraph operator's Webster's *Blueback Speller,* tore out a few pages, and paid to have the wire operator transmit the content of those pages to tie up the wires until he had written and transmitted his stories. Thus, the *Atlanta Constitution* and *New York Herald,* for which he was stringing, scooped the nation on the big news.[101] Months after Hayes took office, Grady continued to poke around in Florida to prove that the election was stolen. In a Tallahassee hotel, he recognized a Washington detective who had previously worked for Hayes but now was collecting confessions of fraud for anti-Hayes forces. Grady drew from the detective information that the former chairman of the Florida canvassing board, now a broken and guilt-ridden man, had signed a statement admitting he threw the Florida vote. That gave Grady another major scoop in the *New York Herald.* With an equally eyebrow-lifting story a few days later, Grady did as much as anyone to deflate the legitimacy of Hayes's presidency. But this meant little, because the South was satisfied that Hayes was withdrawing federal troops in a secret arrangement to give him the questionable election. Grady's reporting of the entire affair was sharp and emotional.[102] After his coverage of the election of 1876, James Gordon Bennett Jr. at the *New York Herald* offered Grady a job, but Grady instead stayed to make his strong imprint at the *Constitution.*

The career of another reporter, Lafcadio Hearn (1850–1904), also turned on covering the fraudulent voting of 1876. Hearn, a brilliant writer, was as peculiar as Poe was reputed to be. He was a dwarfish, near-blind "wandering ghost," as he called himself, born on the remote Greek isle of Lefcada (hence his name, which also meant "wanderer") to a dark-skinned Mediterranean mother but raised and educated by a wealthy aunt on his British father's side. By a strange tangle of misfortune, he found himself reporting for the *Cincinnati Enquirer* at age twenty-two. His literary ambition, his gift of observation (with the help of a magnifying glass and telescope), and his fascination with shadowy subcultures made him an odd sort of journalist in the urban America of the 1870s. He pushed to grotesque extremes the new style of lurid, sensational news reporting, with stories on slaughterhouse workers, the black Bucktown section of Cincinnati, a black ghost-seer, and, of course, violent crime. His account of a notorious murder in which the murderer half cremated the victim is like something out of a Poe short story: "The brain had all boiled away, save a small wasted lump . . . and the yellow fibers seemed to writhe like worms in the Coroner's hands. The eyes were cooked to bubbled crisps in the blackened sockets, and the bones of the nose were gone, leaving a hideous hole." This sort of thing made him the city's star reporter, whom the editor called his "best writer." But when it was discovered that he had married a mulatto woman, which was illegal and a scandal, the *Enquirer* fired him. The rival *Cincinnati Commercial* took a chance and hired him, giving Hearn more room to write longer pieces. But he hankered for a richer setting. In his imagination, that meant venturing south, specifically to southern Louisiana. He was intrigued by the work of the New Orleans journalist and novelist George Washington Cable on Creole culture.[103] An opportunity to drift down to those flowering latitudes came with the controversial Hayes-Tilden election. Louisiana, apart from the other two southern states with disputed returns, could have swayed the election by itself. Hearn secured an assignment from the *Cincinnati Commercial* to follow up in late 1877 with a series of articles on the politics of Louisiana.

Hearn was captivated.[104] Coming from "gray northwestern mists into the tepid and orange-scented air of the South, my impressions of the quaint city, drowsing under the violet and gold of a November morning, were oddly connected with memories of [Cable's short story] 'Jean-ah Poquelin.'" He said Cable's picturesque tale helped him idealize "everything peculiar and semi-tropical that I might see."[105] From his riverboat, the sight of decayed plantations fueled his romanticism: "O, fair paradise of the South, if still so lovely in thy ruin, what must thou have been in the great day of thy greatest glory!" Hearn wrote splendid travel pieces for the *Commercial* about New Orleans, its people, its weather, its legends, and its distinct neighborhoods. But he wrote little about politics, and almost nothing that could be called news, which bored him. He was fired again.

He stayed in New Orleans, in ragged poverty, until he landed a position at the *New Orleans Item* as an assistant editor with a chance to express his range of artistic energies. He wrote editorials on art, philosophy, and even politics, essays and articles that veered between ethnographic studies and impressionistic tone poems. He sketched illustrations and translated French and Spanish literature for the *Item*. After virtually saving the *Item,* he moved over to the larger *Times-Democrat* while freelancing for major national magazines such as *Harper's Weekly* and the *Atlantic Monthly.* In all, Hearn spent ten highly productive years in New Orleans. His work there effectively invented New Orleans, by laying the literary foundation for subsequent writers.[106] The American studies scholar Simon J. Bronner argues that Hearn represented a romantic rebellion against the homogenizing forces of America's Gilded Age.[107]

The southern press of Hearn's day, meanwhile, had to face the issue of race. The next chapter will look at how this issue confronted, confounded, and eventually banished two of the most liberal southern journalists of the era—Hearn's mentor, George Washington Cable, and the North Carolina native Walter Hines Page.

FOUR

GENTEEL LIBERALISM

They were called fire-eaters. By the 1850s, the term applied mostly to the southern newspaper editors and magazine writers who rejected any compromise with antislavery forces.[1] Compromise had been the old way of the early republic—the spirit in Congress and the White House that navigated the young nation through clashes between North and South over economic interests. A rise in cotton prices in the 1850s boosted the southern planters' attachment to the slave system. This is when the fire-eaters flourished as the proslavery theoreticians for the planter class.[2]

Robert Barnwell Rhett Sr. (1800–1876), a politician and owner of nearly two hundred slaves on two South Carolina rice plantations, voiced the ultra dogmas of southern independence in the *Charleston Mercury,* which his son Robert Barnwell Rhett Jr. edited in the 1850s and which perhaps lit the fuse for secession with its editorials in 1860.[3] The elder Rhett's rants against "submission," "consolidated empire," and the "tyranny of the numerical majority" became so obnoxious that even his friend and fellow planter William Gilmore Simms recoiled, calling Rhett "rash, arrogant and a surface man, with one idea only."[4] Edmund

Ruffin (1794–1865), a Virginia planter with an encyclopedic mind, launched and edited one of the South's many popular agricultural newspapers, the *Farmer's Register* (1833–42). But his later work as a long-haired fire-eater eclipsed his career as an agronomist. He read all of the proslavery journals and added his own arguments for secession to their pages.[5] Ruffin ostentatiously fired the first cannon shot on Fort Sumter to start the Civil War in 1861, and he committed suicide after the surrender in 1865 rather than endure the consequences of defeat.[6] Even the distinguished *Southern Literary Messenger,* which John R. Thompson had edited with literary quality through the early 1850s, began to favor sectional polemics as its finances sputtered.[7]

James D. B. De Bow (1820–67) started his influential *Commercial Review of the South and West* in 1846 in New Orleans. Originally, it carried lively articles and opposing viewpoints on agricultural reforms, transportation improvements, and regional manufacturing. But the defense of slavery, on moral and legal grounds, slowly took over its pages, until by 1860, De Bow's *Review* was the South's main soapbox for secession.[8] One of the premiere writers in this campaign was the Virginia planter and lawyer George Fitzhugh (1801–81), whose apologetics for slavery filled two books and many magazines in the 1850s. Fitzhugh, steeped in the writings of contemporary British magazines and economic theories, detected new forms of slavery in every economic system known to the nineteenth century, especially free-market capitalism and utopian socialism. Thus, he framed his argument in favor of the South's race-based version of slavery this way: it was more civilized and historical than all the other forms of slavery. After defeat, Fitzhugh watched Reconstruction with growing despair for the future of the South and the future of southern blacks. He wrote in a letter to De Bow's *Review* of October 1867:

Obliterate all distinctions of race, and the negroes at the South, like those at the North, would become outcasts, pariahs, paupers and criminals. They would be confined to the most loathsome and least lucrative employments, and spend half their time in prisons, workhouses and poorhouses. They know that mere political equality would at once condemn them to social slavery—and they see at the North, that this social slavery, or slavery to skill and capital, of an inferior to a superior race, is the worst possible condition in which human beings can be placed. You, and your readers, must see that the negroes will not be satisfied with a nominal, but deceptive equality, but are everywhere determined to become masters of those who lately owned them as slaves. We admire their pluck. They are all armed and ready; all burning for a fight.[9]

Dissent from this orthodoxy was rare, and hard to sustain. How the South lost its mind—that is, its Jeffersonian mentality of rational discourse and moral reflection—is an interesting question. The southern historian Clement Eaton, in his 1940 book *Freedom of Thought in the Old South,* offered many reasons, from economic self-interest and fear of a slave revolt to the region's evangelical reflexes. "The liberal ideas of the eighteenth century were in large part discarded, as the queues, the tight breeches, and silk stockings were outmoded," Eaton wrote. "The eighteenth-century cosmopolitanism of the Tidewater gave way to an intensely local point of view. In place of the appeal to reason the suppression of radical criticism was substituted."[10] O'Brien, who has made a more recent and more refined examination of nineteenth-century texts, argues that slavery was not the debilitating obsession earlier historians made it seem, nor was evangelical Christianity as inhibiting to intellectual life as had been previously assumed. O'Brien puts some blame, rather, on the antebellum tradition of anonymous

authorship and the lack of a book-publishing industry, which together kept the South from developing professional writers and a
more robust culture of criticism.[11]

W. J. Cash's *The Mind of the South*, which is discussed in Chapter
6, offered a highly impressionistic answer from an artistic journalist, not a historian, but its insight is worth mentioning here: the
white southern mind, forged at all class levels by frontier individualism, crystallized around a set of myths that ensured white unity
but permitted no opposition. Cash called this cluster of myths "the
savage ideal," and he argued that the ideal was savagely enforced.
"Criticism, analysis, detachment, all those activities and attitudes
so necessary to the healthy development of any civilization, every
one of them took on the aspect of high and aggravated treason,"
according to Cash.[12] To be a dissenter in this madhouse culture, in
Cash's view, implied a kind of reverse insanity—a different form
of madness. Indeed, one of the boldest antebellum southern critics of slavery, Hinton Rowan Helper, veered from radical critic
to rabid racist to psychotic suicide. This son of an illiterate North
Carolina farmer had written a book about the gold rush, which
was all he had to show for his three years of prospecting in California. His Maryland publisher edited out a minor assertion in the
book—that slavery was an inefficient economic system—fearing
a state law that banned statements "having a tendency to excite
discontent . . . amongst the people of color of this state" or other
states or territories. Helper was so outraged by this muzzling that
he resolved to write an entire book on the stupidity of a slave
economy. *The Impending Crisis of the South: How to Meet It* used
statistics, logical arguments, and militant zeal to make a powerful
case against slavery, stirring North and South on the eve of the
Civil War like a sequel to *Uncle Tom's Cabin*. But the Civil War and
its aftermath somehow refocused Helper's mind. In 1867, he pub-

lished perhaps the most pathologically antiblack book imaginable, calling for the extermination of the "Negro" and all of "mixed blood" from the face of the earth (one chapter is titled "Black: A Thing of Ugliness, Disease").[13] In 1908, elderly and insane, Helper killed himself in a cheap Washington, D.C., rooming house.[14] One historian speculated on a pattern of self-slaughter among southern dissidents. "A fatal frustration seems to come from the struggle to find a way through the unfathomable maze formed by tradition, caste, race, poverty," wrote V. O. Key Jr. in his seminal *Southern Politics in State and Nation*.[15] Clarence Cason, an Alabama native and professor at the state university, killed himself in 1935 just before the publication of his haunting critique of southern culture, *90° in the Shade*. Cash met a similar end, hanging himself in Mexico City in 1941.[16]

A more common fate for southern writers who ran afoul of the savage ideal was self-exile. This was the path chosen by George Washington Cable (1844–1925), the New Orleans chronicler of Creole culture who confronted the white southern dogma on race starting in 1885. Newspapers and readers from all across the South widely counterattacked Cable. Around this time, Cable was on a literary tour with Mark Twain. In Louisville, Kentucky, where he, Twain, and the *Courier-Journal* editor Henry Watterson met with the local press club, Cable saw the visible expression of the savage ideal on the faces of journalists discussing "the negro question." "It makes one's teeth ache to get once more among a typical group of Southern men who steal glances at each other but not a man Jack of them will venture an opinion," he wrote to his wife in 1885. "Freedom of speech has yet to come to us of the South."[17] Later that year, he moved with his wife and six children to Northampton, Massachusetts. Then his mother, two sisters, and one of his sister's three children also left New Orleans to join Cable in

Northampton. He would live there for the next forty years until his death, writing about the South from a safe distance.[18]

In the decades that followed the Civil War, the destitute black—some four million of them former slaves—presented what W. E. B. DuBois called "a labor problem of vast dimensions."[19] What would be the economic role of this dispossessed "other," if any at all? Attached to that question were more disturbing psychological questions of what would be the African American's social, political, and cultural place in southern life, if any. By the turn of the twentieth century, blacks had settled their own debate over these questions, in their own churches, newspapers, and agricultural-mechanical schools. Two prominent African American figures articulated the black debate well. Booker T. Washington (1856–1915) espoused the dominant view, which was that blacks, if given a modicum of safety and friendly support from whites, would concentrate on self-improvement, practical training, farming, and their own churches and family life while abjuring any claim to social equality or political participation. This position was, for a time, overwhelmingly favored by southern blacks—though not by the black intelligentsia or black press in the North—and quite a few paternalistic and wealthy whites in the North and South endorsed it. Clark Howell, editor of the *Atlanta Constitution,* for example, helped sponsor Washington's famous "Atlanta compromise" speech at the Cotton States and International Exposition in 1895; immediately after the speech, Howell told the applauding audience the speech was "the beginning of a moral revolution in America."[20] The dissenting black view was that of W. E. B. DuBois (1868–1963), a Massachusetts native who taught sociology at Atlanta University, helped promote the NAACP after its start in 1909, and for twenty-five years edited that organization's magazine, *Crisis.* DuBois, an intellectual, an exquisite writer, and an unyielding critic of white supremacy, insisted on full political participation without regard to race and a truly intellectual education for the "talented tenth" of black society.[21]

The white South, in the decades following the surrender of the Confederacy, developed several conflicting theories about the role of "the free Negro." The historian Joel Williamson, drawing on his twenty-year study of the period, delineated these racial theories in *The Crucible of Race: Black-White Relations in the American South Since Emancipation.*[22] Williamson associates each theory with a particular social class and identifies the ideological struggles between the theories as a "rage for order." The first group he calls the conservatives, consisting mainly of the ruling class, either former planters or New South professionals. The conservatives' racial attitude was paternalistic, believing that "the Negro" had a place in the postwar South, but that place was at the bottom of the social scale, presumably forever. The second group was minuscule, the liberals—southern dissenters who called for reform, amelioration of the social conditions of black life, and some measure of political or social equality, at least in the fullness of time. The third group, the radicals, consisted mainly of poor whites and populist Democratic politicians such as Tom Watson and "Pitchfork Ben" Tillman. They rather suddenly overtook the conservatives in dominating race relations in 1889, and their reign lasted until about 1915, according to Williamson. The radicals believed that there was no place for "the Negro" anywhere, though here and there in the 1890s some of them envisioned a black-white populist alliance of common grievances rising up to join the western populists, as with Tom Watson's unsuccessful campaign for reelection to Congress in 1892 and in the Fusionist Party in North Carolina. The radicals' antiblack field of action was violence, from grotesque communal lynching to urban riots such as those that ended the fusionist movement in Wilmington, North Carolina, in 1898 and bloodied downtown Atlanta in 1906.[23] Finally, a new kind of conservative emerged out of a younger generation, born too late to fight in the Civil War. Williamson calls these the *Volksgeist* ("folkways") conservatives. Their theory of race was shaped by the experience of Jim Crow segregation since the 1890s, a total separation that made paternalistic relationships impossible, and by a kind of Hegelian idealism about folkways and the "science" of race. The latter notion, imported from German research universities, pointed toward what Williamson calls a "white communion" that supported reforms and medical missions to help poor whites.[24]

George Washington Cable, the New Orleans newspaper columnist and popular novelist-turned-reformer, represented the liberal in this grouping. One who embodied the *Volksgeist* conservative was Walter Hines Page (1855–1918), a North Carolina native who pushed progressive reforms for the South from his editorial chairs at magazines in Boston and New York. These two men are a perennial fascination to historians and literary critics interested in the South and its writers. Cable and Page, after several years of fighting on their home turf, both reluctantly transplanted themselves to the North, where they found great success. Coincidentally, both departures occurred in 1885. Today, both Cable and Page are largely forgotten, but in their time they strode gigantically and originally across America's cultural Mason-Dixon Line. Their writings—newspaper reporting, editorial essays, and fiction—hold up well on close examination a century or more after they left their mark. Yet the historians and literary critics who make such an examination tend to admit, despite their admiration, that something hobbled these two talents as writers and reformers. The South nourished the genius of both Cable and Page, but the times limited what they could achieve, between Reconstruction and World War I. The verdict of historians is that the crucible of race held them back.

Cable was born and raised in New Orleans at a time when the city was one of the busiest ports in America. His father was an entrepreneur, originally from Virginia. At one time, the elder George Washington Cable was wealthy enough in New Orleans to own eight slaves, but after flood and failure, he sent his wife and children back to a previous home in Indiana. The father died in 1859, forcing the fifteen-year-old son to take his father's dreary job as a customhouse clerk in New Orleans. From his mother, Rebecca, the son inherited a Presbyterian rectitude that was deeply offended by social injustice, as well as by sinful pleasures like theater. After the Union siege of New Orleans during the Civil War, the widow Cable and her children were allowed to flee to Mississippi, where the diminutive G. W. Cable joined the Confederate army, fighting in several battles, in which he was twice wounded. He returned to New Orleans in his gray uniform, feeling that he had served an honorable cause and owed no loyalty to the United States.[25]

In his youth, before and after the Civil War, Cable absorbed the romance of New Orleans like sunshine. He was also something of a natural social scientist, and this side of his nature saw the city's rich mix of people and history with a luminous clarity. He was especially drawn to the old French aristocracy and Spanish holdovers, mixtures of Latin and Gallic blood known as Creoles. After President Thomas Jefferson's purchase of the Louisiana Territory from Napoleon in 1803, an Anglo-Protestant culture began competing for dominance. Other European immigrants poured in. Meanwhile, slaves and free people of color added more variety, including additional mixed-blood rankings of mulatto, quadroon, and octoroon. Ninety-three years after the Louisiana Purchase, an octoroon, or one-eighth black, named Homer Plessy lost his case in the U.S. Supreme Court claiming a right to ride in trains with white passengers.[26] Cable by then had become an outspoken liberal on "the Negro problem," daring to oppose the rigid dogma of racial segregation. But in the beginning, in the 1870s, he made his name as a fiction writer who popularized Creole culture.

Cable had literary ambitions, a keen eye, a moral temperament, and a gap in his formal education—all the usual equipment for a journalist of the era. He became a weekly columnist for the daily *New Orleans Picayune,* the closest thing to a penny paper in the South. (A *picayune* was a Spanish coin worth about three cents.) Like Lafcadio Hearn a decade later, Cable filled his columns with local history and odd sociology, much of it gleaned from old newspapers and archives he searched out.[27] The newspaper hired him as a full-time staff writer but when assigned to review a play, his religious scruples prompted him to quit. By then, he was turning his literary journalism to short stories based on Creole culture, much as Joel Chandler Harris was doing with African slave culture in Georgia. Cable admitted he left the *Picayune* for another reason as well—because he was more interested in well-written prose than in just-broken news. He had "neither the faculty for getting mere news, nor the relish for blurting out news for news' sake after it was got."[28] Cable returned to his customhouse job at the New Orleans Cotton Exchange, but he freelanced historical sketches for the *Picayune* and atmospheric short stories for one of the most popular magazines of the era, *Scribner's Monthly.*

His tales in *Old Creole Days,* published in 1879, exploited the romantic haze of a vanished antebellum culture, but with a sense of human tragedy and folly tempered by Cable's postwar experience. His blend of local color with the gothic, in stories about falling aristocratic mansions and cross–cultural tensions, harks back to Poe and foreshadows Faulkner. His portrayal of change is finely observed, as in this description from the Nathaniel Hawthorne–like tale "Jean-ah Poquelin": "The alien races pouring into old New Orleans began to find the few streets named for the Bourbon princes too strait for them. The wheel of fortune, beginning to whirl, threw them off beyond the ancient corporation lines, and sowed civilization and even trade upon the lands of the Graviers and Girods. Fields became roads, roads streets. Everywhere the leveler was peering through his glass, rodsmen were whacking their way through willow-brakes and rose-hedges, and the sweating Irishmen tossed the blue clay up with their long-handled shovels."[29]

Cable, like many southern writers, had a good ear for the music of the spoken language around him. He was himself a musician and wrote about indigenous music of black and white Louisiana for magazines in New York. He carefully rendered dialect in his stories, and his descriptions rise above ordinary reporting like literary gems. A single sample: the floor of a French Quarter mansion rotting into boardinghouse decay "was of wide slabs fastened down with spikes, and sloping up and down in one or two broad undulations, as if they had drifted far enough down the current of time to feel the tide-swell."[30] Northern and European critics hailed his short stories as the work of a newly discovered giant—"no mere talented writer [but] a genius in his way," said the reviewer in *Scribner's Monthly*.[31] Yet the strength of Cable's early stories was not so much in their gothic and romantic elements, notes literary historian Louis D. Rubin Jr.: "The art of the stories in *Old Creole Days* is founded upon realistic social observation," in other words, careful reporting.[32]

Cable was studying the problem of race in New Orleans and in the wider South. But for most of these years, before 1884, he avoided preaching against the doctrine of white domination. The stories in *Old Creole Days* were only indirectly about race, carrying an implied criticism of the social rules that made outcasts of people having the slimmest black ancestry. His first novel, serialized in *Scribner's Monthly* and published in 1881 as *The Grandissimes,* went further; it was so frank and serious in its portrayal of black-white relations in New Orleans that Rubin calls it the first "modern" southern novel.[33] But for the most part Cable kept his liberal views on race out of the public arena, so he enjoyed local popularity along with his growing national success. He made his first explicit political statement quietly, in two letters to the local papers in September 1875 arguing in favor of racially integrated public schools.[34]

Privately, Cable later wrote, he was "very slowly and painfully guessing out the riddle of our Southern question."[35] As his thinking grew more independent, Cable took advantage of two opportunities to ground his ideas in hard data. One was an assignment from a project of the U.S. Census Bureau. An official was compiling a supplement to the census of 1880 with reports from the largest cities. Having read *Old Creole Days* on the train to New Orleans, the official located Cable and gave him charge of the city's report. For more than a year, Cable expended his literary energy digging up statistical information on the city's economy, drainage, sanitation, and public health—all the rational systems that the Crescent City tended to neglect in its tropical hedonism. The literary artist was turning social reformer. Cable's New York publishers asked him to expand his government report into a more colorful book on the Creoles of Louisiana. His second opportunity in fact gathering began around this time. Appointed to head a grand jury, he led an investigation of local corrections and charities.[36] He examined prisons and asylums in New England for comparison and was shocked by how brutal New Orleans appeared in contrast. After making his grand jury report, Cable helped the city set up the independent Board of Prisons and Asylums Commissioners.[37] The *New Orleans Times-Democrat* assigned Cable to write a series of exposés on local jail conditions. Leading citizens formed the Prisons and Asylums Aid Association, with Cable as secretary.

His investigations of parish jails led to the discovery of a leased-prison-labor system that was, in effect, an extension of slavery across the South.[38] The statistics and state reports he gathered clearly showed that blacks were being given absurdly longer sentences for minor offenses and being leased out disproportionately under brutal working conditions in mines, lumberyards, and railroad projects. In 1883, Cable rolled out his indictment of this system in a two-hour speech in Louisville, Kentucky, and in an article in *Century Magazine* in 1884.[39] Here was an example of the crusading journalism that was just emerging in the *New York Sun* of Charles Dana, the *New York World* of Joseph Pulitzer, and magazines like *Century*.[40] Cable expected his appalling facts to stir the best people of the South, such as the prominent citizens serving with him on the prison-reform association.[41] But it was not that simple. The "facts" carried hidden dynamite that threatened to blow up the whole cherished system of discrimination against blacks in southern courts, schools, jobs, trolleys, trains, restaurants, and hotels. Cable now understood, as well as anyone, how all these inequities were bound together in one Gordian knot. But he was not ready to make an all-out attack on white supremacy, at least not until something happened to him on the train to Louisville.[42]

He noticed a young mother and child, neatly dressed in summer muslins, confined to a separate coach because "they were of African blood." At one station, two chain gangs of filthy black convicts, in stinking rags and shackles, filled the separate coach.

The young woman and her daughter could not leave their corner in that frightening space because of Jim Crow laws. "Had the child been white, and the mother not its natural but a hired guardian," Cable later wrote, "she could have sat anywhere in the train, and no one would have ventured to object, even had she been as black as the mouth of the coalpit to which her loathsome fellow passengers were being carried in chains."[43] He resolved that he would break his silence on the South's underlying sickness.

He did so in a commencement address at the University of Alabama on June 18, 1884, later adopted in an address to the American Social Science Association and in an article in *Century* called "The Freedman's Case in Equity." At a time when the North and South seemed content to declare the wearisome race question settled, or marginal, Cable declared it the "greatest social problem before the American people today." The South's defense of slavery had deformed the region's morals and culture, and it had ended in a massive bloodletting. Now, if neglected, the same inequity in a different form would again seed, root, and sprout, he said, yielding "the red fruits of revolution."[44] The evil had worked itself deep into the southern soul because of the "discipline of the plantation," an assumption that "we were dictators." From this arose a moral laxness and a host of vices in the post–Civil War era: "Shameless hard drinking, the carrying of murderous weapons, murder, too, and lynching on its heels, the turning of state and county prisons into slavepens, the falsification of the ballot, night riding and whipping, and all the milder forms of political intolerance." He predicted that Christian moral outrage would someday cry out in shame against these things, "though it split every social circle and every church and every family in the land."[45]

Cable had crossed the line. The local press, for the first time, had nothing good to say about his message. When his full-bore attack was published in *Century* in January 1885, Cable was denounced in editorial pages throughout the South. *Century* received so many rebuttals that the editors assigned Henry W. Grady of the *Atlanta Constitution* to speak for the entire region against Cable's assertions. Grady said that Cable did not understand the South because of his mother's New England ancestry. "There may be here and there in the South a dreaming theorist who subscribes to Mr. Cable's teachings," Grady wrote. "We have seen no signs of one."[46] Cable knew that the white South would not tolerate criticism of its racial orthodoxy.[47] But he nursed a quixotic belief in a latent goodness he called "the Silent South." In a lengthy article responding to Grady in the *Century*, "in a spirit of faithful sonship to a Southern state," Cable attempted to arouse this silent South. This article was "written not to gratify sympathizers, but to persuade opponents; not to overthrow, but to convince." It starts with a lyrical interpretation of the statue of Robert E. Lee high atop a column in Tivoli Circle in New Orleans, surrounded by the city's streetcar tracks. Lee was a silent symbol of everything that was noble and good about the South. "So this monument, lifted far above our daily strife of narrow interests and often narrower passions and misunderstandings, becomes a monument to more than its one great and rightly loved original. It symbolizes our whole South's better self; the finer part which the world not always sees; unaggressive, but brave, calm, thoughtful, broad-minded, dispassionate, sincere, and, in the din of boisterous error round about it, all too mute."[48]

But his hopes proved futile. By the time "The Silent South" was published in September 1885, Cable had moved with his family to Northampton, where he continued to write and speak out for nearly forty years until he died while wintering in St. Petersburg, Florida, in 1925.

It would be too simplistic to say that Cable was chased out of the South because of his liberal stance on race. His relationship with the North and the South was tied to a more complicated tension between Cable's southern identity and a national literary market. The arbiters of that market were genteel editors and writers in the Northeast with whom Cable established strong ties. For example, Richard Watson Gilder, the editor at *Scribner's* and later at *Century* when these magazines were publishing Cable's fiction and social criticism, encouraged him to take on the subject of racial discrimination in the South.[49] A Cornell University professor of literature named Hjalmar Hjorth Boyesen, whose journalism, poetry, and essays were widely published in magazines, realized on a visit to New Orleans around 1870 that the place was a perfect setting for a novelist. When he read "Belles Demoiselles Plantation" in *Scribner's,* he felt Cable was that novelist. He said so in a letter to Cable in 1877, which helped the freelancing clerk decide to throw himself into being a full-time writer. Boyesen promoted Cable among the publishers in New York, and he encouraged Cable to aspire to a publishing market that had not developed in the South. "I mean no disrespect to the South," Boyesen wrote, "but I have been there and know how uncongenial its atmosphere must be to a true artist."[50]

Cable was welcomed like a celebrity in the North's editorial offices, opera halls, and salons. He was the guest of his census-project publisher in Newport, Rhode Island, where he met another publisher who offered to bring out his next novel.[51] At the Century Club in New York, he posed for his portrait a few feet from where William Makepeace Thackeray once sat, as he wrote home to his wife. He socialized in Hartford with Harriet Beecher Stowe and her next-door neighbor Mark Twain. In his well-attended public readings with Twain, Cable's natural voice was said to be pleasing in its Louisiana drawl. But he received voice lessons in New York to help him project in large halls.[52] At the New York home of his editor Gilder, he met Andrew Carnegie and Matthew Arnold. Visiting New York, he learned to love the theater he had once avoided as sinful.[53] In Boston, the elderly poet John Greenleaf Whittier visited him, while the *Boston Herald* was on hand to record their dialogue.[54] In a letter to Boyesen, he confessed that he was bedeviled by an ambition that he could not keep under control when his northern literary patrons stimulated it. "I yearn toward the North," he wrote. "To me *that* is the South. There is the sunlight and flowers and fruit—there is Boyesen" (italics in original).[55]

Cable's success with the northern publishing crowd embittered other New Orleans writers rooted in the region's older standards of belles lettres. The novelist Grace King, although she was pleased to welcome him back to an appreciative audience in 1915, wrote in her memoirs that native-born Cable "had been well treated by its people, and yet he stabbed the city in the back, as we felt, in a dastardly way to please the Northern press."[56] Charles Gayarré, a respected Louisiana historian of Creole descent who befriended Cable, felt a similar betrayal, of the city and of himself.[57] Major E. A. Burke, manager of the *New Orleans Times-Democrat,* made it impossible for Cable's friends on the newspaper to remain his friends.[58]

Cable's exile may have saved his skin, but it damaged his artistic imagination, according to critics of his later work. It was as if he needed to be close to his subjects and landscapes, notes Alice Hall Petry. "Perhaps, indeed, he was already so much an outsider in New Orleans that to live in Massachusetts made him doubly one—sequestered from New Orleans' allures and surrounded by appreciative northern critics, to be sure, but so out of touch with his material that he became oddly dry and preachy," Petry writes.[59]

Rubin's explanation for the decline of Cable's genius was that he "disappeared into the Genteel Tradition" of lesser talents like Hamlin Garland.[60] On another level, Cable's departure marked the limits to which the South could go—the limits of its press—in self-analysis and indigenous reform.

Walter Hines Page presents a parallel case of expatriation, but with two significant differences. Page was eleven years younger than Cable, and he experienced the Civil War as a boyhood romance rather than a traumatic reality. And he was from North Carolina, a state that lacked the large-scale slavery, historical cities, or peculiar pride of Virginia or the Deep South. These two factors alone help explain the contrast between Cable's liberal sympathy for the plight of "the Negro" and Page's equivalent sympathy for the plight of the poor white southerner. Page was a moderate in his racial attitudes, insisting on capitalizing the word *Negro* in his North Carolina newspaper in the mid-1880s and sitting at dinner tables with black professionals without concern for how it looked.[61] But he believed that the southern race problem was better left alone to solve itself, in keeping with the self-help strategies of Page's close ally Booker T. Washington. Page was far more focused on the "forgotten" white man who was being driven from farm to town, and from town to city, in search of opportunity. (Or in the case of restless talents like Page, driven to New York or Boston for lack of professional challenges in the South.) Page envisioned a Jeffersonian revival of what he called "the old commonwealths," which was closer to the small-farm and small-city South of his state than to the industrializing New South of Grady's Atlanta.

His *Volksgeist* racial views reflected a pseudoscientific, neoromantic belief in an inherent virtue in the white race. He believed that a natural "race instinct" confirmed racial segregation.[62] Page was enamored of the German thought that supported such ideas. He had spent a summer studying in Berlin, and he was in the first elite group of graduate students at Johns Hopkins University when it introduced the German research university model to the United States in 1876. Poor whites were the primary concern of his editorial crusades for practical education, hookworm eradication, and agricultural modernization. He helped implement such reforms as a leader of the philanthropic Southern Education Board from 1901 to 1913. Josephus Daniels, a former newspaper junior partner of Page's whose *News and Observer* in Raleigh became the voice of North Carolina's antiblack Democratic Party, railed against Page for demeaning his native state. But Page believed he was merely giving scientific explanations for why this once-noble race of independent yeomen had become so washed out. It was hookworm, he wrote in his weekly news magazine *World's Work* in 1912, "not the warmth of the climate, . . . not the after-effect of slavery, . . . not a large 'white-trash' element."[63]

Page is best known historically as President Woodrow Wilson's ambassador to the Court of St. James during World War I. For this service he earned a memorial tablet in Westminster Abbey as "the friend of Britain in her sorest need." But before shipping out for London in 1913, his enormous energies were mainly expended as a prominent journalist in the North with the outlook of the South. Like Cable, he insisted throughout his life that he was a true southerner, despite his self-exile and political differences with the late-nineteenth-century South. Even after leaving in 1885, he usually visited the South two or three times a year until he died in 1918, in North Carolina as he had wished.[64] As the first non–New Englander to take control of the stuffy *Atlantic Monthly* offices in Boston, he shook things up with his cigar smoke, messy piles of reading material, and "nigger stories," a phrase that horrified the sons of abolitionists at the magazine.[65] As a graduate student in philology, he felt the South was naturally fitted to make her great contribution in literature, not in science.[66] Page wished to see the South advance by developing a literary culture, as New England had enjoyed in the past. At the beginning of his journalism career, he was writing poetry and developing a distinctive prose style that one biographer described as "plainspoken pungency."[67] "The poets, the novelists, the magazines, and the newspapers have done more than all the schools to stimulate the intellectual life of New England," he wrote in an essay of 1881 on the South's educational problem.[68] That same year, at age twenty-six, he also published an article in the *Atlantic Monthly* on the struggle between the past and modernity in small southern towns, "Study of an Old Southern Borough," and visited Cable in New Orleans and Joel Chandler Harris in Atlanta to talk about southern literature for letters he published in the *Boston Post*.[69] He was already becoming a native interpreter of the South for the North.

Page was raised in a twilight South; he was suspended between times and between social classes. His paternal grandfather, Anderson Page, qualified as a gentleman planter, at least by North Carolina standards, with twenty slaves on the "Old Place" where young Wat Page played around the cotton gin and family cemetery.[70] His father, Frank Page, was more mercantile, an antisecessionist who milled timber and developed the town of Cary, North Carolina. His mother, Kate, a sensitive, bookish graduate of a girls' classical academy, was Wat's tutor until he began formal schooling at age ten.[71] Page's most objective biographer, John Milton Cooper, paints Page's mother and father as symbols of two competing forces in his character: the artistic-feminine and the pragmatic-masculine, or culture versus capitalism, or even nostalgic South against un-

sentimental North. Cooper also dramatizes Page's search for vocation as the historical struggle of a rising generation of Americans
who came of age after the Civil War. After attending a military
academy called the Bingham School, Page veered from Trinity
College (later renamed Duke University for a tobacco tycoon)
to Randolph-Macon College to Johns Hopkins University to the
University of North Carolina, where he taught a summer session
in English literature.[72]

Wavering between the Methodist ministry and a life of writing, Page agonized in a search for meaning that characterized this
period of American history, according to Cooper. In the end, the
pen won, and religion, especially the southern variety, henceforth represented for Page a hindrance to southern progress. In
Louisville, where he was teaching at a boys' school, he landed a
job at the new magazine *The Age.* The weekly was modeled on
E. L. Godkin's Republican New York journal, *The Nation,* except
that *The Age* was southern and Democratic in outlook. Young Page
became a half owner of the magazine, which died three months
later.[73] Unable to find a permanent job back in North Carolina,
he went to work at the *St. Joseph Gazette,* a Democratic paper in
Missouri, and soon became its editor. In 1881, he took a leave to
travel the South writing for northern papers, such as the *New York
World,* and national magazines. With a wife and a child, he moved
to New York to work for the *World* until Joseph Pulitzer bought
it in 1883. Page was ready to give the South one more chance to
support his journalistic ambitions: he launched the *State Chronicle,*
a weekly in Raleigh that embraced the modern idea of a newspaper surviving on advertising and circulation, not government
printing contracts for political payback. Cooper calls this the first
attempt in American journalism to cover an entire state in the new
style of metropolitan journalism.[74] Two years later, he left it in the

hands of Josephus Daniels, his junior partner, and moved back to New York. From there, he wrote letters critical of the South for the *State Chronicle,* more scathing than anything he had written while in Raleigh. One, called "the mummy letter," was particularly offensive to locals. He said that an aging elite as sleepy, or dead, as a bunch of mummies controlled North Carolina. The state was "the laughingstock among States," losing its most promising young men to the North, or to alcohol. It was his farewell letter to the South, and it was not pretty.[75]

The South pushed Page out, finally, because of money—that is, how much he could make in the evolving magazine and newspaper industry. Daniels could not keep the *State Chronicle* running past 1892, which marked the onset of an economic depression that was especially hard on the South. (Partly as a result of that depression, Daniels in 1894 was able to buy the leading Raleigh daily, the *News and Observer,* and several other papers, to combine them into what eventually became the most successful Democratic paper in eastern North Carolina.[76]) For Page, southern literary ambition always led to New York. When he was barely twenty-four years old and teaching Shakespeare to boys in Louisville, Page secured a literary agent in New York.[77] The magazine he joined in Louisville, *The Age,* was launched to show that the South and West were able "to do their own thinking in national affairs, and to pass their own judgments on the World's literature."[78] It survived seven months. This was the dawning of America's magazine age, but not in the South. Page, writing later in New York, noted that two fellow Tar Heel journalists who had complained of his being "Yankeeized" had themselves sought unsuccessfully to land jobs in New York. "Their work [in North Carolina] had killed their chances," Page wrote, "because they are neither scholars nor men who know modern things."[79]

Page gained his footing in the modern magazine revolution by joining the *Forum* in 1887 as business manager. The *Forum* was a successful new monthly in New York that followed an original formula that blended the seriousness of the older "quality" magazines like *Harper's*, edited by poets and essayists, with the lighter, more timely style of mass-circulation magazines like *Munsey's* and *Cosmopolitan*, which were mostly in the hands of former newspaper editors.[80] When Page became editor of the *Forum* in 1891, he pushed the reform-minded discussions in the magazine to a higher level. It ran no fiction or poetry but carried articles on literature, education, politics, world affairs, and of course, "the Negro question" in the South.[81] Page cut the newsstand price in half, to twenty-five cents, helping boost circulation to a peak of forty thousand.[82] This was well below the numbers of the larger mass-circulation magazines but higher than those of the musty old reviews. "Effective style is changing," Page wrote in *World's Work*, a weekly magazine he started with publisher Frank N. Doubleday in 1900 to gain, finally, full control of his own publication. "The man who would write convincingly and entertainingly of things of our day and our time must write with more directness, with more clearness, with greater nervous force."[83] He hated dullness, twice rejecting ponderous pieces written for him by Henry James.[84] His own novel, *The Southerner*, is engaging enough as thinly disguised autobiography but not as great fiction.[85]

Page was on the cutting edge of what would become muckraking journalism. He assigned the pediatrician-writer Joseph M. Rice a nine-part series in the *Forum* that described Rice's visit to thousands of public school classrooms to prove that American education was scandalously lacking in any scientific, that is, progressive, basis for childhood happiness and mental development. S. S. McClure, the famous magazine publisher of the muckrakers, briefly hired Page as an editor. Page knew McClure's famous staff of writers well and published them. Ray Stannard Baker's best-selling *Following the Color Line,* an eyewitness account of conditions among blacks in the South in 1907, was assigned by Page and published by Doubleday, Page and Company in 1908.[86] But Page pulled back from the core journalistic principle of this age of reform, the conviction that exposure was the best medicine. He considered the exposé a good correction for criminals but said that "it makes dreary literature."[87] To Page, the proper way to improve society was through well-expressed ideas and debate.

The generation of southern writers after the war could not get around the problem of race, with its dying echoes of the fire-eaters before the Civil War. New South newspaper editors Henry Grady, Henry Watterson, and Frances Warrington Dawson embraced advancement through rapid industrialization while declaring the race problem safely "settled" by disenfranchisement and Jim Crow laws. But statistics belied their optimism. By the 1880s, the South still languished pathetically in capital accumulation, manufacturing output, literacy, public health, and every other social measure, as a Richmond shoe manufacturer demonstrated in a scathing 1889 book titled *A Southern Prophecy: The Prosperity of the South Dependent upon the Elevation of the Negro.* The writer, Lewis H. Blair, sarcastically deflates the happy picture seen through newspaper lenses. He argues that the newspapers were "circulating a vast amount of misinformation about the growth and prosperity of the South," particularly the *Manufacturers Record* in Baltimore. (Three years after this charge was made, Walter Hines Page acquired a controlling interest in the *Manufacturers Record* with financial help from the Duke family.[88]) The underlying cause of the South's impoverishment, Blair argued, was the degradation of blacks. And this aristocratic scion of old Virginia more boldly argued that the solution was to grant black southerners equality, the vote, and access to a unitary public school system. Unlike Cable's writings, Blair's book was virtually ignored and forgotten, until the historian C. Vann Woodward edited and wrote the introduction to a new edition in 1964. Furthermore, before his death in 1916, Blair renounced his prophetic views, concluding in an unpublished manuscript of unknown date that "the only logical position for the Negro is absolute subordination to the whites."[89] If Blair was what the historian Joel Williamson classifies as a southern "liberal" on race, at least in 1889, when the region tipped toward the anti-black "radicals," Page followed a third way. He sought to revive the Jeffersonian spirit of the agrarian white South but freed from old-time religion and infused with the intellectual vitality of the modern world.

Page's hope was that the race problem would eventually take care of itself, as long as the violent demon of white reaction was not provoked. But his strategy proved impotent, as Page himself seemed to recognize in a few rare instances when his outlook darkened. Page probably regretted publishing the novels of Thomas Dixon, who had been a fellow reformer in Raleigh but whose best-selling novels *The Leopard's Spots* and *The Clansman* romanticized white supremacy and lasciviously sexualized the black male.[90] A race riot in Wilmington, North Carolina, which was calculated to throw the election of 1898 to the Democrats, gave Page "very deep concerns" about remaining silent, he admitted privately in a letter to black writer Charles W. Chestnutt.[91] White mobs had killed at least thirty black residents and destroyed the presses of the black *Wilmington Daily Record*. Page's enthusiasm for segregated education reform through the Southern Education Board was occasionally shaken by the realization that blacks were getting little from the effort. "In most places the poor devil is simply forgotten; in some places he is deliberately swindled," he wrote in a confidential letter in 1910 to the Hookworm Commission. "I have no sentimental stuff in me about the Negro, but I have a lot of economic stuff about the necessity for training him." But such philanthropic agencies refused to risk their credibility by exposing the inequality, and so Page let the matter drop.[92]

Page felt the forces holding the South back were evangelical religion and the paternalism of the Bourbon class—a derogatory label for the South's postwar gentry, the name taken from a European royal dynasty. He "hewed to a materialistic, democratic viewpoint," according to biographer Cooper. But Page had little to offer for racial change. Perhaps he was right to fear white reaction, judging from the antiblack demagoguery that would continue to flourish in southern politics for the next fifty years. Nor did liberals like Cable or Blair seem to make much real difference, except as honest writing has its place of honor above the turmoil of history. "By the end of the century the South had reached a consensus on race policy," Woodward writes, "its mind was closed."[93]

But an opening would come through another window—that of freethinking against the habits of puritanical religion. This was Page's core crusade. "I doubt if there has come a week in twenty years but some Southern man has told me or written to me of his sense of suffocation—his longing for fresh air," Page wrote the New Yorker who led the Southern Education Board in 1903: "Their troubles have come oftener from church parties than from political parties."[94] It would be a more thundering writer than Page who would barge through that opening in the mind of the South—H. L. Mencken, the "Sage of Baltimore."

FIVE

THE MENCKEN CLUB

Every normal man must be tempted, at times, to spit on his hands, hoist the black flag, and begin slitting throats.
— H. L. Mencken, *Disturber of the Peace: The Life of H. L. Mencken*

Imagine a dinner party where the hosts are hypersensitive, and all the guests understand that good manners and flattery count for everything. All the guests, that is, except one cigar-puffing, beer-swilling charmer, whose brilliant verbosity insults the hosts—and most of the guests, though quite a few are titillated—by loudly exposing the bad taste and hypocrisy just below the party's surface. Such was the cultural life of the South in 1920 when H. L. Mencken published his flamboyant critique of the region's beaux arts in an essay he playfully misspelled as "The Sahara of the Bozart."

Henry Louis Mencken (1880–1956) was a gifted, ebullient "prince of journalists" who flourished in his hometown of Baltimore as newspaper reporter, magazine editor, self-taught scholar, and critic of the nation's prudery and what he termed its "booboisie."[1] His attack on the South's Kultur (Mencken was proud of his German American heritage) seems to have started as a lark. But it excited so much reaction in the South that the response stirred the writer's love of a good fight and involved him with the region as a sideline for more than a decade. He did not back down from his original conceit that the South was a vast wasteland of the arts, but he soon found a more delicious target in the South's lowbrow and puritanical Christianity. Mencken, more than anyone else, made the 1925 so-called monkey trial (a label he invented) in Dayton, Tennessee, the landmark case and comic opera it became.[2] But Mencken also inspired a generation of southern journalists to find a new role for themselves as indigenous critics, social liberals, and literary stylists.

"The Sahara of the Bozart" twisted around the South's belief that it was still a region of refined sensibility. On the contrary, Mencken roared, it is a vacuity so blank that it staggers the imagination. "Down there a poet is now almost as rare as an oboe-player, a dry-point etcher or a metaphysician," he wrote. "If the whole of the late Confederacy were to be engulfed by a tidal wave tomorrow, the effect upon the civilized minority of men in the world would be but little greater than that of a flood on the Yang-tse-kiang. It would be impossible in all history to match so complete a drying-up of a civilization."[3]

The essay packed enough historical insight and twinkling intuition to make up for what serious historians would call its flaws: for instance, Mencken's sentimental and racist assumptions about the South's antebellum gentry, blacks, and "white trash." Another element of "Sahara" to make pedagogues wince was its rhetoric of exaggeration, "truth magnified by ten diameters," as Gerald W. Johnson put it, approvingly, many years later. Johnson, a former editor at the *Greensboro (North Carolina) Daily News* and

briefly a journalism professor at the University of North Carolina before joining Mencken at the *Baltimore Evening Sun* in 1926,
was one of a dozen or so notable southern journalists infected
by this new style.[4] "I believed that the South, immediately after
World War I, was ten percent as bad as Mencken said it was—
and bad in precisely the ways that he described," Johnson wrote
decades later.[5]

Mencken had been toying with his theories about the South
for years. In 1907, in the *Baltimore Evening Sun,* he mourned "the
passing of a civilization" below the Potomac. Over the next few
years in the *Smart Set,* a sassy New York magazine he coedited,
Mencken attacked the quality of poetry and prose coming out
of the South. In other columns, he noted a revival of puritan-
ism not primarily in its native New England, but in the modern
South. "If you doubt it, turn to prohibition and the lynching-
bee (the descendant of the old Puritan sport of witch-burning),
or run your eye over any newspaper published South of the
Potomac."[6]

In the essay published in his *Prejudices—Second Series* in November 1920, Mencken calls the South a "stupendous region of
fat farms, shoddy cities and paralyzed cerebrums." For all its pride
and size, the entire South could really claim no critics, compos-
ers, painters, sculptors, historians, sociologists, philosophers, theologians, or scientists, he said. Not one! Mencken goes on to say
that this barrenness is particularly astonishing when one considers that the South was once the only civilized part of America,
with gentlemen of "delicate fancy, urbane instincts and aristocratic
manner." It gave birth to the nation's enlightened political theories. Mencken suggested that the Civil War had drained the South
of its "best blood." His faith in an aristocratic ideal was always one
of his cleverest weapons against America's satisfaction with itself

as a democracy. In an essay in 1930 titled "The Calamity of Appomattox," he says a turn of fate in 1865 would have saved the North from the disastrous "moral victory" of its moneygrubbing patrons and created an independent South based on the concept of human inequality, which Mencken considered a better bet.[7]

Nine months after "Sahara" appeared, Mencken published "The South Begins to Mutter" in the magazine *Current Opinion*. He was beginning to revise his appraisal of Dixie, reporting news of an incipient uprising of intelligent life. But the insulting tone of his original essay remained.[8] The Arkansas press led a counterattack, accusing "Herr Mencken" of having ties to the German enemy lately defeated by the Allies. Readers, informed of this outsider who called them "dead brains" and "idiotic patriots," denounced the scoundrel. The president of the Arkansas Advancement Association called for his deportation, and Congress looked into this possibility until it was discovered that Mencken was, in fact, a native and citizen. Southerners finally began reading "Sahara," and the reaction grew. The *Richmond (Virginia) News Leader* berated Mencken for his ignorance of history and "spiritual indigestion." An "ignorant critic of a great people," the *Danville (Virginia) Register* called him, "typically German."[9]

It should not have shocked the southern press to hear that the region was resistant to serious poets and writers, and rife with the fourth rate. Poe had harped on the same theme, and it had been a common complaint of aspiring southern letters ever since. "In no country in which literature has ever flourished has an author obtained so limited an audience," lamented Henry Timrod (1829–67), the official poet laureate of the Confederacy and one of its best war correspondents.[10] Most of what passed for southern writing was so sappy, Joel Chandler Harris had complained, it was "a disgrace to the people whose culture it is supposed to represent."[11] Hjalmar Hjorth Boyesen, the northern literary figure who encouraged George Washington Cable to write as a serious artist for an audience outside the South, used the phrase "literary Sahara of the South" in a letter of 1877.[12] By 1920, industrial development was modernizing the South, but the region had yet to develop much of a literary audience, or any other cultural life comparable to that of, say, Philadelphia, New York, or Newport, Rhode Island. So Mencken was hitting the side of a barn long sullied by other hurlers.

The difference was not only that Mencken was an outsider and a literary pugilist. It was also in the timing. The South, always somewhat resentful of moral comparisons with the North, was increasingly defensive about its relative cultural worth in the early decades of the new century. By 1910, southern writers had produced a twelve-volume celebration of southern culture pointedly titled *The South in the Building of the Nation,*[13] and had begun publishing a serialized *Library of Southern Literature,*[14] which showcased the flowery, emotion-clotted confections that Mencken would later attack. Nothing riled Mencken like false pretense—"a wobbly axiom" or "sham virtue"—and it was the South's pretensions to high culture that originally inspired his assault.[15] In addition, the growth of lynching and the revival of the Ku Klux Klan caught national attention following the end of World War I. Indictments against the South in such liberal magazines as *The Nation* and the *New Republic* tightened the region's defensive crouch.[16]

The firstborn of four children, Mencken revered his father, August, a successful Baltimore cigar manufacturer who died in 1899 and had doted on his mother, Anna. Henry Mencken lived with his mother, and after she died in 1925 he continued living in his childhood home at 1524 Hollis Street, a sociable bachelor, for the rest of his seventy-five years (except for five equally happy years in a childless marriage with a much-younger wife until she died in 1935).[17] His formal education had been blandly local and technical, but he shone as a precocious star student and greedily consumed the higher literature of his father's library. When he was only eighteen years old, with his father dead and his formal education complete, he threw himself into the clattering chaos of his first newspaper job, reporting for the *Baltimore Morning Herald*. He loved everything about it—the grubby street wisdom of his city and the thrill of banging out effervescent prose on deadline. The work was hard, but it was heaven to be a reporter in what seemed to him a golden age of reporting. Mencken's love of old-fashioned newspaper reporting kept him associated with one or another daily paper for most of his life—mainly the *Baltimore Evening Sun* from 1906 until 1941, with a last hurrah in 1948 covering the national political party conventions.[18] But he also delighted in slashing the daily press for its low standards. What the reporter of his day needed, he felt, was more skepticism, courage, and intelligence. When Mencken had an idea for reforming something, he was usually original and facetious. To reform newspapers in the 1920s, he proposed making journalism schools as difficult to enter as medical and law schools, and abolishing all city press clubs. "They are the resorts of idler and blackmailers," he huffed.[19]

He found a more satisfying venue for his journalism of wit and taste in magazines such as the *Smart Set,* where he served as coeditor until 1923, and the *American Mercury,* which he launched with his *Smart Set* colleague George Jean Nathan in 1924. During his fifteen years with the *Smart Set,* he performed an invaluable cultural service much like Poe's at the *Southern Literary Messenger*—he reviewed about two thousand books, giving the mediocre ones a merciless lashing and discovering originality where it would otherwise be overlooked. His *American Mercury* set a tone of carefree sophistication in the 1920s that inspired a generation of college students and spawned dozens of iconoclastic campus magazines. A third literary field of endeavor, after newspapers and magazines, was philology. Mencken, like Samuel Johnson in eighteenth-century London, wrote an original dictionary with thousands of examples of usage and quirky analyses of word histories. Mencken's *American Language* was first published in 1919 and became a lifelong project with expanded editions and two supplements. As journalist, critic, or scholar, Mencken was never far from merriment and assault, creating literary hoaxes and then writing about the gullibility of the American public for being put on or puncturing a big, bloated target such as the South.

But Mencken's relationship with the South was not simply one of enmity. He would occasionally find it convenient to praise the South, particularly the historical and mythic South, and to identify with it: "In so far as I am an American at all, I am a Southerner, and have a high veneration for the character of General Robert E. Lee," he wrote in his 1921 sequel to "Sahara," "The South Begins to Mutter."[20]

Baltimore, his beloved home, also bore an ambivalent relationship with the South. Although Maryland did not secede from the Union, it was below the Mason-Dixon Line and had always had something of southern manners in its genes. At the outbreak of the Civil War, Baltimore citizens were fired upon after they mobbed Massachusetts soldiers marching southward, which inspired a southern editor-to-be to write the poem later adopted as the state song, "Maryland, My Maryland."

> The despot's heel is on thy shore, Maryland!
> His torch is at thy temple door, Maryland!
> Avenge the patriotic gore

That flecked the streets of Baltimore,
And be the battle queen of yore,
Maryland! My Maryland![21]

An old-fashioned southern classicist named Basil Gildersleeve, en-
sconced at Johns Hopkins University in Baltimore, elevated southern letters by inspiring his most influential students (Edwin Mims,
editor of the *South Atlantic Quarterly* at the future Duke University;
William Peterfield Trent, founding editor of the *Sewanee Review*
at the University of the South in Tennessee, and Walter Hines
Page).[22] Mencken, an anti-democratic curmudgeon who fancied
that his ancestors had been among Germany's nobility, wrote that
Baltimore was greatly enriched by the presence, in his youth, of
Virginia aristocrats who arrived in the city after the Civil War
with nothing but "good manners and empty bellies."[23] It was also
southernized by the influx of freed slaves and the beginning of the
Great Migration of blacks from the South. "I am myself somewhat
gifted as a professor of Confederates, white and black, for I have
lived among them all my life," he wrote.[24]

Although "Sahara" was obviously not the work of a true southerner, a few lonely souls scattered around the region recognized
it as a lively expression of their own thoughts and feelings. In
Richmond, for example, three young alumnae of a ladies' seminary decided to start a "little magazine" of cultural criticism called
The Reviewer. They seized on the idea at a party, in a spirit of pure
fun and in reaction to a local newspaper's abolishing the local
book review page. Emily Clark and her two cohorts were young
members of a particular class of educated southern women who,
after the shattering waste of World War I, no longer felt satisfied
with the sheltered life and its magnolia-scented myths. They were
beginning to feel empowered by the success of the suffragette

movement with ratification of the Nineteenth Amendment in August 1920, giving women the vote. And after the Eighteenth Amendment made liquor illegal starting in January 1920, they enjoyed defying the ban at upper-class parties with plenty of booze. Clark, a member of the Colonial Dames and daughter of an Episcopal clergyman, wrote to Mencken to assure him that, despite their "cumbrous inheritance" of things southern, they were "fearfully dissatisfied with Virginia," which is why they had started their magazine. Mencken responded with the first of many encouraging letters to Clark about *The Reviewer.* "The South is beginning to emerge from its old slumber," he wrote her. "You have a capital chance to lead the way."[25] Mencken was also privately writing to encourage other upstart southern magazines, such as the *Double Dealer* in New Orleans and *All's Well* in Fayetteville, Arkansas. Publicly, he began announcing in his newspaper columns and magazine essays that he had discovered such oases in the Sahara, and he had found a stirring of critical thought below the Potomac.[26]

Mencken's perspective began to change, as documented in Fred Hobson's *Serpent in Eden: H. L. Mencken and the South.* Starting around 1921 he began to be drawn into a crusade waged from within enemy territory. He became the master patron of a movement that, as Hobson points out, would evolve into the southern literary renascence of the 1930s. But by then, that movement and Mencken had both veered in other directions. The first stage of any renascence, Mencken believed, requires the dynamiting of the old through new magazines. With the emergence of the new little magazines, the kind of verbal fireworks that Mencken had displayed in "Sahara" was showing up within the old Confederacy. *The Reviewer's* first issue, in February 1921, carried a favorable review of "Sahara." Other lesser-known magazines were launched in the same spirit: *The Southerner* in New Orleans and *Bozart* in

Atlanta. These magazines also published poetry and fiction from a new breed of southern writer—early modernists such as Ellen Glasgow and James Branch Cabell in Virginia, and little-known younger writers such as William Faulkner, Allen Tate, and Robert Penn Warren (all three of whom appeared as poets or critics, not as fiction writers).[27]

In his evolving role in the southern insurgency, Mencken directly shaped the magazines and the movement. He urged that the journals favor new southern writers, not traditional voices such as the conservative Richmond writers Thomas Nelson Page, Henry Sydnor Harrison, and "eminent lady authors of Virginia."[28] Mencken praised the *Double Dealer* for how it "struts a bit and doesn't give a damn for the old gods." But he felt it should be judged, finally, by its success at unearthing authentic regional writers with something to say, and it failed to achieve this goal to Mencken's satisfaction before shutting down in 1926. He found *The Reviewer* far more engaged in nurturing indigenous talent. To that end, he directed writers and ideas toward the Richmond editors.[29]

The Reviewer broke all the rules for how to start and run a magazine. Its editors conducted their business at parties, had no prior experience with publishing, and laughed at their lack of cash. They paid contributors "in fame, not specie," according to a note in the magazine written by the novelist James Branch Cabell. The ghost of Poe's *Southern Literary Messenger* seemed to haunt *The Reviewer,* both as the deadweight of a past that *The Reviewer* rejected and as a kind of living legend it was re-creating. Thomas Nelson Page, the novelist, suggested that the editors make their magazine a revival of the *Messenger* in name as well as spirit, which was not the only advice from the old gentleman that they ignored. A great-grandson of Thomas W. White, the *Messenger's* original owner who had hired and fired Poe, offered to become *The Reviewer's* business manager without pay. The editors accepted—and nearly drove him crazy with their lackadaisical policies. When Cabell—Mencken's favorite southern writer—donated his services as editor for three issues in 1921, Emily Clark thought of Poe. "We believe that in the future," she wrote coyly in her memoir *Innocence Abroad,* "it will be as well remembered that James Branch Cabell edited [*The*] *Reviewer* for three months as that Poe edited the *Southern Literary Messenger* for a much shorter period than is generally known."[30] The national press took notice. *The Reviewer* was "blazing a way through the literary sand flats of the South," wrote the *New York Times.* The *New York Tribune* predicted that future historians would date the start of a "great Southern literary renaissance" to the launch of *The Reviewer.*[31]

Many of the southern writers inspired by Mencken, in *The Reviewer* and elsewhere, were literary amphibians like Mencken himself—part journalists, part creative writers or cultural critics. All felt emboldened by Mencken's leadership, and all suffered some ostracizing on the home front. Julia Collier Harris, who ran the *Enquirer-Sun* in Columbus, Georgia, with her husband, Julian LaRose Harris, wrote social criticism for *The Reviewer* after the playwright Paul Green began editing it in Chapel Hill in December 1924.[32] She and her husband crusaded against antievolution bills and the mistreatment of blacks, regardless of what it cost them in advertising and subscriptions.[33] But she declined Mencken's invitation to write an article critical of Georgia in the *American Mercury* out of concern for local reaction, and Mencken agreed that her "job is in Georgia, and it is a big one." She and her husband, the son of Joel Chandler Harris, were engaged in an editorial crusade against the Ku Klux Klan, which earned them a Pulitzer Prize in 1926. Julian Harris credited their work, and prize, to Mencken, who had "even if unwittingly, made himself the benefactor of the South."[34] Nell Battle Lewis, a Sunday columnist for the *News and Observer* in Raleigh, took up Mencken's cause with a vengeance, calling him "an effective purgative for intellectual inertia and dry-rot complacency and asinine self-glorification and pathetic 'artistic' clap-trap." Mencken, in his tireless reading of southern papers, discovered Lewis and promoted her with *The Reviewer.* Sara Haardt, a writer from Montgomery, Alabama, who would become Mencken's wife in 1930, also began appearing in the magazine thanks to Mencken. Two more female writers Mencken discovered for *The Reviewer* were Frances Newman of Atlanta and Julia Peterkin of South Carolina. Newman would eventually write a satirical novel of southern manners, *The Hard-Boiled Virgin.* Peterkin, writing in isolation on her plantation in South Carolina, published fourteen short stories in *The Reviewer,* largely based on the black Gullah culture of the state's Low Country.[35]

Although poets and short-story writers were part of this movement of social criticism, it was largely made up of journalists. Newspaper editors led the way, even if not directly connected to Mencken. Among these, Hobson includes Louis I. Jaffé of the *Norfolk Virginian-Pilot,* Charlton Wright of the *Columbia (South Carolina) Record,* and W. O. Saunders of the feisty weekly *Elizabeth City (North Carolina) Independent.*[36]

No writer was more forceful or prolific for Mencken's cause than the North Carolina journalist Gerald W. Johnson (1890–1980). Although both of his grandfathers were slave owners and three uncles had fought for the Confederacy, Johnson came from a moderately progressive Southern Baptist family. His progressivism was characteristic of the Tar Heel State. Johnson's father edited a Baptist newspaper, *Charity and Children,* which covered politics as well as religion. The younger Johnson enrolled at Wake

Forest College, a Baptist institution then under the liberal presidency of William Louis Poteat, a German-educated Darwinian who kept the local fundamentalists at bay. The college poured light over a darkening land, as Johnson recalled, and exposed him to a literature professor named Benjamin Sledd who had a gift for "de-educating" students of "the nonsense with which the romantic idolaters of the Lost Cause had stuffed them."[37]

While still in college in 1910, Johnson started a newspaper in his hometown of Thomasville. The following year he joined a larger North Carolina paper, and then in 1913 he began an illustrious ten years at the *Greensboro Daily News.* He ignited like dry tinder when he read Mencken's "Sahara" in 1920, for it gave him leave to express the same wild notions. For example, in 1922, in a student magazine in Chapel Hill, he advised a new poetry society in the state to start by exterminating "the maundering imbecility, the sniffling puerility, the sloppy sentimentality, and bunk, bosh and tommyrot that pass for poetry in North Carolina."[38] Mencken, having read the article, praised Johnson in the *Baltimore Evening Sun.* Johnson in turn wrote Mencken a fan letter. Soon, Mencken was touting Johnson as the best of his southern protégés, passing him on to *The Reviewer* and trying to lure him to the *Baltimore Evening Sun*—which he finally did in 1926.[39]

Johnson's essays were as stylish and slashing as Mencken's, but from a southern perspective. In some ways, they were better than the master's, as Hobson argues.[40] Johnson was able to tap into the deep roots of southern oratory and rhetoric, whether in a serious or a satiric mode. His metaphors were more poetically sensitive than Mencken's bombastic comparisons. And even though Mencken was inexhaustibly erudite, Johnson's references were more learned, Hobson claims. Johnson employed Menckenesque irony in full measure, but he was fairer and his love of the South was more genuine than Mencken's. He knew his Bible well and could thwack the revivalists as one who was steeped in the Baptist faith.

A good illustration of these stylistic differences is the first essay Johnson wrote for *The Reviewer,* a mock argument with "Sahara" that puts forth the notion that Mencken's geographic metaphor was all wrong. "The Sahara, as I am informed and believe, is for the most part a treeless waste, denuded alike of animal and of vegetable life," Johnson wrote. The South is more like a sub-Saharan jungle, he says. "And if Mr. Mencken presumes to doubt it, I invite him to plunge into the trackless waste of the Library of Southern Literature, where a man might wander for years, encountering daily such a profusion of strange and incredible growths as could proceed from none but an enormously rich soil." The South, culturally, is not sterile but altogether too luxuriant, he writes; not the Sahara, but the Congo. Writing by southerners pulses with the hot blood of emotionalism and a strange obsession with sound over sense, he says. The reason white southerners express themselves this way, he continues, is because of their proximity to "the most potent personality on the continent"—the African American. He predicts that a new southern literature, once it overthrows the false sonorousness of the old school, will also be loud and outlandish, like jazz, "the flaming colors of the jungle in its eyes."[41]

In the Roaring Twenties, America was ready for Mencken, and the South was ready for its own minor rebellion. Nationally, as William Manchester notes in a biography of Mencken, the young doughboys returning from World War I were fed up with the paranoid patriotism of the Palmer raids, the "don't" of Anthony Comstock, and the "dry-as-dust fifth-carbon-copy Ralph Waldo Emersons." Mencken was the literary expression of their backlash against the elders.[42] In the South, the intellectual ground was prepared for its own liberalism that scoffed at Bible-thumpers, the Anti-Saloon League, the United Daughters of the Confederacy, and the Ku Klux Klan. This was the Mencken club of Gerald W. Johnson and the other writers filling the pages of *The Reviewer.* Two books from the period fleshed out an intellectual history of this uprising—one by Edwin Mims, an English professor then at Vanderbilt, and the other by Virginius Dabney, a promising young newspaper journalist in Richmond.

Mims, whose old-fashioned teaching style was remembered fondly in Ralph McGill's memoir, published *The Advancing South* in 1926 "to reveal and interpret the individuals, institutions, and organizations that are now carrying on a veritable war of liberation in the Southern States." Mims noted the growing number of southern newspapers willing to take a stand apart from the Solid South's Democratic Party machinery. He cited the *Nashville Banner, Columbia State, Macon Telegraph, Chattanooga Times,* and *Asheville Citizen.* He noted that Pulitzer Prizes were awarded to the *Memphis Commercial Appeal* in 1923 for its exposure of the Klan and to the *Charleston (South Carolina) News and Courier* in 1925 for an editorial lamenting the South's lack of political ideas.[43] Mims was a Victorian-style professor who embraced modernity with exuberance, as some of his chapter titles suggest: "From Romance to Realism" (new writers), "The Revolt Against Chivalry" (the new southern woman), "The Ebbing Tide of Colour" (new cross-racial councils such as Will W. Alexander's Commission on Interracial Cooperation), and "Ecclesiastics and Prophets" (southern liberals like William L. Poteat who could mediate between religious fundamentalists and agnostic modernists). Mims was perhaps overly optimistic about how smoothly the South could update its best-known features. Mencken complained that Mims should have more vigorously attacked the contemporary South.[44]

Dabney was less sanguine in his 1932 book covering a broader sweep of history, *Liberalism in the South.* The son of a prominent history professor at the University of Virginia, Dabney was a Mencken disciple who was feeling restless as a reporter at the *Richmond News Leader* and *Times Dispatch* in the 1920s. He was freelancing articles about Virginia for Mencken's *American Mercury* and the *Baltimore Evening Sun,* though Mencken had to coach the serious-minded Dabney to "let some irony and some humor" into his writing.[45] Louis I. Jaffé, the Pulitzer Prize–winning editor in Norfolk whom Dabney trusted for guidance, told him to remain at the paper while he wrote the book as his "passport to a better job in the North."[46] In *Liberalism in the South,* Dabney finds the liberal tradition rooted in Jefferson, considers the Civil War an aberration brought on by hotheads, and views the current liberal uprising as a return to the true and honorable South. He condemns Democratic Party politics of the South not only for maintaining a one-party system but also for being reactionary. He notes that southern Democrats invoke states' rights when it serves their interests but give up liberty when it comes to Prohibition, the poll tax and other voting restrictions, and the authority of the clergy. Dabney bemoans the rabble-rousers of the Democratic Party who look to "the lower class whites" for support and who rejected the party's presidential candidate of 1928 on account of his being Roman Catholic. The southern reactionaries, in his view, were not worthy of the aristocratic Jefferson, who happened to be a distant relative of Dabney.[47]

Religion in the South was an easy target for Mencken's southern disciples, up to a point. But Mencken took far more latitude than did his disciples in attacking religion. His position was "heathen," as he liked to call it, a stance that was not an option for southern newspaper journalists like Dabney, Johnson, or the Harrises. Mencken came to his atheism early through the writings of two European freethinkers, the playwright George Bernard Shaw and the philosopher Friedrich Nietzsche. Mencken's first two books were on Shaw's plays (*George Bernard Shaw: His Plays,* 1905) and Nietzsche (*The Philosophy of Nietzsche,* 1908). Liberal journalists in the South tended to keep their faith private, which was easy enough for an old-line Episcopal Jeffersonian like Dabney, or literary, as Johnson managed to do with his stirring biblical references and images. They followed Mencken's lead in thrashing the backwoods revivalists, know-nothing biblical literalists, and blue law puritans. Dabney, for example, wrote many columns attacking the "Methodist Pope" of Virginia, James Cannon, and eventually published a biography, *Dry Messiah: The Life of Bishop Cannon* (1949), criticizing the bishop's role in state politics. But Mencken's followers never attacked faith in God. The sort of atheistic sneering that a Smith College professor slipped into the Chapel Hill journal *Social Forces* in January 1925 almost killed the journal.[48] "In the South heresy is still heresy with the vast majority of people," wrote one of the more liberal divines in 1935. "This is to say that the religious South exhibits a more homogenous quality than any other section."[49]

The liberal critique of fundamentalism in the South reached a theatrical climax in a sweltering courtroom in Dayton, Tennessee, in July 1925. A young teacher named John T. Scopes was tried for teaching in a public school biology class Charles Darwin's theory of natural selection, in violation of a fresh-minted Tennessee law and contrary to the Genesis account of creation. Scopes was not exactly the ostracized, truth-seeking young Galileo portrayed in the fictionalized version—the play and movie *Inherit the Wind.* Historical interpretations vary, but he was apparently playing a cooperative and friendly role in an event put on by local civic boosters, the American Civil Liberties Union (ACLU), and the *Baltimore Evening Sun*. It was, in a way, the world's first media event and the "trial of the century." It drew more than one hundred reporters and Teletype operators from throughout the United States and Europe and featured the first live radio broadcast from a courtroom—by WGN, the *Chicago Tribune's* station. Mencken was not only the most famous of the reporters; he dominated the coverage. This was his show, as Scopes put it.[50] While visiting the novelist Cabell in Richmond earlier that year, Mencken had met with the lawyer Clarence Darrow, renowned for defending controversial causes, and persuaded him to represent Scopes without cost. Mencken even suggested legal strategies (he would later claim that these were mapped out in his house in Baltimore) and committed his newspaper to provide bail for Scopes.[51]

All eyes were on Dayton as the trial crystallized deep conflicts that were dividing social classes, generations, and worldviews in the America of the 1920s. The South, being the slower, poorer, and more rural "other" America, brought these conflicts into high relief. Darwin's theory of the descent of man had long blazed its intellectual tracks through the educated classes of Great Britain and the United States. What was on trial in Tennessee in 1925 were the unseen forces that Darwin's theory symbolized—the power of science to chip away at religious faith and to trump parental control in tax-supported classrooms, as well as the attitude of superiority imputed to urban elites and advocates of social progress. At root, it was about the conflict of traditional values against modernity, with traditional values having their strongest hold in the rural South.

Galvanizing this conflict was the famous silver-tongued orator from Nebraska, William Jennings Bryan, who rushed to Dayton to lead the prosecution of Scopes as a grand finale to his quixotic political career. Bryan, who had three times been the unsuccessful Democratic candidate for president, embodied the traditional values of the common folk of the rural South. He had been their Populist Party candidate in 1896, with Georgia firebrand Tom Watson as his running mate. (In that hopelessly muddled campaign, Bryan was also the Democratic Party nominee with a different running mate, and he carried the South as such.) He had stood for the little guy against the big trusts, for free silver against the gold standard, for peace against U.S. imperialism, and for Prohibition. Now, at age sixty-five, Bryan believed that defending a literal interpretation of Genesis against naturalistic science would be his finest hour in fighting back the evils of the modern world. Mencken was delighted. He sensed an opportunity to make Bryan a buffoon and thus lay waste the religious bigotry, ignorance, superstition, and hatred he believed were embodied in Tennessee's antievolution law. He urged Darrow to concentrate on Bryan, not Scopes. "Nobody gives a damn about that yap schoolteacher," he said. "The thing to do is make a fool out of Bryan."[52]

What Mencken did not fully grasp was sectional resentment. The conflicts over religion, education, science, and morality that played out in the Rhea County Courthouse were merely interesting to the curious shopkeepers and farmers who came to the trial for entertainment. They obviously favored Bryan, but they cheered wildly for an ACLU lawyer's best speech. They were not the imbeciles Mencken had assumed. Locals had a book club and knew of Mencken because they had read his *American Mercury*. Some stood on either side of the evolution dispute, and to Mencken's surprise the two camps were indistinguishable and on the best of terms. A Dayton drugstore, where local boosters had decided to persuade Scopes to test the law, displayed a large banner boasting WHERE IT ALL STARTED. The town was not nearly as weird or devout as were the colorful evangelists whom the trial attracted from the distant hollows. But Mencken and the nonsouthern press wanted to see extremes. They "fed upon a thousand different ideas of the south," the *Chattanooga News* complained. Locals obliged the visitors' appetites. A young female reporter with the *Chattanooga News* led Mencken and an *Evening Sun* colleague to a Holy Roller meeting in a cornfield outside of town. Mencken's long report in the *Evening Sun* was devastating comedy, later published in *Prejudices— Fifth Series* as "The Hills of Zion." He covered the trial with a predatory gusto, taking the best views atop desks or slouching in a corner with the *Science Services* reporter, mopping his eager face of sweat, scooping the other reporters, and setting a tone of mockery. As Mencken's widely syndicated dispatches came back to Dayton from Baltimore in the airplane-carried editions at the local drugstore, the local citizenry began to feel their bumptious guest was being rude. It was the worst publicity they could get, one businessman complained. Locals did not like being quoted phonetically or called morons. Even Scopes did not approve of Mencken's coverage, because those covered were his friends. The insult was not so much to their religion or education level. It was to their being southern and judged by outsiders. Ministers in southern pulpits, the governor of Tennessee, and newspapers across the South echoed the same complaint.[53]

By the end, what had started as a publicity stunt for Dayton and high comedy for Mencken was open to more troubling interpretations. Mencken went back to Baltimore early, before Darrow's brilliant surprise of putting Bryan on the stand as an expert on the Bible. The princely journalist denied he was run out of town by a mob but admitted he was disappointed by what he had witnessed. "I set out laughing and returned shivering," he said. "The Fundamentalists are on us!"[54] Indeed, several other southern states defiantly began to pursue their own antievolution laws.[55]

Julian Harris, who covered the trial for his paper in Georgia, campaigned vigorously against such a law in his state, and according to Mencken, he successfully stopped it.[56] Mencken's bitter turn after he left Dayton colored the Bryan obituary he wrote several days afterward. The stress and heat had triggered Bryan's death, following his disappointment with being made a fool and having Scopes fined a mere $100 (paid by Mencken's paper). The obituary was insightful but meaner than typical Mencken meanness. What motivated Bryan, he wrote, was not religion but hatred, burning pathetically for his enemies, and hatred of all learning, beauty, and nobility. "He was a peasant come home to the dung-pile. Imagine a gentleman, and you have everything that he was not." The uproar over this obituary was so immediate that Mencken had time to edit the meanest words out of a late edition. But the *Evening Sun* turned to Gerald Johnson to write a more sympathetic piece on Bryan for balance.[57]

Another southerner who witnessed the trial, the sociology professor Howard Odum, lamented that the trial was more tragedy than comedy. He cautioned his fellow social scientists against taking Mencken's side and labeling the other group ignorant. "The difference between the two groups is not intelligence, but vast, yawning distance." Odum was the leader of an emerging movement of scholars based in Chapel Hill who would become known as the regionalists, writers engaged in a respectful study of southern folkways through Odum's journal *Social Forces*. Writing in that journal after he attended the *Scopes* trial, Odum worried that Bryan, Darrow, and Mencken had inflamed a latent misunderstanding between the nation's fundamentalist majority and the "professional folk" of more experience into outright battle. An inveterate quantifier, Odum estimated that the trial had become the number-one topic for some 2,310 daily newspapers, 13,267 weeklies, and 392 quarterlies, not to mention the pulpits in 237,945 churches. What troubled him was the rhetoric of the discourse: the basic conflict between these two groups of Americans had been turned into a "duel to the death" before social scientists had any real understanding of either group.[58]

Meanwhile in Nashville, on the other side of the Appalachian range from Chapel Hill, Vanderbilt University was home to a more literary group that had been publishing a journal concentrating on poetry in the New Criticism vein. The *Fugitive,* which began in 1922, carried verse and criticism from the southern poets Allen Tate, John Crowe Ransom, Robert Penn Warren, and Donald Davidson.[59] Most of these bohemian southerners read and admired Mencken's literary criticism. Davidson, the book editor for the *Nashville Tennessean,* sent his book-review pages from that newspaper to Mencken. Tate and Davidson, in their correspondence in the early 1920s, referred often to Mencken in a positive light.[60]

But the *Scopes* trial changed everything. The so-called Fugitives were indignant at the depiction of their region as a land of yokels and religious fanatics. They ceased publication of the *Fugitive* and began reexamining their understanding of the South. The trial, "with its jeering accompaniment of large-scale mockery directed against Tennessee and the South," hit these poets like a fire alarm, Davidson said. "It was not the sole cause of change, but from about that time Ransom, Tate, Warren, and I began to remember and haul up for consideration the assumptions that, as members of the Fugitive group, we had not much bothered to examine."[61] Although they were in no way biblical fundamentalists, they believed that religion in the South signified a noble resistance to certain destructive forces of modernity. For them, religion, myth, poetry, and community all supported a robust alternative in southern life.

They began to see attacks on the South in the national press as not only irritating, but dangerous—a propaganda campaign that broke what Davidson called the "Gentleman's Agreement" of 1876 running from Henry Grady to World War I. Mencken, to their new thinking, was the noisiest expression of this campaign. "We rubbed our eyes and looked around in astonishment and apprehension," Davidson wrote. "Was it possible that nobody in the South knew how to reply to a vulgar rhetorician like H. L. Mencken?" On a high intellectual level, this scholarly group began to formulate a defense of the South quite different from Odum's call for a program of sociology and uplift. The Vanderbilt group began to view the South as a last bastion of old European civilization against corporate capitalism, atheism, industrialism, and social science. They chose one word to sum up the nature of the South that explained the myriad ways it was in conflict with these modern elements: *agrarian*. The result of their ruminations was a book of twelve essays published in 1930 called *I'll Take My Stand*.[62]

The Fugitive-Agrarians had driven a wedge into the Mencken insurgency, and the reaction rumbled across the South. Odum found the book elegant and artistic but out of touch with the real South—"as a fact and not as an ideal."[63] The editors of the *Sewanee Review* and the *Virginia Quarterly Review* debated representatives of the Vanderbilt group in a series of public performances around the region. The debate in Richmond, sponsored by the *Times Dispatch* and attended by more than three thousand citizens, occasioned several articles by Dabney, who sympathized with the Agrarians' dislike of commercialism but felt that their back-to-the-land dream would be a "disastrous experiment."[64]

Mencken allowed that the book deserved respect and showed "a free and bold spirit." But he disagreed with its romantic rejection of industrialism. Instead of denying the inevitability of the factory, Mencken said, the South should "seize industrialism by the horns, and try to shake some measure of justice and decency out of it." The South will get nowhere, he said, "following sufferers from nostalgic vapors; its deliverance lies in the hands of such realistic and indomitable fellows as, say, Julian Harris, Gerald W. Johnson and Grover C. Hall Sr."[65] Johnson, for his part, felt that the nostalgia of the Fugitive-Agrarians came out of books by Joel Chandler Harris and Thomas Nelson Page, and blinded them to the reality of race-baiting demagogues and disease-ridden farms in the actual modern South. "Have they been completely oblivious to the Vardamans, the Bleases, the Heflins, the Tom Watsons, who are the delight of Southern agrarianism?" wrote Johnson in a review of four books on the South for the *Virginia Quarterly Review.* "Are they unaware of pellagra and hookworm, two flowers of Southern agrarianism?"[66]

For most of Mencken's liberal followers in the South, the question had become how to "seize industrialism by the horns." The bloody strikes of 1929 in the North Carolina textile cities of Gastonia and Marion were still fresh in the mind of Johnson when he wrote another critique of *I'll Take My Stand,* in *Harper's.* Underpaid and overworked, the southern millworkers were violently put down when they sought to unionize. Several strikers and a police chief were killed, but only strikers were prosecuted. Johnson saw in Marion and Gastonia the shame of unpunished murder and free opinion suppressed. For fifty years, the South had found excuses for every ill and outrage in blaming the Civil War and Reconstruction. Now the South had "no more excuses." Johnson admitted he disliked the brash millionaires, the fouled land, and the frantic tempo that industrialism was bringing to the South. But he welcomed the money it brought for universities like Duke and the University of North Carolina, for paved roads, reduced illiteracy, state boards of health, and state prison reform. His call for facts over emotion, for reform over nostalgia, signaled a new role that a critical, independent press could play in the troubled South of the 1930s.

But the southern press was ill prepared to address "the concrete evils and workable remedies" that Mencken saw in 1931. Most of the 527 daily newspapers in the fourteen southeastern states from Maryland to Texas (including Kentucky) were uncritical supporters of the sacred cows of the New South: industrial development, real estate, banking, civic boosterism, and the whites-only state Democratic parties. A young journalism professor at Mercer University in Georgia, John D. Allen, was selected by the University of North Carolina Press to write a critical assessment of southern journalism in 1933.[67] Allen's laconic report describes an industry in which the typical publisher "has no perverse impulse to disturb his patrons by transgressing the bounds of propriety." Like newspapers in other regions, he reports, the average southern newspaper flatters its community by mirroring local prejudices and beliefs and "deviates scarcely at all from the stereotypes and formulas of journalism." He divided the southern press into three types. The largest group, typical of perhaps 75 percent of the dailies, applauded uncritically the proliferation of textile mills that were drawing workers off the farms and into mill towns. The *Atlanta Constitution,* which with the *Charlotte Observer* in North Carolina was the most advanced of such probusiness organs according to Allen, insisted that the new mills and their villages were a great benefit for thousands of these transplanted families.[68] The *Constitution* argued that cheaper power and lower wages were the natural endowments of a southern climate, so northern complaints about working conditions "should be made to God and not to the southern industrialists and workers."[69] A second group, about 18 percent of the dailies, reflected the old agrarian culture. Editors of these papers were

"backward-turning" conservatives and "in a bad sense provincial."
But Allen accords them some of the virtues of nineteenth-century
southern editors—dignity, integrity, and a paternalistic sense of ob-
ligation to their "inferiors." The third and tiniest group comprised
young independent-minded editors and their papers, a group that
viewed the conservative agrarian-aristocratic newspapers as "irrelevant farce" and the dominant probusiness newspapers as "moral
prostitution." The *Virginian-Pilot* of Louis Jaffé exemplified this
type. Other "liberal" papers in this group were less consistent. Examples of this sometimes-liberal type, according to Allen, were
the *Raleigh News and Observer, Richmond Times-Dispatch, Columbus (Georgia) Enquirer-Sun, Charleston News and Courier, Louisville
Courier-Journal,* and *Macon Telegraph.*[70] Allen's verdict, overall, was
despairing. "The great majority of southern newspapers are smug
class organs," he wrote, "standardized, often unfair in the presenting of news, and worse than useless as interpreters of the present
scene or as guides of the future."[71]

At the same time, newspapers in the South were losing much
of the personality that editors were once able to imprint on them.
They had become businesses like any other, and more like newspapers elsewhere. Power had shifted to the publishers and business
managers, though sometimes these individuals were also editors.
The publishers and owners of thirteen of these newspapers had
organized into the Southern Newspaper Publishers Association
(SNPA) in 1903, in Atlanta, to advance the cause of profitable
growth for the region's newspaper industry. Expanding rapidly
with the spread of telephones and advent of the automobile, and
meeting annually in such plush watering holes as the Grove Park
Inn in Asheville or the Greenbrier in White Sulfur Springs, West
Virginia, the SNPA helped modernized the news business in the
South. It pursued the viability of southern spruce pine for news-

print and the establishment of a southern paper mill. Its committees reformed advertising policies that had given too much
privilege to quack medicines, fought for lower second-class postal
rates, and tempered the publishers' antiunion biases with guide-
lines for relatively genteel relations toward unionized typesetters.
Too often, the SNPA saw its larger business interests as exactly the
same as those of the textile, power, and other industries. Thus, in
1928, the *Nashville Tennessean's* publisher proposed that the organization launch a $300,000 publicity campaign in cooperation with
southern railroads and publicity agencies promoting economic
development in the South. The SNPA might have approved had
not one of the old stalwarts of personal journalism, Major Edward
Bushrod Stahlman, appeared before the assembly in a wheelchair
like a long-haired ghost from the 1880s (when he had first taken
over the *Nashville Banner*). "The Major" warned against getting in
bed with other businesses, especially profit-greedy power trusts.
He reminded them that the Federal Trade Commission had recently exposed the publicity agents of power companies who were
slipping their propaganda into some newspapers nationally.[72]

The following year, the International Paper and Power Company went further by gaining control, through a front, of the *Columbia (South Carolina) Record,* the *Spartanburg (South Carolina)
Herald and Journal,* and the *Augusta (Georgia) Chronicle.* The company's low-interest "loan" to the sham owners bought it guaran-
teed customers for its newsprint, at those three papers, and many
suspected it also bought a mouthpiece for its power interests.
When the SNPA met later that year, in 1929, the International
Paper and Power Company president waited in the lobby of the
Grove Park Inn to make his case before the publishers. But he was
never invited in. Instead, the publisher of the *Shreveport (Louisiana)
Times* won unanimous approval of an angry resolution saying the

purchase of newspapers by power or paper company interests "is contrary to sound public policy and to sound journalistic policy and is a menace to a free press and free institutions of these United States."[73]

Still, southern newspapers proved reliable boosters of their own cities, even in the diminishing number of cities with competing papers. There were exceptions to this, such as an exposé of municipal corruption that won a public service Pulitzer Prize in 1931 for the *Atlanta Constitution.* More typical was New Orleans, where the triumvirate of the *Times-Picayune, Item-Tribune,* and *State,* despite their rivalry, could be counted on to help the New Orleans Association of Commerce control bad news like a case of bubonic plague or a controversial port policy. John M. Barry, in his history of the Great Mississippi Flood of 1927, *Rising Tide,* recounts how the three editors of these papers met in a time of panic as members of a Safe River Committee to "avoid . . . alarming information" as the river rose to dangerous levels. When the flood swept away hundreds of shacks of "river rat" dwellers on April 13, nothing appeared in the papers. When the local U.S. Weather Bureau issued flood bulletins, the papers did not run them. At one point, James M. Thomson, editor of the *Item-Tribune,* suggested the shocking idea of illegally dynamiting the levee elsewhere, sacrificing the livelihoods of thousands of people to save New Orleans. Eventually, with bankers worried about financial ruin, the levee was indeed dynamited and neighbors downriver washed away— unnecessarily for New Orleans, it turned out.[74]

Mencken's effect on the best southern journalists of the 1920s was mainly about style—a fresh literary and critical pose. It was a style that put on aristocratic airs and a bohemian slouch simultaneously, while also incinerating all the conventional courtesies that kept the South from seeing itself. It was both smart and smart-alecky. It drew on literary traditions and trashed them. Mencken, in 1909, lamented the effect on southern writers of that "ignorant and pretentious man" Edgar Allan Poe. "The spell of Poe reveals itself in a liking for ponderous and sonorous words ... a vast excess of parts of speech, a surfeit of polysyllables, an appalling flapping of wings." Some would say this describes Mencken's writing at its most outrageous, and indeed he confessed he was infected by the loathsome "Southern malady" or "bacilli" of Poe.[75] Mencken also followed Poe's slashing style of literary criticism. Johnson called this "mule-skinning," adding William Hazlitt's reviews to the examples of Poe and Mencken. "All three were such superb craftsmen that anything they wrote has a certain interest, if only for the workmanship," Johnson wrote. "But their blasting arouses no emotion today save a mild wonder that such splendid ammunition was wasted on such piffling targets."[76]

SIX

THE MIND OF THE SOUTH MEETS THE MOVEMENT

The South was a puzzle to some of its more sensitive souls, and to none more so than Wilbur Joseph Cash (1900–1941) of Boiling Springs, North Carolina. Cash, the son of a Southern Baptist sock-factory superintendent, was driven to ponder his environment so deeply that it hurt him. A plump, balding figure in the dingy city room of the *Charlotte News,* he was preoccupied with trying to figure out the conundrum of the South and generally willing to talk out his ideas with anyone willing to listen. Cash read books greedily from early on, earning his nickname "Sleepy" when he fell off a porch while dozing under a book. He moved from romance and history to the great dissidents of past and present—Michel Montaigne, John Stuart Mill, Voltaire, François Rabelais, Edward Gibbon, William Hazlitt, and to his deep delight, H. L. Mencken. Underneath his churning intellect lay physical and psychological vulnerabilities—a lifelong curse called "neurasthenia" at the time, which seems to have been a combination of hyperthyroidism, depression, hypochondria, and a choking sensation.[1]

The puzzle that obsessed Cash was one that was becoming sharply pertinent in the 1930s, when the South's continuing problems of ignorance, disease, race hatred, poverty, and low-wage industry frustrated so many would-be reformers. Blaming the Civil War and Reconstruction was less persuasive as time rolled on. If the South had finally rejoined the nation, why did it remain, according to a presidential commission in 1938, the nation's number-one economic problem?[2] Why were the southern states consistently at the bottom of the rankings that Mencken devised for a series in *American Mercury* in the early 1930s called "The Worst American State"? (Categories ranged from "tangible property per capita" to "farms employing tractors" to "telephones.") There were really several puzzles wrapped up here. Why was the antiblack feeling among whites not only persistent and total but also still given to grotesque violence? Why did poor whites fail to fight for their own economic interests through labor organizing and voter campaigns? Why was the white South so "solid" politically? Why was it so romantic, religious, and unable to address its problems realistically?

One of the puzzles of the South before World War II—why such independent, wordy, or at least loudmouthed people could be so homogenous in their thinking—seemed to stultify, in particular, the theory of a free press in a democratic American society. According to this basic American theory, dissent, discussion, and outsiders' viewpoints were the public's essential means of checking power and moving forward. Why was dissent from within the South considered heresy and criticism from outsiders an insult?

Cash, who was one of those solitary southern writers in direct contact with Mencken in Baltimore, sought a modern theory or theories to make sense of the puzzles. He read widely in sociology, drawing on such works as Broadus Mitchell's 1921 classic *The Rise of Cotton Mills in the South* and, at one point, desperately running out of postage for scholarly books borrowed from the university library at Chapel Hill.[3] Cash disdained the Fugitive-Agrarians at Vanderbilt and admired the regionalists at Chapel Hill, but he was not satisfied with the regionalists' sociological answers or with their specialized terminology.[4] Cash was a thinker, but his true originality lay in his prose style. He was a literary craftsman of the highest order, with the music of southern romanticism and the drumming of southern oratory in his veins. For most of his life he dreamed of publishing literary novels. He secretly produced manuscripts of fiction in his youth and pitched various ideas to the Guggenheim Foundation for travel in connection with novel writing. At one point, he sketched out an idea for a literary biography of Lafcadio Hearn, retracing Hearn's wanderings from Europe to New Orleans to delineate "the anatomy of a Romantic." As a stylist, Mencken was his model, at least in the beginning.[5]

So, with a blend of Mencken's throat slashing, Howard Odum's sociology, and Thomas Wolfe's prose style (if Wolfe had been the self-editing perfectionist Cash was), the sad, bookish writer chiseled away on his theory of the South. Early on, bolstered by readings in Sigmund Freud, Cash was determined to lodge his theory in the South's mentalité, as the rising *Annales* school of French historians would call it. The "mind" of the South, to Cash, meant not intellectual history but the psyche of an entire people—or at least of the people he projected from the Babbitts and "lintheads" he knew and loved (or hated) from the Piedmont uplands of the Carolinas.

Cash worked out his thinking by freelance writing. His major vehicle for this was the *American Mercury,* beginning with an article in the July 1929 issue called "Jehovah of the Tar Heels." It was what his first biographer, Joseph L. Morrison, called a "gorgeous and virtuoso writing display" and a later biographer, Bruce Clayton, called "brilliant pyrotechnics."[6] The article was on the anti-Catholic demagogue senator Furifold M. Simmons. By now, Cash had returned from a sabbatical in Europe and had left the *Charlotte News* for the lighter work of a semiweekly in Shelby, North Carolina. He was thrilled to receive a $200 check signed by Mencken himself.[7] After that, Mencken published one article after another from Cash in the *American Mercury*. In October 1929, the magazine ran one titled "The Mind of the South," which laid out the writer's trademark themes of the South's raw individualism, foggy-headed nostalgia, plantation-style industrialism, and pinched religious piety. The article slashed away at the South with such ruthless gusto that nearly fifty editorials in southern newspapers squalled in protest. The article also brought Cash an invitation from Knopf, the New York publishing house that shared offices with the *American Mercury,* to write a book. Over the next five years Cash continued to refine his ideas in the *American Mercury,* with Odum's counsel and Mencken's approval and editing: "War in the South," a sympathetic account of the Gastonia strike in February 1930; "Paladin of the Drys," an ironic sainting of Senator Cameron Morrison, a Charlotte prohibitionist in October 1931; "Close View of a Calvinist Lhasa," on the dominant business and religious ethos of Charlotte in April 1933; "Buck Duke's University," on the anti-intellectual influence at Duke University of its rough-hewn founder in September 1933; and "Holy Men Muff a Chance," a sarcastic sneer at preachers for not profiting more from the Depression in January 1934. At this point, Mencken, who was losing his zest for some of his old battles, gave up editing the *American Mercury.* Cash, around the same time, began freeing himself from the excesses of Mencken's rhetoric. He reined in his prose and clarified his hypotheses.

"Genesis of the Southern Cracker," his next piece in the *American Mercury* in May 1935, unveiled a key insight in a mere sixteen paragraphs. It was this: "The cracker," or poor white, was not the descendant of weak bloodlines, as Mencken had argued, for he came from the same Scots-Irish and Anglo-Saxon stock as most of the planters. Rather, he was the weaker brother driven to the hills and swamps by the nouveau planter's rapacious gobbling up of land for cotton. After fighting bravely in the Civil War, typically loyal to his captain and a static economic order, worsening poverty forced the poor white to replace independent farming with cash-crop cotton, this time on land even less suited for it than was the Low Country. Such planting required the use of fertilizer at usurious rates that turned the baffled cracker into a pathetic cropper and tenant. Still, the poor white thought of the planter, the Confederate captain's son, as his friend, an error helped by the boss's "genial, expansive, hand-on-the-shoulder manner which would be ideally calculated to draw the sting from the rising contempt for the cracker." No matter how low he fell, or how much he felt that contempt, he retained the bond of race with the boss— "that other all-dwarfing distinction between the white man and the black."[8]

The worse things got for the poor white, the more violently he would direct his bitterness at the black. Instead of developing class consciousness, Cash writes, he remained a sometimes hedonistic, sometimes fanatically religious, sometimes deadly individualist, "at his worst a dangerous neurotic, a hair-trigger killer, a man-burner, a pig quite capable of incest." The poor white's hatred of black, perversely, was tied up with his maintaining a sense of kinship with the white boss, who according to an interpretation Cash accepted, had developed the cotton mill as a sincere act of charity for his poor white brother. This brotherly feeling Cash would later designate as the "proto-Dorian" bond or convention, referring to the esprit de corps of ancient Spartan soldiers.

Cash's next freelance article, "The Reign of the Commonplace," published in the fall 1936 issue of the magazine Lillian Smith coedited, *Pseudopodia,* elaborated on a second key insight. Here he calls this second axiom "the savage ideal," which is the enforcement of conventional thinking by common courtesies or, if necessary, by violence. The excerpt was almost verbatim as it would appear in Cash's book five years later in a section called "Of the Frontier the Yankee Made," on how the South's destitution from 1865 to 1895 served to harden rather than overturn the more primitive impulses established in the frontier South before the Civil War: "Any questioning or doubting of the South in any respect (and in this atmosphere of boiling emotion merely to stand aloof a little was *ipso facto* to be convicted of such questioning and doubting) was inevitably felt by each loyal Southerner as a questioning and doubting of his immediate ego."[9]

The book *The Mind of the South* was a staggering achievement, but the intellectual and literary challenge was not the only reason that twelve miserable years stretched between the invitation from Knopf in 1929 and the publication in 1941. Cash's health problems, some of them probably real, his perfectionism, and his poverty combined to override Knopf's deadlines year after year. Soon after getting the big assignment, he was hospitalized in Charlotte for several months with nervous exhaustion and ordered to avoid certain unsettling activities, such as reading and writing.[10] In the darkest years of the 1930s, crammed back in his parents' home in Boiling Springs with jobless siblings, he banged away at his book in a frigid office behind the post office. He asked a friend in New York for money for typing paper. He returned to the *Charlotte News,* first as a contributing book reviewer, then in 1937 as an editorial writer. Warning readers about the rise of Adolf Hitler produced some strong newspaper columns, but this too became a debilitating obsession. His writer's block was, in part, a growing feeling that, in getting to the bottom of the South's psychic puzzle, he saw no way out. "I have never been able to approach the task of continuing it without extreme depression and dislike," he admitted to Alfred Knopf.[11]

Yet he finally completed the work, all 160,000 words, on July 27, 1940, and saw it published the following February, to nearly universal acclaim.[12] Southern newspapers pronounced the book brilliant, with surprisingly few complaints, "whooping it up almost to a man," as Cash's new wife Mary Bagley Ross Cash put it. The national reviews were even more fawning, bowled over by what seemed, finally, the right way to understand the wild and woolly South. "Anything written about the South henceforth must start where he leaves off," *Time* magazine proclaimed.[13] Most reviewers recognized that *The Mind of the South* was an odd sort of history, more a work of art than of scholarship, authorized by the writer's imagination. The writing was occasionally rhapsodic but also gently intimate—guiding the reader along with phrases like, "Perhaps the reader is thinking . . ." or, "Nor have we done yet"— and mixing lapidary prose with earthy idioms. It was no longer Mencken's echo but a distinctly southern voice compounded of love and despair for his region, of tradition and modernity. Yet the ideas in Cash's analysis had more lasting impact than the book's literary style. A generation later, young foot soldiers going into Alabama and Mississippi for the civil rights movement carried *The Mind of the South* in their knapsacks as a field guide.[14] Journalists and historians of the region would continue to reflect on the book for decades. In 1965, the *Greensboro Daily News* associate editor Ed Yoder allowed that Cash had deepened regional self-consciousness not only for writers but also for the common country boy with greased hair and a hot rod. George Wallace, then governor of Alabama, understood how to play to Cash's proto-Dorian convention with poor whites.[15] In 1978, the book was still eliciting serious analysis in the *Journal of Southern History* in an article by southern historian Michael O'Brien. "Historians are notoriously severe toward journalists, but Cash has proved an exception," he wrote. "Many of his ideas, and even more of his striking phrases, have passed into common usage."[16] On the fiftieth anniversary of the book's publication, Cash's alma mater, Wake Forest University, held a symposium on *The Mind of the South* that drew hundreds of people to hear some dozen scholars wrestle with the continuing legacy.[17]

When the book was first published, the civil rights protests for racial equality were still some fifteen years away. But any analysis of how that social movement came into focus and how the press covered it should begin at least as early as 1941, when certain fateful wheels and levers began to rumble and creak below the public's attention.[18] World War II brought defense-dollar prosperity and a new mobility to the South. Although black southerners did not benefit appreciably, the changes stirred their aspirations. They took pride in their sons' fighting in all-black units against the fascists and Nazis of Europe. Black leaders pushed harder for rights, such as an end to segregation in the military and a fair portion of military contracts. To avoid a march on Washington planned by A. Philip Randolph of the Brotherhood of Sleeping Car Porters, President Franklin Roosevelt signed an executive order banning discrimination in defense work. Some half dozen weekly black newspapers stoked the hopes of southern blacks by covering such developments.[19] Metro daily newspapers in the South and elsewhere, most of them without a single black reporter, seemed oblivious to these stirrings. A few white liberal editors were paying attention. But these editors, who had crusaded against lynching, the Klan, and discrimination against "the Negro," were disturbed by what they saw as a rising black militancy. Virginius Dabney, in the *Saturday Review,* worried that "drastic revolution overnight" would only invite violence and bitterness.[20] Mark Ethridge, the liberal publisher of the *Louisville Courier-Journal,* put a brake on black aspirations when Roosevelt named him head of the board to carry out the antidiscrimination executive order, the Fair Employment Practices Committee. At a hearing in Birmingham, Alabama, in June 1942, Ethridge asserted that no armored power in the world, Axis or Allied, "could now force the Southern white people to the abandonment of the principle of social segregation."[21] The historian John Kneebone contends that white liberal journalists reacted this way because their liberalism always assumed that whites would control the pace and strategy of progress in race relations.[22] They were also afraid of what poor whites, aroused, might do if change came too quickly.

"I have been for a number of years studying and thinking about the problems of the South," the president of the University of Texas wrote Cash, inviting him to give the commencement address in Austin on June 2, 1941. "But in all of my reading I have not found any analysis that I think is so courageously penetrating and so fundamentally sound as the analysis which you have given."[23] Cash spoke at that commencement, ditching his prepared text for an improvised summary of his book.[24] He and Mary then proceeded by train to Mexico City on the Guggenheim grant he finally won. A month later, within a twenty-four-hour period on July 1, Cash was deluded into thinking that Nazi agents were trying to kill him and refused medical help, moved furtively from hotel to hotel, and apparently hung himself in a bathroom by his necktie.[25]

After *The Mind of the South,* other talked-about books on the puzzle of southern history came forth, beaming more and more light into the shadows. The most important of these was *An American Dilemma,* the massive, Carnegie Foundation–funded study of "the American Negro" by the Swedish sociologist Gunnar Myrdal published in 1944.[26] Myrdal did not stress southern history so much as a psychological contradiction between the American creed of equal opportunity and the reality of poverty and discrimination under which many blacks lived, especially in the South. Myrdal concluded that the majority of people in the North, in particular, were not bothered enough by this contradiction because they were ignorant and unemotional about the plight of most blacks in the South. The best strategy to force northerners to confront the inconsistency, Myrdal wrote, was publicity—coverage in the national press of the political and economic conditions of blacks. Gene Roberts and Hank Klibanoff, in their 2006 book *The Race Beat,* consider Myrdal's insight prophetic, given the way the news media eventually helped stir the nation's conscience and prod Congress and a president to produce the Civil Rights Act of 1964 and the Voting Rights Act of 1965. But Roberts and Klibanoff, both of them newspaper journalists from the South, admit that "publicity" is a rather simplistic way to describe what turned out to be the evolving, dynamic, and multiple roles that journalists would play in the civil rights epic. It is tempting in retrospect to view the story as entirely about race and the development of an effective race "beat." But in the 1940s, the struggle was viewed more as a sectional phenomenon, certainly with race at the center but tangled up in southern history and southern identity. Cash's book gave clarity and voice to a cadre of southern writers who were seeking to understand and explain how change might come about in this land within a land, "sharply differentiated from the rest of the American nation, and exhibiting within itself a remarkable homogeneity," in Cash's words.[27] Their view, like Cash's, was pessimistic. There was nothing crusading or muckraking about it, except in the courage required to speak out in the face of the "savage ideal" of conformity. It was a historically conscious mind-set, cautious and conflicted, best framed in a suitably literary-journalistic style of restraint and irony.

Harry Ashmore, who took Cash's long-vacant editorial chair at the *Charlotte News* in 1945, was a master of this literary-journalistic style. Even at the age of twenty-nine, he impressed older liberal southern editors with his independence, his intelligent prose, and his flair for cocktail-fueled bonhomie. He fell in with older editors such as Dabney, Ethridge, McGill, and Jonathan Daniels, covering the political circuses of backcountry demagogues and meeting at conventions of the American Society of Newspaper Editors (ASNE). At the ASNE convention in 1947, Ashmore gave a snappy presentation about the stresses of filling a one-writer editorial page every day. At the time, new owners at the *Charlotte News* had disappointed Ashmore by elevating his title but not his salary. He was looking elsewhere, and other publications were interested in him. *Time* magazine, which had recently called Ashmore "one of the South's most realistic and readable editorial writers," inquired, but Ashmore rejected the idea instinctively. "I had a deep distaste for *Time*'s assembly-line journalism, and an even deeper distaste for New York's abrasive life-style," he wrote years later.[28] He interviewed at the *Richmond News Leader* and at the *Atlanta Journal,* but management at both papers left him cold. John N. Heiskell, the rare-book-collecting, elderly editor of the *Arkansas Gazette,* was far more appealing. His family had owned the paper since 1902. Heiskell, who had been impressed with Ashmore's talk at the ASNE, was looking for an editor who would guide the paper as a public trust. Ashmore felt this was a good fit, and so he moved with his family to Little Rock in 1947.

Ashmore continued to attract attention, regionally and in New York. He believed that the best hope for southern blacks lay in their securing and exercising voting rights and in the gradual outlawing of discrimination at the state and local levels. Segregation could not be attacked head-on or by force, he felt, for there was little support for such a radical change without years of preparation. He worried that President Harry Truman's push for civil rights in the South was counterproductive, but he urged southerners to remain loyal to the Democratic Party in 1948, as he would continue to do in the presidential election years of 1952 and 1956. Truman's earlier push against discrimination, such as desegregating the military, did indeed help stimulate a southern backlash, which swelled to a wave of sectional pride and resentment in the 1948 bolting of the Dixiecrat third party. In editorials and in a radio-broadcast debate with the Arkansas governor, Ashmore attacked the Dixiecrats for giving the national Republican candidate, New York Governor Thomas Dewey, an easier shot at the White House. But Truman won, thanks to Arkansas and six other southern states sticking with the Democratic Party. Ashmore continued to fight for his "moderate" position on race and civil rights, urging the South to avoid rebellion while explaining to national audiences, in speeches and magazine articles, the historical complexity of the South's resistance to change and federal intervention.

Southern editors like Ashmore and Hodding Carter Jr. were becoming the great explainers of the South to national elites. They were not crusading against segregation. Indeed, Ashmore told the Southern Governors' Conference meeting in Hot Springs, Arkansas, in 1951, "The practical problem before the South . . . is to preserve social segregation" while at the same time meeting the demands of civil liberties and equal opportunity.[29] Three years earlier, Ashmore and Carter had debated two antisegregation opponents in a town-hall performance in New York. Ashmore said that the fact that black voters had helped elect Truman "declared race a dead issue."[30]

To northern foundations, Ashmore represented the decent, intelligent southerner. The top two officers of a Ford Foundation offshoot, the Fund for the Advancement of Education, came to know Ashmore during visits to Arkansas for an experiment they were funding in teacher education. In 1953, the fund was looking to underwrite a larger, more controversial project. The goal was to investigate and quantify the differences between white public schools and segregated black public schools throughout the South. Five cases brought by the NAACP Legal Defense Fund were pending before the U.S. Supreme Court charging that black students were getting unequal schooling in five particular districts. The cases were consolidated to become the historic ruling of May 17, 1954, *Brown v. Board of Education of Topeka*. The fund's proposed study of some 3,700 school districts in the seventeen legally segregated states would show just how earthshaking the *Brown* decision could be, in terms of the practical problem to be remedied. The fund's officers asked Ashmore to direct the research project. He reminded them that he was not an academic scholar, only a journalist. They assured him that this would not be a problem, because they would pay for as many social scientists as he needed for the research. Being a journalist, they told Ashmore, was an advantage because he would be able to make deadlines and write well. As the *Brown* decision loomed, this report needed to be completed quickly. Ashmore agreed to take the job of writing, while the fund recruited some forty-five scholars, most of them from southern universities and the interracial Southern Regional Council, to do the research. "Son," an old politician told Ashmore when the project was explained, "it sounds to me like you have got yourself in the position of a man running for sonofabitch without opposition."[31] The book that the Ashmore project eventually produced, *The Negro and the Schools,* was published the day before the *Brown* ruling, a lucky accident that gave it wide coverage.

Meanwhile, as the *Brown v. Board* ruling drew near, prominent southern editors were forming an unusual news service to report whatever developments might follow. They knew the ruling would trigger a powerful running story and that southern news organizations would be ill equipped or reluctant to cover it alone. Ashmore was a central figure in the launching of this agency, the Southern Education Reporting Service (SERS). In a smoky room of the Statler Hotel in Washington, D.C., during the ASNE convention of April 1954, Ashmore huddled with fellow southern editors to plot out this unprecedented experiment in American journalism. Money would come from the Fund for the Advancement of Education. The secret of success, they all felt, was balance. Dabney, a moderate, would be chairman of the SERS board. They believed it was important to have a die-hard segregationist as vice chairman. McGill suggested Thomas R. Waring of the *Charleston News and Courier.*[32] The *Nashville Tennessean's* liberal editor Coleman A. Harwell would be balanced on the board with the *Nashville Banner's* conservative editor Charles Moss—and so on. The SERS, which would operate out of a house at the edge of Vanderbilt University in Nashville and publish specialized periodicals for the next two decades, carefully defined its beat in the awkwardly paired phrase "segregation-integration." It complained to *Time* magazine about a brief, complimentary reference saying that it reported on "the progress of desegregation"—the SERS was afraid that *progress* implied that it favored the *Brown* decision.[33]

The first director, selected by his friend Ashmore, was C. A. "Pete" McKnight, the droll, bespectacled editor of the *Charlotte News*. Years earlier, McKnight had been close to W. J. Cash as a young reporter at the *News* and a resident of the same cheap rooming house as Cash. Back then, when McKnight would hear a phonograph record of Beethoven or Wagner repeating itself past midnight, he would let himself into the room to put Cash to bed after he had collapsed from drinking too much booze.[34] McKnight became a journalistic rarity in his first year of running the SERS in Nashville—a white editor who was on top of the race issue and cared about it intensely. He selected seasoned correspondents in each of the seventeen *Brown v. Board* states to report for the monthly *Southern School News,* which he edited for the thousands of readers whom he called the "latent leadership" of the region. This ideal—the assumption that rational adjustment to the Supreme Court's order would come from moderate white leaders guided by objective news and information—was the corporate-style, Eisenhower-era reappearance of George Washington Cable's hoped-for "silent South." McKnight and the SERS became the most trusted sources of objective information on the race story, a crossroads and clipping service for the hundreds of reporters visiting the South to cover it, as well as for a number of historians.[35]

One problem with this model of balance was that all the correspondents of *Southern School News* and all the staffers working in the SERS offices were white. Simeon Booker, a black correspondent for *Jet* magazine who was covering the rising anti-Negro

violence in Mississippi in 1955, complained about this and suggested several black correspondents who might contribute to
Southern School News.[36] The SERS responded that it could not find
qualified black reporters to meet its needs at that time. McKnight
and his successors said they would like to hire black correspondents but saw no serious problem with not doing so. Their faith
in journalistic objectivity assured them that the race of a reporter
was irrelevant. The two black board members of the SERS—
P. B. Young Sr., editor of the Negro-oriented *Norfolk Journal and
Guide,* and Fisk University President Charles S. Johnson—tried
behind the scenes to integrate the SERS but failed.[37] The news
service did hire one black female researcher, the sociologist Bonita
Valien, who had worked for Charles S. Johnson. But the SERS
never gave her an office, and when the board member Waring discovered that she had made a speech in Boston giving her opinions
on school desegregation, he made sure she was let go for violating
the news service's strict neutrality.[38]

McKnight did not consider himself an expert on race as knowledgeable as, say, Gunnar Myrdal or a black sociologist like Charles
S. Johnson. But he safely assumed he knew more on the subject
than any of the other 350 or so white editors of America's major
daily newspapers meeting in Washington at the April 1955 convention of the ASNE. And he felt compelled to let them know
that their relative ignorance and smugness on the subject was a
disservice to their readers at this moment in history, and not just
in the South. McKnight made his case that this was a bigger, more
important news story than current newspaper coverage indicated,
and that their "minimal" coverage since *Brown v. Board* "has all
too often been unbalanced, and frequently distorted." In cold war
terms, the poor state of race relations was "the chink in our diplomatic armor" in trying to win people of color around the world to

democracy against communism. Other editors from Dixie, in the question-and-answer period, let slip the firecracker passions and views that McKnight's professionalism had smoothed over. Harry M. Ayers, considered a liberal editor at the *Anniston (Alabama) Star,* bewailed the Court's rejection of the separate-but-equal idea, which he believed was the real solution and one the South was making progress on. Fred Sullens, the arch-segregationist editor of the *Jackson (Mississippi) Daily News,* said that any effort to put Negro children with white children in his state would mean bloodshed. Southerners will resist, Sullens said, because "mixed schools mean mixed marriages and mixed marriages mean a mongrel race."[39]

To explain the white South's resistance to *Brown v. Board,* national magazines turned to southern journalists just as they had in the past. *Harper's* monthly, in January 1956, published "The Southern Case Against Desegregation" by the *Charleston News and Courier* editor Thomas R. Waring, an article so toxic in its "facts" against Negro intelligence, morals, and hygiene that the magazine ran a disavowal from the editors explaining why they were publishing the article. The Boston-based *Atlantic Monthly,* in November 1956, ran an article by another Charleston journalist, Herbert Ravenel Sass, "Mixed Schools and Mixed Blood," justifying the southern resistance on the grounds that America should not abandon its 350-year tradition of "keeping our races pure." McKnight, having left the SERS to become editor of the *Charlotte Observer* after the Knight newspaper chain bought it in 1955, was invited by *Collier's* magazine to explain the situation from his perspective. His article, unlike those of Waring and Sass, sought to describe the plight of the white southern "moderate," as the subhead put it, "caught between powerful forces." Apparently, Americans were hungry for this perspective, for McKnight received more positive reader response than he had ever enjoyed.[40] The same was true for Dabney when he wrote a similar article, as a moderate southerner, for *Life* magazine two years later (republished in *Reader's Digest* and *U.S. News and World Report*).[41]

Reading the *Collier's* article today, one might be surprised at how pessimistic the moderate position seems to be. McKnight starts off blaming *Brown v. Board* for interrupting "the most promising, most fascinating stage of regional history" in a long time—a period he eulogized as a slow, steady improvement in the economy and in race relations. The Court's decisions of 1954 and 1955, he said, changed everything. Suddenly, the South was seized by "ugly race tension stirred by hatred, bitterness and fear; incidents of individual and mob violence; political demagoguery of the shabbiest kind; the eruption of a vast and angry resistance movement; the passage of a great bulk of frenzied, unwise and unnecessary legislation; and a very real, though yet intangible, threat both to the region's system of public education and to its continued economic progress." McKnight did see some hope in the long run, given the slow evolution of white attitudes as the younger generation grew up and churches became more active. White southerners, he predicted hopefully, will eventually learn that they can practice segregation off the books, as in the North, and that if they do not settle the issue, businesses will stop coming south. McKnight, like most white southern liberals at this time, was blind to the possibilities of the civil rights movement. He did not see a solution in "the approach of the militant Negro," which included the NAACP, nor in the extreme resistance of the white Citizens' Council, though he owned to having considerable sympathy for the viewpoint "of its more respectable leadership."[42]

The SERS tested the power of the news profession's highest standards—objectivity, balance, courage, and social responsibility.

In some ways, the agency distilled the best qualities of American journalism. McKnight spoke the truth about the school desegregation story to his fellow editors in 1955. Another talented director of the SERS was Reed Sarratt, who ran the agency from 1960 to 1965. He was idealistic, bookish, and straitlaced. Sarratt was the teetotaling, hair-parted-in-the-middle cub reporter who, with McKnight, helped make up the energetic staff at the *Charlotte News* when W. J. Cash worked there in the late 1930s.[43] At the ASNE convention in 1956, when Harry Ayers of the *Anniston Star* once again stunned the other editors with comments from the floor, this time asserting that black men are driven to ravish white women, Sarratt stopped him with a procedural move.[44] In 1966, when Sarratt had moved on to run a journalism project at the southern governors' agency called the Southern Regional Education Board, he published a definitive book about the first decade of the turmoil in the South, *The Ordeal of Desegregation.*[45]

But the SERS model of unadorned, factual journalism also proved inadequate, as the "latent leadership" it sought to inform became increasingly silent in the face of a powerful white backlash. Once a continuous civil rights movement got under way in 1960, the evenhanded, plain-style approach seemed obsolete. The lack of black journalists in mainstream newsrooms, and especially in editorial offices, continued to belie the claim of balance. McKnight was troubled by this dilemma as his understanding of racial issues evolved in the 1960s. As a member of the ASNE, he pushed for more black reporters in the industry, and when he became the ASNE president in 1971, he appointed the Minority Employment Committee to investigate the problem. The ASNE itself had been lily white. The first token black member was admitted in 1965. The 1972 report, under McKnight's leadership, found that less than 1 percent of newsroom employees in the United States were nonwhite.[46] But while newsroom segregation and white backlash confounded the effectiveness of the SERS, its idealism drew many of the best and brightest of the South's journalists. *Southern School News* included two Nieman Fellows and a Rhodes Scholar among its correspondents. Among the writers who got their start at the SERS or its successor, the Race Relations Information Center, were southerners who later flourished in the national press: the Nashville-based author John Egerton, the Charlotte-based reporter and book writer Frye Gaillard, the *Time* magazine editor Jack E. White, and the *New Yorker* staff writer Lawrence Wright.

On an April morning in 1935, Adolph Ochs, the seventy-seven-year-old patriarch of the family that owned the *New York Times,* was visiting the city room of a Tennessee newspaper—the *Chattanooga Times*—that he had owned since 1878, long before he bought his New York paper. For lunch that day, he walked to a nearby Chattanooga coffee shop with a brother, a couple of staffers, and his nurse. At the table, he slumped over his menu, dead from a stroke. "He was one of the strong men," wrote Gerald W. Johnson in a biography, "who in the latter half of the nineteenth century riveted together the fabric of American civilization."[47] Perhaps it was a legacy of Ochs's reconciling spirit that gave the *New York Times,* after World War II, a special sense of responsibility for what was happening in the South. The three managing editors who dominated the *Times* during these years were all southerners: Edwin L. James of Virginia, with his fancy vests, cane, and cigars; Turner Catledge, a courtly gent from Mississippi; and Clifton Daniel, the North Carolinian who had married President Harry Truman's daughter.[48] In 1947, Catledge, then the assistant managing editor at the *Times,* opened the first southern bureau of a national paper, in Chattanooga, and staffed it with an affable southerner named John N. Popham. Willing to drive all day and listen to anybody to synthesize a generally optimistic view of the South's prospects, Popham was as much a roving ambassador as he was a reporter. "There was hardly a cow patch or a shade tree mechanic below the Mason-Dixon line he did not know or a mayor or sheriff who did not know him, his Jim Dandy hat, and his extraordinary Tidewater Virginia accent," wrote *Times* veteran Harrison E. Salisbury in *A Time of Change: A Reporter's Tale of Our Time.*[49] Popham was especially fond of economic reports and non-profit agencies such as the SERS and Southern Regional Council. Like Ashmore, he felt that race relations in the South would inevitably be resolved because of massive social forces slowly lifting the South in every way. This was the cautious conclusion of an eight-page special report by ten *Times* reporters in 1956, a team led by Popham that started with a few days of research at the SERS headquarters. But the *Times* recognized that Popham's diplomatic journalism was not adequate for the violent white backlash signified by the white Citizens' Council and the Little Rock crisis. The newspaper hired a younger Georgia-raised, wire-service-hardened reporter named Claude Sitton to join Popham in 1957. Within a year, Sitton had become the *Times*'s one-person regional bureau out of Atlanta. He covered his beat in perpetual motion, by airplane more than car, an apt symbol for the altered perspective.

In 1960, a new spiritual dimension of that story arose with the black student sit-ins that started February 1. From then on, the big story was the civil rights movement and new forms of police and thug violence that the movement's nonviolence intentionally provoked. The spark that set the dry-tinder fire happened with no reporter present, on that afternoon when four freshmen from a local black college sat down at a whites-only lunch counter in Greensboro, North Carolina. Sitton led the national coverage as the protest spread quickly to Nashville, Atlanta, and scores of other southern cities. The sit-ins gave way to freedom rides and voter registration drives, filling jails, and risking shotgun blasts and firebombs. Sitton became the lifeline of many young movement operatives. The SNCC workers usually carried Sitton's Atlanta phone number to call before they would call the FBI or their own organization. "Sitton would take [their] calls quickly, laconically, efficiently," Salisbury wrote in another one of his memoirs. "Where were they, who were they, what was the nearest town. Then he would call back the local sheriff, the mayor, the police chief, the highway patrol. It became almost a routine. Sitton would bluntly tell them so-and-so was the son or daughter of a very well-known family. 'If a hair of her head is touched,' he would say, 'there will be hell to pay. You will have all the newspapers in the USA down there.'"[50]

Eventually, the South got all the newspapers down there anyway, and television and radio too. The movement worked because it successfully surfaced oppression into vivid accounts and images of violence that made the national television networks, *Time* and *Newsweek,* and especially picture magazines such as *Life.* Martin Luther King Jr. understood the importance of the media bearing witness to the mistreatment of nonviolent protesters. He once scolded a *Life* photographer who had assisted children whom police were shoving to the ground in Selma, telling the photographer that he should have been snapping pictures instead. He was neglecting his "duty as a photographer," King told him.[51] The nation saw the oppression, and its conscience was greatly troubled. Sitton's part in this moral epic was to write it straight for the elite readers of the most influential paper in the world. He used his southern accent and country knowledge to get into the action or out of jams. But his writing style could not be called southern. It was plain and meticulous. Still, by being as close to the center of the story as any reporter, Sitton conjured up vivid images worthy of Hollywood's most gothic take on the violent South:

> As the seventy-year-old peace officer spoke, his nephew and chief deputy, M. E. Mathews, swaggered back and forth fingering a hand-tooled black leather cartridge belt and a .38 caliber revolver. Another deputy, R. M. Dunaway, slapped a five-cell flashlight against his left palm again and again. The three officers took turns badgering the participants and warning of what "disturbed white citizens" might do if this and other rallies continued. . . .
> *[July 26, 1962, on a raid by a sheriff's posse of a black voter-registration rally in a country church in Terrell County, Georgia.]*

> As he turned to walk into a side entrance opening into a carport, the sniper's bullet struck him just below the right shoulder blade.
> The slug crashed through a front window of the home, penetrated an interior wall, ricocheted off a refrigerator and struck a coffee pot. The battered bullet was found beneath a watermelon on a kitchen cabinet.
> *[June 13, 1963, on the murder of the NAACP leader Medgar Evers in Jackson, Mississippi.]*

> None of the 50 bombings of Negro property here since World War II have been solved. . . .
> . . . The four girls killed in the blast had just heard Mrs. Ella C. Demand, their teacher, complete the Sunday school lesson for the day. The subject was "The Love That Forgives."
> *[September 15, 1963, on the Sunday-morning bombing of Birmingham's black Sixteenth Street Baptist Church that killed four girls and set off disturbances in which two young black males were fatally shot.]*

Sheriff L. A. Rainey, a burly, tobacco-chewing man, showed little concern over the report that the workers were missing.

"If they're missing, they just hid somewhere trying to get a lot of publicity out of it, I figure," he said.

[June 22, 1964, on the disappearance of three civil rights workers in Neshoba County, Mississippi, who were later found to have been abducted, murdered, and buried under a dam. Rainey was implicated in the killings but never tried. He died in 2002.]

While the story was being reported for the national press (mostly by southerners like Sitton, *Newsweek's* Karl Fleming, and the most reliable source in Mississippi, *Times-Picayune* reporter Bill Minor), the southern press was giving desegregation and civil rights only spotty coverage. Still, ambitious young reporters moved south to work at any paper because they felt that history was taking place there. The New York–born David Halberstam, for instance, took his experience as an undergraduate at the *Harvard Crimson* straight to a small Mississippi newspaper in 1955 and then to the *Nashville Tennessean,* before joining the *New York Times* in 1960. Fred Powledge, who covered the movement for the *Atlanta Journal* and later wrote a history of the movement, recalled his urge to leave the Associated Press in New Haven, Connecticut, in 1960 to go south because this "clearly was going to be the biggest story of my time."[52] But most southern newspapers and television stations looked the other way, or worse. Die-hard segregationist editors such as J. B. Wall at the *Farmville (Virginia) Herald,* Carter Glass II at the *Lynchburg (Virginia) News* and the *Daily Advance,* and the members or hirelings of the Hederman family at the *Clarion-Ledger* and *Jackson (Mississippi) Daily News* slanted and shortchanged news coverage to match their editorial passions. A journalism review in 1967 called the Jackson papers possibly

the worst in the nation.[53] Roberts and Klibanoff characterize the
papers' news on race, apart from the rabid editorials, "vindictive,
poorly written, and error-ridden."[54] It later came out that the se-
cretive state-sponsored Sovereignty Commission had suggested or
fully written a number of stories in the Hedermans' newspapers
(and in a conservative black-run weekly in Jackson). The editors
also quashed stories at the commission's bidding. Calvin Trillin,
who had covered the South for *Time* magazine at the time, saved
for his own amusement a typical *Daily News* story that has all the
markings of an official plant. It began: "Mississippi authorities have
learned that the apparently endless 'freedom' rides into Mississippi
and the [S]outh were planned in Havana, Cuba, last winter by officials of the Soviet Union."[55] The station WLBT-TV in Jackson was
so blatantly antiblack that local civil rights activists were able to
get the Federal Communications Commission to pull its license, a
penalty the FCC had never exacted in its history.[56]

Segregationist editors like Wall and Glass in Virginia and Fred
Sullens and Jimmy Ward at the Hederman papers in Mississippi
were throwbacks in the southern tradition of bare-knuckled,
feisty editors who cared little for credible or well-crafted writing. But a few segregationist editors stood out as embodiments
of a more refined archetype of the southern press: the flashy or
pompous wordsmith whose independence was a matter of honor.
Among these were Thomas R. Waring of Charleston and John
Temple Graves II of Birmingham. Two more such figures merit
special attention here: Grover Cleveland Hall Jr. (1915–71), editor of the *Montgomery (Alabama) Advertiser* and the *Alabama Journal,* and James Jackson Kilpatrick (1920–), editor of the *Richmond
News Leader.*

Grover C. Hall Jr. was a dandyish, free-spirited writer-editor
who might have been one of the best of Mencken's band of

southern liberal editors. Sadly, though, he was born twenty-five years too late for that, and so squandered his gift trying to be like his father, Grover C. Hall Sr. The elder Hall, in fact, was one of Mencken's protégés as editor of the *Montgomery Advertiser* in the 1920s and 1930s, fighting Alabama mossbacks, prudes, and bigots with a rambunctious style that won a Pulitzer Prize in 1928. The younger Hall, the only child of this spunky editor and a mentally troubled mother, idolized his father. G. C. Jr. had been working at the *Advertiser* since he was twenty. By the time he was named editor in 1948 at age thirty-three, he had developed a frisky writing style, a brave independence, and a lust for Alabama politics. In the 1940s, he was a southern liberal (in the manner of Virginius Dabney) on race, Roosevelt, and religion. In the 1950s, he was one of the last of the colorful southern editors with a stylish editorial voice and direct control of crusading news coverage.[57] Corporate management be damned!

Hall's city, the capital of Alabama and first capital of the Confederacy, became the focus of national press coverage during the black boycott against segregated seating on Montgomery's buses, starting in December 1955. Hall enjoyed playing host to the hordes of Yankee and European journalists who came to cover the protest. His position on integration, at first, was nuanced; his focus was avoiding civil violence, which led him to oppose *Brown v. Board* but also the white reaction to it (he called the white Citizens' Councils "manicured Kluxers" and the Ku Klux Klan "albino gangsters"). He understood the central role of race in all southern politics, having closely read the standard text on this, V. O. Key's 1949 *Southern Politics in State and Nation*.[58] But the bus boycott forced him, by his dislike of mass action, to side with the doomed "Southern way of life" segregation.[59] More significant is that he developed an argument in his columns that the press visitors were foolishly ill informed about the story, the South, and race relations. "For the most part these tourists have come here with pre-conceived notions of the South seemingly derived from *Uncle Tom's Cabin* or abolitionist literature they found in an old trunk," Hall wrote in the third month of the boycott.[60] He proposed to New York editors that he be given a tour of the ghettos there by *New York Post* writer Murray Kempton, for whom he had played the knowledgeable cicerone in Montgomery. He launched a series of staff-written articles in the *Advertiser* highlighting racial incidents outside the South, each article pointedly stressing the hypocrisy of the national press giving little coverage to such stories. The series, with the biblical title "Tell It Not in Gath, Publish It Not in the Streets of Askelon," won a National Headliner journalism award, was widely praised and picked up in other papers (especially in the South), and caused Hall to boast that the series had done more for race reporting than had the Associated Press with all its vast resources.[61] The old southern resentment against the moral judgments of the North since the days of the abolitionists steadily consumed Hall, draining his sense of humor and balance.

In 1960, the resentment flared out in an editorial Hall wrote on April 7 against a full-page ad in the *New York Times* the previous week. It was only by slender chance that a city editor at the *Alabama Journal* saw the ad, for only thirty-five copies of the *Times* came by mail to Montgomery County. The ad sought contributions to a defense fund for Martin Luther King Jr. with an account of harassment and brutalities by unnamed "Southern violators" against King and the student sit-in movement in Montgomery.[62] It contained several factual errors that struck Hall as outrageous as soon as the ad was brought to his attention. "Lies, lies, lies," he wrote, "and possibly willful ones on the part of the fund-raising novelist who wrote those lines to prey on the credulity, self-righteousness and misinformation of northern citizens."[63] The ad and its "lies" quickly became the cause of a $500,000 libel suit against the *Times* led by Montgomery County police commissioner L. B. Sullivan. This developed into the celebrated *New York Times v. Sullivan* decision of the U.S. Supreme Court in 1964, the unanimous ruling, overturning an all-white Alabama jury's maximum damages against the *Times,* that protected the press from libel suits filed by public officials in cases of honest mistakes. No law or ruling, outside of the First Amendment, has given the American press more privilege.[64] Little attention has been given to Hall's role in the case. Not only had he done as much as any editor to stir local and regionwide resentment of the growing national coverage. He also encouraged the lawsuit, giving his newspaper's attorney permission to represent Sullivan and offering himself as the first witness on Sullivan's behalf.[65]

After new owners took control of the Montgomery papers in 1963, Hall's career wobbled downward. The new owners cut staff, imposed petty rules on cleanliness, and confined Hall's job to the editorial page. He disparaged the cost-cutting owners as "strip-miners" and fought a guerrilla war against them for three years. When Hall refused to endorse the publisher's liberal candidate for governor in 1966, he was fired. He left in bitterness, refusing to accept the time-beaten desk that he and his father had both used at the paper. Ray Jenkins, an admiring colleague who later moved to the *Baltimore Sun* papers, felt Hall was a victim of his own refusal to accept that "the age of individualism was over, the age of the institution had come."[66] Things got worse for Hall. His peers in Richmond, Dabney and Kilpatrick, helped him land a job replacing Kilpatrick as lead editorial writer at the *News-Leader* so that Kilpatrick could focus on his national syndication. Hall's work in Richmond flubbed—he could never whip up as much interest in Virginia politics as he still had in Alabama politics. The publisher D. Tennant Bryan, too polite ever to fire anyone, nevertheless became so exasperated with Hall that he told him to leave in November 1968, after only a year.[67] Hall then tried his hand at a syndicated column out of Washington, D.C., but in September 1970 he decided to join George C. Wallace's campaign for president. He shipped his furniture, packed up his big old Chrysler, and headed for home. On September 18, around three o'clock in the morning, an officer stopped him around Charlotte. Detecting no alcohol, the officer threw him in jail for driving without a license. In fact, Hall was delirious with an undiagnosed brain tumor. He had been missing for a week on the South's highways, had lost his wallet, and when jailed was unable or unwilling to identify himself. Thus he remained, in a Kafkaesque nightmare in the Mecklenburg County Jail, for seven days—a mute victim of inattentive jailers and doctors—until he told his captors he knew Pete McKnight, then publisher of the *Charlotte Observer* (which at the time ran Hall's syndicated column). McKnight, the same fellow who had sometimes put a drunken W. J. Cash to bed more than thirty years earlier, sent a reporter to rescue Hall. "I still cringe," McKnight wrote Hall later, "when I think that you spent a week in our detention house in need of medical attention."[68] In Montgomery, the tumor was removed, but the malignancy was terminal. He spent a year dying, "surrounded by books and roses, family and friends."[69]

Kilpatrick's story also twists through the South's racial passage but bends more toward redemption. He came from Oklahoma City, Oklahoma, by way of the University of Missouri to the heart of old Virginia, where he began as a reporter for the *Richmond News-Leader* in 1941. Kilpatrick was a facile writer, with a restless curiosity about everything, especially history. Politically, he leaned to the right. All this made him one of the few journalists in the South qualified to replace Douglas Southall Freeman (1886–1953) as editorial-page editor in 1949.

From 1949 to 1966 Kilpatrick ran a lively and combative editorial page. Among the writers who got their start under Kilpatrick at the *News-Leader* were the political journalist Richard Whalen, the historian Garry Wills, and the literary scholar Louis Rubin Jr.[70] Kilpatrick's position on *Brown v. Board* began calmly enough. "This is no time for rebellion," he advised readers in his first editorial on the decision of May 17, 1954. "It is not time for a weak surrender either. It is a time to sit tight, to think, to unite in a proposal that would win the Supreme Court's approval."[71] His thinking became more and more rebellious as he thumbed through constitutional theory and American history. Finally, in November 1955, he landed on a legal theory that would provide the South, and especially Virginia, with an excuse for resisting *Brown,* rigidly and violently. That theory was "interposition," the notion that a sovereign state can interpose itself between an act of the federal government and the people of that state. Kilpatrick exhumed the idea from Jefferson, Madison, John C. Calhoun, and the thorny history of federalism from 1788 to 1830.[72] His account downplayed the Civil War and cast some doubts on the legitimacy of the Fourteenth Amendment.[73]

Kilpatrick's brief for interposition was full of historical references, but its mode was good old fire-eating rhetoric.[74] His editorials on the subject were relentless and clever, and other Virginia newspapers followed his lead.[75] Kilpatrick not only legitimized the massive resistance stance of his friend Senator Harry Flood Byrd, a small-town newspaper publisher who ran the dominant political machine in Virginia, but also inspired politicians in all the Deep

South states to concentrate their fight through the state's power to shut down entire school systems if a single black student breached the wall of segregation. Several school systems in Virginia, in fact, were closed as a result, forcing Kilpatrick and his newspaper to shift their strategy from massive to "flexible" resistance. Kilpatrick's words seemed to give intellectual weight to the South's defiance. Such legalism was the basis for the so-called Southern Manifesto, a declaration signed by 104 of the South's congressmen in March 1956 in support of all efforts to resist "forced integration by any lawful means."[76] Kilpatrick would continue arguing forcefully, sometimes brilliantly, for states' rights and southern apartheid. As late as 1962, he published his last-ditch argument in a book titled *The Southern Case for School Segregation.* "When the Negro race proves itself, in terms of Western values of maturity and achievement, it will be time enough to talk of complete social and economic integration," he wrote in that book. "Until then, it is pointless to argue sociology; it is more useful, in every way, to meditate upon the transcendent issues of the law."[77]

Even his critics had to admire his talent and conviviality. "Kilpo," as he was called, claimed a southern identity based on a branch of his family with New Orleans roots. Having played adviser to the doomed fight against school desegregation, he proceeded to become a leading spokesman for three favorite subjects of the old southern elite: classical conservatism, the history of the Supreme Court, and the beauty of the mother tongue. He began writing a syndicated column called "A Conservative View" in 1964. From his farmhouse near Scrabble, Virginia, he wrote columns and books on domestic life, folkways, and tall tales.[78] In an introduction to one of his books on English usage, his friend William F. Buckley Jr. said that it was hard to argue about syntax with "a man whose ear is a Stradivarius."[79] Kilpatrick continued well into his eighties writing widely syndicated columns covering the Supreme Court and the state of the English language.

Kilpatrick did confess the error of his ways, if not the magnitude of his influence. By 1970, he wrote later, he had come to recognize "the terrible evils of state-sponsored racism." He admitted he was slower to come to that realization than some others, such as McGill, Ashmore, and Dabney; but the fault, he said, was in his southern roots. He was of a generation for whom segregation was mother's milk, the natural order of mankind. "It was no more to be challenged than the morning tide. Racial equality? We never even thought about it. It was simply the way things were."[80] The cynical view is that Kilpatrick needed to drop his segregation baggage around 1964 to become an American conservative celebrity with syndication. Whether his conversion was heartfelt or expedient, he enjoyed national success for the next four decades in his columns and, in the seventies, as the "Point-Counterpoint" conservative on 60 *Minutes*.[81]

Scholars have sought to know why white southern liberalism "failed"—that is, why prewar liberals took so long to attack Jim Crow segregation that the civil rights movement eventually surprised and preempted them. Their hesitation might be explained by "the mind of the South"—the notion that they were up against the savage mentality that Cash described. But once the black protests began filling the churches, the streets, and the jails in the 1960s, the question became why some old-style liberals like Dabney held back, while others like McGill and Gene Patterson, though nervous about the headlong pace of events, sided with King. One historian suggests that religion could be the answer. Dabney, like Cash, held to Mencken's distrust of evangelical Christianity. McGill, like Lillian Smith, found moral answers in evangelical-style repentance, confession of sin, and the embracing of all God's children.[82]

McGill, Smith, and others found support and friendship with more explicitly evangelical liberals in organizations such as the Fellowship of Southern Churchmen. James McBride Dabbs, a member of that group, was also an English professor, South Carolina planter, and president of the Southern Regional Council. Dabbs wrote books about the soul, rather than the mind, of the South and found a more optimistic outlook than did Cash.[83] The dismantling of segregation, Dabbs felt, would renew the southerner's frontier spirit but on a new frontier of "social relations, a space of unsettled intersubjectivity."[84] Like the Fugitive-Agrarians, he saw southern history and religion forging certain virtues that were not those of the standard American individualist. But to Dabbs, they pointed toward transformation, not stasis. "These virtues now begin to appear publicly," he wrote in 1964, "most clearly in the lives of the Negroes, who have suffered the most and have therefore lived the most. The Southerner who is true to his religious heritage will be inclined to say that this has happened because of the grace of God. The South has been God's project."[85]

Some of the hardened white reporters who witnessed the spiritual electricity of the movement's mass meetings underwent a kind of conversion. Their accounts of this experience Fred Hobson has called the "white Southern racial conversion narrative."[86] One of the writers he examines, journalist Pat Watters, begins a book on the movement by trying to describe the impact on him when he was reporting for the *Atlanta Journal* in the early 1960s: "Sometimes, covering events, crises in the onward sweep of the southern Negro movement during its early, greatest days, I would lie in my motel bed, half asleep, half yet with senses heightened, and hear all night the echo in my mind of the singing in the church, that incomparable music. The mass meetings and demonstrations that I saw in the early 1960s were foremost for me a deep, personal awakening, in the real sense of a religious experience."[87]

Watters left commercial journalism to join the Southern Regional Council, for whose periodicals he worked as reporter and editor. When the 1960s ended he felt let down but not in what he experienced. He wrote that if Americans could truly understand the breakthrough that happened with the movement, "then we might know better what to do in the name of decency now and in the future." The media failed to express what was really happening because the movement was on a level that was outside the culture. It was "extra-cultural," Watters wrote, this power of love that broke through the old conundrums of the South.[88]

Left: Edgar Allan Poe—J. H. Ingram photograph of Stella daguerreo-type, c. 1848. JOHN HENRY INGRAM'S POE COLLECTION, SPECIAL COLLECTIONS, UNIVERSITY OF VIRGINIA LIBRARY

Right: Augustus Baldwin Longstreet—lawyer, editor, university president, and author of *Georgia Scenes.* EUPIX COLLECTION; MANUSCRIPT, ARCHIVES, AND RARE BOOK LIBRARY, EMORY UNIVERSITY

Top, left: Joel Chandler Harris at his writing desk. J. C. HARRIS COLLECTION; MANUSCRIPT, ARCHIVES, AND RARE BOOK LIBRARY, EMORY UNIVERSITY

Top, right: Lafcadio Hearn—portrait from Simon Studio, New Orleans, 1887. LAFCADIO HEARN, SPECIAL COLLECTIONS, UNIVERSITY OF VIRGINIA

Bottom: Set of dueling pistols used in a series of duels in 1822 between Augustus Baldwin Longstreet's friend George McDuffie and Augusta lawyer and army colonel William Cumming. Such a set was standard equipment for some southern newspaper editors. PISTOLS IN POSSESSION OF AUTHOR'S FAMILY; PHOTOGRAPH FROM *GEORGIA HISTORICAL QUARTERLY* 44, NO. 1 (MARCH 1960)

Mark Twain and George Washington Cable—two popular writers who together made a speaking and reading tour of American cities, 1884. CLEMENS/CABLE, SPECIAL COLLECTIONS, UNIVERSITY OF VIRGINIA

Left: Walter Hines Page—editor of *Atlantic Monthly.* RANDOLPH-MACON
COLLEGE

Right: Henry Grady—the last photograph taken of the managing
editor of the *Atlanta Constitution* before his death in 1889, at the age of
thirty-nine. HENRY GRADY COLLECTION; MANUSCRIPT, ARCHIVES, AND RARE BOOK LIBRARY,
EMORY UNIVERSITY

H. L. Mencken at his typewriter at the *Baltimore Sun*. ENOCH PRATT FREE LIBRARY

Alfred Knopf (*left*) and W. J. Cash (*right*) in the restaurant of the Hotel Charlotte in March 1941. WILBUR J. CASH COLLECTION, SPECIAL COLLECTIONS DEPARTMENT, Z. SMITH REYNOLDS LIBRARY, WAKE FOREST UNIVERSITY

Top: The poet Carl Sandburg (*left*) and Ralph E. McGill of the *Atlanta Constitution* (*right*) with his son Ralph Jr. (*center*) at Sandburg's farm in Flat Rock, North Carolina, 1953. EMORY UNIVERSITY SPECIAL COLLECTIONS

Bottom: Harry Ashmore, editor of *Arkansas Gazette,* 1957. PHOTOGRAPH FROM THE ONLINE *ENCYCLOPEDIA OF ARKANSAS HISTORY AND CULTURE,* COURTESY OF BARBARA ASHMORE

Top: Tom Wolfe in his office, New York City. PHOTOGRAPH © 1980 BY PATRICK HINELY, WORK/PLAY®

Bottom, left: Marshall Frady. COURTESY OF BARBARA GANDOLPHO–FRADY

Bottom, right: Willie Morris in Yazoo City graveyard. PHOTOGRAPH BY JACK BALES

SEVEN

THE SOUTHERN ROOTS
OF NEW JOURNALISM

On a passenger train called the *Southerner* in 1949, a hapless, pimply seventeen-year-old Italian American from Ocean City, New Jersey, made his way to the only college that did not reject him—the University of Alabama. Although he was a mediocre student, Gay Talese had his own definite ideas of the kind of journalism he wanted to practice. He was drawn to the losers, the luckless characters on the edges. Rather than the objectivity and five Ws that his journalism professors would push, Talese favored the singular experience of the private individual most affected by a news event, or the social history found in a newspaper's back-page advertisements, not its front-page news.[1]

After graduating in journalism from Alabama in 1953, Talese followed his subjective literary impulses to New York. He made a slow start at the *New York Times* covering sports, state politics, and obituaries, but he eventually found his natural habitat writing feature stories for the *New York Times Sunday Magazine* and *Esquire.* His feature writing incorporated some odd elements out of keeping with the news-reporting standards of the day. He would hang out with his subject, sympathizing even with the unlikable, recording dialogue and scenes that showed action, character, and arresting detail. These were the elements of fiction. The difference was that Talese was writing nonfiction molded out of patiently gathered facts. The way he used his techniques in articles such as "Joe Louis: The King as a Middle-Aged Man" (*Esquire,* June 1962) or "Frank Sinatra Has a Cold" (*Esquire,* April 1966) gave definition to a movement that would be called New Journalism. Its leading apostle, Tom Wolfe, later described his amazement at reading Talese's "Joe Louis" piece in *Esquire.* For Wolfe, it was an epiphany, discovering this frontier stakeout of a movement that was just starting to shake the world of journalism. The excitement was to come pouring out of certain slick magazines published in New York. Within a year, Wolfe was publishing his own creative nonfiction in *Esquire* and in the Sunday magazine of the *New York Herald-Tribune,* which would soon transmute into *New York* magazine.[2]

This New Journalism movement, in the years since, has drawn plenty of commentary from celebrity practitioners and media scholars—and so it should. New Journalism deserves the large share of praise and blame it has received for influencing American news writing and nonfiction literary books since the 1960s. This chapter offers a new argument overlooked in all this commentary: much of the movement drew on traditions of the southern press and was advanced by a disproportionate number of talented journalists marked by southern culture. The point is not that this New Journalism was "southern" in any direct way. It was the combustion of complex and accelerating forces—the social revolutions of the 1960s, a certain literary community gathered in New York, and trends in magazine advertising that reflected a dazzling new affluence. Nor does it prove anything to find mere geographic connections with the South, such as Talese's four years at the

University of Alabama or the fact that *Esquire* writer and novelist Terry Southern hailed from Texas and attended Southern Methodist University there in the 1940s. The argument here is that certain aesthetic sensibilities and "outsider" attitudes characteristic of southern writers and southern intellectual history were imported, in vivid color, into the movement. This happened, in part, because it was a natural fit. Historically, the South had a unique ability to bemoan, satirize, or resent the dominant American culture. Its rebellious or reactionary viewpoint was originally at home in the southern press of the nineteenth century, which was more committed to argument and storytelling than to the reform-minded idealism or mass-market neutrality of big-city American journalism. In the 1960s, a number of talented southern-bred journalists brought their attitudes and energy to New York, to the very magazines that created New Journalism. At *Esquire,* the managing editor Harold Hayes, alumnus of Wake Forest University and son of a Southern Baptist pastor, nourished writers such as Tom Wolfe, alumnus of Washington and Lee University in Virginia and son of a Richmond farm-newspaper editor. The editor at the *Saturday Evening Post* was William A. Emerson Jr., of Charlotte and Atlanta, who had covered the South for *Newsweek.* Out of his San Francisco bureau of *Look* magazine, the Atlanta-raised George Leonard was celebrating hippies and the human potential movement as bright insurgencies against the entrenched Northeast establishment. And editing *Harper's* at the height of all this was Willie Morris, the romantic Rhodes Scholar from Yazoo City, Mississippi, whose literary aspirations seemed as distinctly southern and flawed as those of his hero Thomas Wolfe, the novelist from Asheville, North Carolina.

William Weaks Morris (1934–99) depicts his youth in "Miss'ippi" as a sunny idyll of top-dog frolic and white-boy ignorance. He edited his high school paper, starred in baseball, and made out with the luscious majorette whose family plantation he planned to acquire through marriage. He was Yazoo High valedictorian (class of 1952), local radio sports announcer, and a prankster popular with the boys. He was, in a word, smug—contented to live well in that segregated world of niceness and sudden inexplicable violence. "On any question pertaining to God or man I would have cast my morals on the results of a common plebiscite of the white voters of Yazoo County," he wrote.[3] That, at least, is the image of his boyhood he reports in more than a few of the books he wrote about himself.

Larry L. King, a longtime friend and fellow southern writer, probes the Tom Sawyer boyhood that Morris projects and finds that he left out some vital components of reality. Morris often used words "to conceal as much as to reveal," King writes in his posthumous tribute, *In Search of Willie Morris: The Mercurial Life of a Legendary Writer and Editor.* King, a merry Texan whose many articles in *Harper's* during Morris's editorship included "Confessions of a White Racist," suggests that the autobiographical version of young Willie fails to account for the grown man's sorrows, contradictions, and self-destructive urges. King finds it significant that Morris, in all his literary self-reflecting, never conveys the truth that his mother was a cold, domineering, insecure social climber or that his father was emotionally absent, almost silent. "Yes, I lie a lot," he confessed to King late one boozy night when King had accused him of writing the world greener and sunnier than God had made it. This might have seemed a dark confession after a lifetime of hard-hitting journalism at the University of Texas's *Daily Texan,* at Ronnie Dugger's *Texas Observer,* and then at *Harper's.* Indeed, King was shocked speechless.[4]

But King allows that Morris meant *lie* loosely, speaking as a literary journalist who seeks beyond mere facts for the truth. There are two ways of being a great journalist, and Morris pursued them both with passion. One is to be the crusading, fact-digging slayer of political dragons. In this, Morris's role models were journalists like Lincoln Steffens, S. S. McClure, H. L. Mencken, and William Allen White.[5] Morris was fearless, stubborn, and liberal. As the elected student-editor of the *Daily Texan,* his fights against the university's oil and gas interests and its administration censors won him national hero status. In every office he occupied from then on, including at *Harper's,* he displayed a copy of Joseph Pulitzer's last-will statement printed daily in the *St. Louis Post-Dispatch*—"always be drastically independent, never be afraid to attack wrong, whether by predatory plutocracy or predatory poverty."[6] The other kind of journalist is the storyteller. The storytelling model, as much as the public-interest model, is basic to the news business. It was the other side of Joseph Pulitzer's success, the appeal of crime stories, celebrity news, and other sensationalistic story forms from the days of yellow journalism to today. Even at its most common level, the storytelling model is aesthetic, a form of social ritual.[7] At its highest level, it aspires to the intensity of literature—it is stylish, committed to a higher truth, and capable at certain climactic times of transforming social consciousness. Such was the goal of Willie Morris at *Harper's* in the late 1960s.

His twenty books—including *North Toward Home, Yazoo: Integration in a Deep-Southern Town, New York Days,* two novels, and several meditations on southern sports—in some ways strive to tell a higher truth about America's post–World War II coming-of-age.[8] This may explain why his literary narrative leaves out so many troubling "facts" about Morris's actual life. Morris was writing not reminiscences but of himself as a metaphor for America. He used his experience and his southern identity not for self-aggrandizement but as he might use a character in a novel—sometimes in the role of an innocent abroad, sometimes a good old boy whose eyes were opened by witnessing the racial prejudice of his people and the justice of the black cause. One reviewer of *North Toward Home* noted that the memoir parallels the history of the country as a whole in an attempt "to explain in large part what was happening in America in the forties, fifties, and sixties."[9]

The deploying of subjective experience—whether in the first person or through another—was one of the fundamental innovations of New Journalism. Some critics argue that this violation of journalistic objectivity was a poison that the movement injected into contemporary American news writing. The *Washington Post* book editor Jonathan Yardley indicts Morris for putting himself at the center of his writing and encouraging some of his *Harper's* writers to do the same. Yardley admits that Morris's writing comes close to literature but dismisses the flowering of New Journalism at *Harper's* under Morris as a twinkle remembered only within the "exceedingly narrow bounds of Manhattan magazine journalism."[10]

Whether for good or not, Morris was at the center of Manhattan magazine journalism during these fertile years. In 1967, when he became the youngest editor in chief in the history of the oldest continuously running magazine in America (founded as *Harper's New Monthly Magazine* in 1850), he was hot to make a splash with both kinds of journalism. He did not mind if a good writer participated in events, took as much space as needed in the magazine, and used the techniques of fiction and first-person writing, "so long as the facts and the mood were treated with the utmost truth."[11] He began at the magazine as a subeditor in

1963 and was soon injecting his southern perspective. In a 1965 supplement called "The South Today," on the one-hundredth anniversary of Robert E. Lee's surrender, he published essays by the conservative columnist James J. Kilpatrick, the Louisiana novelist Walker Percy, the North Carolina journalist Ed Yoder (a friend since they had been at Oxford together as Rhodes Scholars), the black leader Whitney Young, the historian C. Vann Woodward, and others. One of these was a meditation by the novelist William Styron of Virginia on a historic slave rebellion of 1831, the subject of a novel he was working on. Morris would later run a forty-five-thousand-word excerpt of that controversial novel, *The Confessions of Nat Turner,* as a cover story in 1967. "We passionately wished to re-establish the connection between the magazine and many of the finest imaginative writers of the country for fiction, essays, and even reportage," Morris wrote. "Styron himself as one of America's two or three foremost novelists was an appropriate choice."[12]

The magazine under Morris drew its voltage from the high-energy era of the Beatles and black power. He felt that the spirit of *Harper's* grew out of the creative personalities he let loose in the magazine's pages, big-name characters he also loved to assemble after dark in loud camaraderie at dinner parties and at "our magnetic grotto at Madison and Thirty-fourth, the Empire Chinese."[13] Swapping lurid tales and brilliant profanities, these assemblies sported the likes of the poet James Dickey, the historian C. Vann Woodward, the *Paris Review* editor George Plimpton, Marshall Frady, Gay Talese, Joan Didion, Norman Mailer, Robert Penn Warren, Styron, and others. And always, there was booze: "Just about every writer I knew then in New York was a drinker, and so were most of the book and magazine and newspaper editors," Morris writes.[14] Larry King recalled southern writers like himself,

Tom Wicker, Ralph Ellison (from marginally southern Oklahoma City but with a strong identity in black southern culture), Styron, and Woodward becoming more southern as the fumes thickened at Willie and Celia Morris's grits-and-biscuit dinner parties. "Late in the evening bogus literary prizes were distributed, the presenters making exaggerated oratorical declamations full of southern rococo and rhythms quoting, likely as not, from Huey Long's 'Evangeline Tree' speech, Faulkner, the Old Testament, and the combined works of those assembled."[15]

Of the four first-string writer-reporters Morris kept on salary as "contributing editors," none was more original or rococo than Marshall Frady (1940–2004). Frady was younger than the others but seemed a tightly compacted remnant of an older type of writer out of W. J. Cash's South. If the techniques of fiction inspired New Journalism, Frady's inspiration came from the least likely model for journalistic prose, the novels of William Faulkner. Back in the 1930s and 1940s, Faulkner had awakened a generation of book-reading southerners, as Warren put it, to "some truth about the South and their own Southernness that had been lying speechless in their experience."[16] Frady's Faulkner epiphany came a couple of decades later but was more intense for the wait, as if the delay had promoted fermentation. The son of an itinerant Southern Baptist preacher, Frady grew up around Augusta, Georgia, seared by the emotional extremes of hellfire and sunlit paradise. It was a common experience in the South, a revival-tent saga featuring a southern Jesus whom Frady describes (in one of those Faulknerian sentences of his) as "an almost Pre-Raphaelite figure of pale languishing melancholy, with a tender, grave, bearded face much like those thin faces of young Confederate officers that stare, doomed, out of ghostly tintypes." But the enveloping culture of his Southern Baptist cocoon was also dull and depleted. He recalls a childhood experience of seeing his father in the pulpit and the gathered congregation all shrinking to a muffled miniaturization. He became detached and entered an interior universe of "grand private expectations." Frady started writing to imitate the effects of the writers he had stumbled upon, such as John Steinbeck and Edgar Rice Burroughs. Then he found Faulkner, and it was like looking into the full face of the sun, he wrote: "Faulkner is an experience that a lot of Southern boys spend the rest of their lives trying to recover from."[17]

Southern boys or girls who pursued the romance of writing through the path of modern journalism were sure to have Faulkner and other eccentricities planed out of them by gruff city editors. Frady was a slender, bright filament proving, to the contrary, that with enough talent and excitement, a genuine southern aesthetic could survive leaden editing. When he was a student at Furman University in Greenville, South Carolina, from 1959 to 1963, he left his distinct imprint in the student newspaper, the *Hornet-Paladin*. A history of the university calls him the most eloquent student ever to write for the campus newspaper and quotes his snappy take on the attempt of local Baptist authorities to control fraternity high jinks at the Baptist college. Frady said these "vigilantes of righteousness" would crank out their prudish resolutions each fall "with the bland squat inevitability of pumpkins."[18] His first editors at the *Greenville (South Carolina) News* and the *Augusta (Georgia) Chronicle and Herald* somehow failed to dampen Frady's writing or his Byronic concept of being a writer. He landed at *Newsweek* from 1964 to 1967, mostly in the Atlanta bureau.[19] The spiritual experience that the civil rights movement flashed upon a number of white southern scribblers also struck Frady, but with an added complex insight into journalism's new potential as art. Captive to these historic events, he lamented that his own "errant star was to be that of a forestalled, unbegotten novelist left with journalism to do it all in." But later he realized that this was not such a bad thing, for it thrust him to the frontier of the new age, after the ages of faith and romance—that of journalistic reality.[20] He left the South to attend the distinguished Iowa Writer's Workshop on a nine-month fellowship. He wrote for the quality magazines of this supposed new age—the dying dinosaurs of the *Saturday Evening Post* and *Life,* the edgy *Esquire* and *Harper's,* the faculty-lounge tabloid *New York Review of Books,* and a last short-lived showcase of New Journalism called *New Times.* His "high" journalism began with a book about the Alabama governor George Wallace that was intended to parallel the art of the southern novelists who created Willie Stark and Flem Snopes, two models in fact for his unique take on Wallace.[21] Later, he would write a biography of the evangelist Billy Graham as the embodiment of a naive, narcotic "American righteousness" whose literary parallel Frady found in Melville's Billy Budd. Profiles and biographies of southerners would continue to be Frady's canvas. After seven years and two Emmy Awards as chief correspondent for ABC News' *Closeup,* he became a regular writer for the *New Yorker.* A series he wrote for that magazine on the black populist-insurgent Jesse Jackson became another book in 1996, lifting the Reverend Jackson out of the joke the media had made of him and into a kind of possessed heroism. In 2002, Frady's long-held ambition to write a book on Martin Luther King Jr. manifested in one of the slender, well-wrought volumes of the Penguin Lives Series. At his untimely death from cancer at the age of sixty-four, Frady had returned to Furman University to teach and was working on a biography of Fidel Castro, circling back to his origins. At age sixteen in 1956, Frady had three times attempted to run off to Cuba to join Castro's jungle fighters, making it only as far as Havana on his third try.[22]

Frady's prose style defies every journalism textbook's advice on writing well. The how-to books say to stick with concrete nouns and active verbs. Frady was a master of polysyllabic abstraction, the kinds of modifiers diligent readers look up (*lambent, licker-ish*), and phrases favoring adverbs and adjectives. A "three-adjective man," his southern bureau chief called him, in admiration.[23] Frady skittered around the usual journalistic editing and "betrayed no scars," as another admiring southern journalist noted, because his writing was too exuberant to be crushed. When Frady pulls off a 255-word sentence, as his fellow southerner Hal Crowther notes, it holds together and surges.[24] When Frady uses three adjectives for a person, place, or thing, it is usually a triangulation of higher accuracy; he nails it. His abstractions and metaphors issue out of a reporter's close observation on the scene of action, transmuted by an artist's effort at what Frady called "ultra-telling." In his biographies, he was not interested in exposure or reform but in getting at the flesh-and-spirit mystery of his male subjects by telling their story "with the deepest possible registers and sensings."[25] Even a production-line magazine like *Life* allowed Frady to get away with two or three adjectives modifying one noun, as in this passage about a high school football game, from a selection in the Library of America's two-volume *Reporting Civil Rights:* "But there was, this particular evening, a discreet surreal alteration in the imme-morial pageant. In the midst of whites in the stands who would release at every long gain by the Panthers those wild abject savage yodels that have lasted from Bull Run and Pickett's Charge, there was a significant population of blacks, students and parents, sitting somewhat more sober and subdued, but producing now and then patterings of circumspect applause."[26]

Although Frady's style of writing was inimitable, his artistic ethic was an inspiration to many magazine-writing colleagues and younger reporters bewitched by his originality. He embodied, first of all, the ethic of total independence so treasured by journalists and artists alike, but Frady's manifestation of this was peculiarly southern and perhaps neurotic. He imagined writers needing to keep miles apart to cover the land as if writing lonely dispatches not to one another but back to Dickens and Shakespeare. He preferred the back roads of the low South to the interstate, as his fellow *Harper's* staffer David Halberstam recalled, "because that was where all the rascals—he was part rascal himself—lived and played."[27] He felt the allure of New York City. But it made him jumpy, and he saw in its publishing and mass communication oligopolies a threat to any writer-reporter's ability to experience American life firsthand. He would swoop in from Israel, Alabama, or California with a mad glint in his eyes to pronounce in half-serious Old Testament tones, "Beware of New York City."[28] Throughout most of his career with New York–based magazines and television news, he lived in Atlanta. Willie Morris recalled that Frady would often vanish from their Manhattan coterie at *Harper's* without explanation, "for he was by deepest disposition nomadic."[29]

A second element of the ethic that Frady practiced, and described with some abashment, was the morally ambiguous turn a journalist makes between the reporting phase and the writing. Frady was almost a method actor in the way he would lose himself in the world of his subjects. Then he would become Faulkner alone with his typewriter, his only loyalty to the story.[30] That shift from reporter to artist, he admitted, often felt like treachery—a betrayal of himself and of his sources and subjects. Wallace and Graham expressed dismay at how they were portrayed. Jackson, on the other hand, hinted that he was pleased with Frady's depiction, and he preached at his 2004 funeral in South Carolina. Using real lives for journalistic art was a perilous ethical problem for New Journalism, or what Frady called the total journalism of "this odd unchurched coupling between the novel and journalism."[31] "Willie," he told Morris (who thought Frady had the most pronounced southern drawl even he had ever heard), "ah luv 'em all when ah'm with 'em. It's when ah sit down to the typewriter that ah make my judgments."[32]

The aesthetic idea Frady passed along to journalism, finally, was that good reporting can be yoked successfully not only to narrative form but also to a tongue that is rich with metaphor, history, oratory, music—all those qualities that have been ascribed to the southern literary renascence. "To my ear," Crowther wrote in his appreciation, "it's a 'Song of the South' sung with near-perfect pitch."[33]

Decades before the 1960s, the South had groomed and given forth some uniquely literary journalists. One brilliant, self-destructive model for later southern literary journalists was James Agee (1909–55). He began his bohemian literary career in the New York offices of Henry Luce's *Fortune* magazine in 1932. Agee was only twenty-two years old, straight out of Phillips Exeter Academy and Harvard College, where his burning ambitions as a writer hatched poems and short stories published in the schools' literary magazines. But the dark-haired, chain-smoking lad occupied the nervous space of the outsider, a rebel to those elite precincts. He was from eastern Tennessee: raised in Knoxville, traumatized at age six by the death of his lusty father in a reckless-driving accident, suffocated by guilt and his mother's fanatical Anglo-Catholic devotions, and mentored by a high-church Episcopal priest at a religious school in the mountain softness of Sewanee, Tennessee.[34] Inspired but feeling cheated by how Thomas Wolfe and William Faulkner seemed to have ransacked his own southern boyhood as literary material, Agee sought out assignments at *Fortune* that allowed him to wax poetical about the South in the depths of the Depression.[35] Luckily, Luce had decided that the best way to celebrate the glories of American capitalism in a magazine was to hire the most literary and creative writers, from Ivy League schools, and to give them scope. In an article on the Tennessee Valley Authority, Agee described the Tennessee River in a ninety-three-word sentence so flowing and complex, his biographer quotes it in full, noting that it took at least an afternoon to craft and was approved, untouched, by the editors Ralph Ingersoll and Archibald MacLeish.[36] Agee brought out a volume of poetry in 1934. In 1936, he and photographer Walker Evans, on assignment for *Fortune,* spent several summer weeks with three dirt-poor, tenant-farm families in Alabama. The book-length account Agee wrote about these families never ran in the magazine but did become one of his most artful, lasting works, *Let Us Now Praise Famous Men.* Evans recalled Agee's rumpled, genteel southern manner, especially his way of talking: "His gestures were one of the memorable things about him. He seemed to model, fight, and stroke his phrases as he talked. The talk, in the end, was his great distinguishing feature. He talked his prose, Agee prose. It was hardly a twentieth century style; it had Elizabethan colors."[37] Agee went on to write book reviews and cover stories for *Time,* autobiographical novels, Hollywood screenplays, and hundreds of influential film reviews for *The Nation;* he was a man for all media.[38]

Another legendary self-exiled southerner writing nonfiction in New York was Joseph Mitchell (1908–96). A soft-spoken, melancholy son of a well-off timber and tobacco grower in the Low Country of North Carolina, Mitchell left the University of North

Carolina and landed in Manhattan in 1929. He became a "district man" for the *Herald Tribune,* the *Morning World,* and then the *World-Telegram,* losing track of his original plan to be a political reporter after falling under the spell of the odd characters he wrote about in New York during the Great Depression. He hated literary pretension, or pretension of any kind. But there was something deeply tender and modernist about his depictions of the daily incoherence of the city and its inhabitants, whom Mitchell said he could not distinguish from the inmates of a psychiatric hospital. In 1938, he joined the *New Yorker,* where he kept a monkish office for the next fifty years. His careful, bittersweet feature stories about dockworkers, bums, burned-out politicos, prostitutes, and dreamers, collected in books such as *McSorley's Wonderful Saloon, The Bottom of the Harbor,* and *Joe Gould's Secret,* came to be considered by many journalists as the gold standard of literary nonfiction. He haunted New York, became its lover and confessor. But his soulful attention to the city's oddness, his sense of lost time and fading courtesies, could have come only from the small-town South of an earlier time. In his last three decades, in which he mysteriously failed to publish anything though he continued coming to his *New Yorker* office, Mitchell retreated several times a year to a timber farm he bought for himself in the flat North Carolina country of his boyhood. He told colleagues he was writing about his roots there.[39]

In the 1960s, the presence of southerners in New York magazine circles was felt as much in boisterous personalities as in writing style. An acclaimed instance of the archetype is William A. Emerson Jr. (1923–). He was raised in Charlotte and Atlanta and started college at Davidson College, in North Carolina. But Emerson's booming, hilarious style—an entirely original southern role he played in New York's editorial offices and among fellow journalists back in the South—could not be explained by his upbringing. Indeed, his colleagues at New York magazines and among the civil rights press corps in the South wondered what springs of life produced this "gargantuan disposition," as Willie Morris put it, out of such an ordinary background. After serving in China during World War II, Emerson enrolled at Harvard, where he was editor of *The Advocate,* the literary magazine, and upon graduation in 1948 he instantly landed a job in New York on the staff of the popular weekly *Collier's.* He opened a southern bureau for *Collier's* in Atlanta in 1951 and then a regional bureau there for *Newsweek,* where he found that his specialties were "riots, revolutions and everyday politics."[40] Ralph McGill and Harry Ashmore were among his favorite drinking pals and rival raconteurs. In 1961, Emerson returned to New York as a senior editor for *Newsweek* and in 1963 joined the giant feature magazine *Saturday Evening Post* as articles editor.

Emerson radiated a haphazard charm that got the attention of people around him and lifted him to the top editorial slot at the *Saturday Evening Post.* It was a charm bordering on offensive, a combination of his large bearlike physicality and a profane, inspired use of English. "I'm going to go on running this magazine just as long as it *amuses* me," he told his second in command, Otto Friedrich, after one of the more disastrous meetings of the dysfunctional board of the company that owned the *Post.* "It *entertains* me. I *enjoy* watching all these pissants f—— around with things. But the minute it stops entertaining me, then I say: F—— the whole bunch of them."[41] Willie Morris describes being involved with Emerson around a project to excerpt a large portion of *North Toward Home* in the *Post* in 1967, illustrated by photographs of Morris's seven-year-old son, David, as a stand-in for the young

Willie in the actual locales of Yazoo City. Emerson told Morris he intended to go for broke on the project. "Let's be inimitable in our approach," he said. "Let's make them remember our compact with the gods. What are we, men or mice?" After several conferences in the *Saturday Evening Post's* offices and a few martini lunches, Emerson said he wanted Morris to take him to the *Harper's* offices so he could "ascertain if yours are equally conspicuous or merely arcane." Morris writes: "[H]e began stalking the secretaries up and down the corridors, shouting 'Pusillanimous!' as he may have tried to pinch them. 'Have you never encountered a hero?' he jocosely asked them. Finally, mercifully exhausted, he departed."[42]

Emerson's style bemused his colleague Friedrich, a Harvard classmate whose private diary later informed his detailed book on the *Post's* slow demise. Friedrich does not blame Emerson for the failure of this once-preeminent weekly, which died in 1969. What killed the *Saturday Evening Post,* Friedrich concludes, had nothing to do with editorial creativity. The fault, rather, lay with incompetent corporate owners who could not adjust to the impact of television. The same change in the mass market would soon kill the *Post's* competitors, *Life* and *Look.* But while Emerson comes across as a lovable victim, if not "the nearest thing to a hero" in the story, Friedrich seems puzzled and annoyed by the man.[43] Emerson was seriously interested in religion—he would later write a storyteller's version of the Synoptic Gospels called *The Jesus Story*—but he resisted having anything about social-activist clergy or "God is dead" theologians in the magazine.[44] His racial attitudes also seemed suspect to Friedrich, who hailed from Boston. Emerson embraced the civil rights movement, for he stayed in touch with his fraternity of white southern reporters with whom he covered the Montgomery bus boycott, Little Rock, and white resistance to school desegregation. But he refused to be defensive as a southern white man in the North, so he adopted what Friedrich called "the pose of a Mississippi sheriff, guffawing and profane over the fate of [blacks]." If Emerson used the *n*-word, as Friedrich implies, it was no doubt to shock stuffy editorial offices the way Walter Hines Page did when he took control of the *Atlantic Monthly*. Emerson would yawp a phrase like "blue-gummed Senegambians," and Friedrich would duly record it in his diary as a sign of racism rather than as Emerson's obscure quoting of Ashmore's account of "Cotton Ed" Smith's stump speech for the redneck vote in 1938 or as his Menckenesque delight in the mere sound of it. Friedrich saw Emerson's self-mocking racism, or what he called a "false hillbilly" act mixed with esoteric learning, as a playful cover for his keen awareness of ethnic and class lines. For all his cussing and cutting up, Emerson would never violate the distinctions between gentlefolk and the rest of society, according to Friedrich. It was hard to read Emerson because of the way he improvised the language like a bebop jazzman. But Friedrich finally ventures a bit of psychoanalysis on Emerson's southern poses and feints: "I could not help suspecting that somewhere at the center of that rambunctious, laughing blustering whirl there was the remnant of a small boy uncertain of his own place in the world—but never mind; if this had ever been a problem, it was one that Emerson had solved to his own satisfaction."[45]

The slow, terminal leakage of national-market advertising from the leviathans of *Life, Look,* and the *Saturday Evening Post,* paradoxically, brought out a fresh spurt of creativity in those publications. Their historic fame attracted creative editors and writers, and the complaints of corporate overseers clutching their tone-deaf consumer surveys only spurred the editors to be more defiant and risk taking.[46] The subjective writing of New Journalism, from talents like Norman Mailer, Styron, Frady, and Wolfe, was in the air, and the big general-interest magazines caught it. *Look* magazine, in particular, sought to be especially creative, because its longer-lead-time and biweekly publication cycle made it much less newsy than its weekly rival *Life*. "It forced us to dig deeper, to approach stories from unexpected angles, to bring additional insights to bear on what other media covered simply as news," wrote George Leonard, a staff editor at *Look* from 1953 to 1970. "We dealt with significant events by printing predictive stories just before they happened, or—more likely—by coming up several weeks later with something that was still fresh and new."[47] A dramatic example from the premovement South was what *Look* did with the well-covered Emmett Till murder trial of 1955. It accepted a "checkbook journalism" story from William Bradford Huie, an Alabama novelist and journalist who thrived on sensational exposés of the South's racial violence.[48] The nation had been shocked by the acquittal of two backcountry whites who were obviously guilty of the savage murder in Mississippi of the fourteen-year-old black boy named Emmett Till. Huie and *Look* paid the two men and their lawyer $4,000 for a confession that Huie crafted with novelistic touches.[49] The story was a journalistic scandal and a popular success, reprinted in *Reader's Digest*. The men, of course, could not be tried for the same crime twice.

A more redemptive encounter with the South's racial demons was the work of George Leonard (1923–) at *Look*. Leonard, a tall, striking figure with intense blue eyes, white hair, and the grace of a dancer, is better known today as a leader of the human-potential movement centered at the Esalen Institute in California. He became president of Esalen, cofounder and master teacher of a school in the martial art of aikido, president of the Association of Humanistic Psychology, and promoter of various new-age blends of spiritual, athletic, and mental practices such as Leonard Energy Training (LET) and Integral Transformative Practice (ITP). Leonard's books delineate his joyous, radical vision of a new consciousness in such basic areas of American life as education, marriage, leisure time, and health: *Education and Ecstasy* (1968), *The Man and Woman Thing and Other Provocations* (1970), *The Transformation* (1972), *The Ultimate Athlete* (1975), *The Silent Pulse: A Search for the Perfect Rhythm That Exists in Each of Us* (1978), *The End of Sex* (1983), *Mastery: The Keys to Long-Term Success and Fulfillment* (1991), and *The Way of Aikido* (1999). After he left *Look* in 1970, he embraced and mastered (or helped invent) practices that issued from the very phenomena he had covered (or discovered, as far as Middle America was concerned) in the 1960s.

The process began when Leonard orchestrated a special issue of *Look* in January 1961 touting the proposition that, as his essay put it, "Youth everywhere is exploding into action," a clairvoyance defying the conventional wisdom that the rising generation was apathetic. Living in San Francisco, where he established a *Look* bureau, Leonard directed other special issues from the windy frontiers of cultural change, giving some thirty million *Look* readers a prescient, vibrant sense of the new meaning of California, hippies, psychedelic drugs, encounter groups, the sexual revolution, hot tubs, and Frisbees. His beat was not merely touchy-feely trends but the whole notion of lifestyle, a term that Leonard introduced into the popular press before *lifestyle* permeated American culture as a section title of metro newspapers everywhere.[50] *Look* magazine's editorial practice was to give one editor or team control over the words, design, and photography of an entire package, so Leonard's evangelizing for the new consciousness included his essays, his choice of artful photographs, and the work of other writers of his choosing. For Leonard to participate in the humanistic revolution he was covering—giving Esalen seminars and experimenting with LSD, for example—was in keeping with New Journalism. A new, more penetrating and personal journalism was needed to cover what was happening. The question was this: what drove Leonard to make that leap into a new kind of journalism and eventually led him to such explorations of the self?

According to his 1988 memoir, *Walking on the Edge of the World,* it was largely his upbringing in a segregated South that gave him his vague longing to break down social barriers.[51] ("Breakdown Is Breakthrough" he titles the final section of the memoir, on the human-potential movement.) As a boy from Atlanta, he spent summers in a small Georgia town with his grandfather, a state senator, undertaker, and farmer. His grandfather took him to see the crowded shacks of the poor black families who worked on his farm. "What do they do at night?" the boy asked. His grandfather assured him that they went to sleep happy. The boy knew this was not the case, but it was forbidden territory and left him feeling very strange. Later, he witnessed a white mob gathered around the town's courthouse as a black prisoner, accused of raping a white woman, was escorted through the crowd past the boy. "Something had happened to me when my eyes had met those of the black man. *I had felt what he felt.*" His heroes would be southerners who questioned this system—Ralph McGill and Leonard's own aunt, the novelist and *Atlanta Journal* columnist Margaret Long, who once edited a liberal journal of the Southern Regional Council. So, for *Look,* he returned to the South several times to witness the nonviolent protests of black students and the march from Selma, Alabama. He hired a young Georgia writer named Bill Hedgepeth to open an Atlanta bureau for the magazine. Leonard liked Hedgepeth because he was a colorful, madcap southern writer who wore an eye patch and white linen suits.[52] In the late

1960s, when ghettos were erupting, Leonard joined a group of fifteen senior editors from America's major news outlets on a jetliner tour, sponsored by Time-Life and the Urban League. They dropped in on the country's most racially troubled cities. Leonard mockingly called the project "seven ghettos in seven days," convinced that the mentality of journalistic objectivity would block any understanding even if these editors could spend a month in the ghetto.[53] At one point in the tour, in Watts, Los Angeles, Leonard nearly exploded with rage, nose to nose with one of the militant black-power advocates who had been haranguing the white editors. Leonard was disgusted with the lack of response from his fellow editors, pathetic not just in their whiteness but in their bloodless, colorless "objectivity." Leonard believed that yelling back was healthy therapy, and his black attacker raised the volume even more. "It was a goddam, all-out black-white confrontation, and what made it wonderful was not the content of the words but the rhythm, the uninhibited release of pent-up feelings. I noticed vaguely during the uproar that my white colleagues were absolutely still and pale."[54] Race, for Leonard, remained a formidable inner wall, and the dream of breaking through that barrier connected his California mind-body trip with his southern roots: "On the matter of race, perhaps more than anything else, I dreamed of things that never were. Race was clearly a powerful searchlight that could illuminate individual neurosis and penetrate to the core of our national sickness. Through heartfelt confrontation and understanding, integration could become a two-way process. Black Americans could gain a fair share of the rewards of the mainstream culture. White Americans could tap into the richness of the black culture, could recognize the spontaneity, the joy, even the ability to perceive reality that we had kept hidden somewhere in the sterile suburbs of our senses."[55]

The 1960s saw breakdown and breakthrough in many forms, not the least of which was the form of the American magazine. The success of magazines such as *Playboy* and *Sports Illustrated,* launched in 1953 and 1954, respectively, suggested that lifestyle magazines had more appeal in the age of color television than did general-interest periodicals. Lifestyle, in a sense, would become just another niche in this new era, as corporations that owned magazines learned to slice readership into narrow, lucrative markets. But lifestyle was also the name of the revolution in culture taking place in the 1960s. In the South of this decade, the civil rights revolution saw a counterrevolution in the suburbs, a flowering of lifestyle enclaves around cities such as Birmingham, Charlotte, Orlando, and Atlanta. The magazine that catered to this lifestyle, with a formula that proved hugely profitable, was *Southern Living.* Started in 1966 by a Birmingham company that also published an eighty-year-old periodical of the agrarian-populist tradition called the *Progressive Farmer, Southern Living* depicted a postfarm, postfactory South of unflagging pleasantness. Its still-life cover photographs and vanilla-flavored articles focused on gardening, travel, southern cooking, and home design, rarely on interesting people and never on political conflict.[56]

Meanwhile, the lifestyle revolution that coalesced around the upheavals of the 1960s presented a different sort of business opportunity for national magazines. No magazine would embody the 1960s like *Esquire,* a monthly that had moved from Chicago to New York in the early 1950s. When *Vanity Fair* in 2007 looked back forty years at *Esquire* in the sixties, it concluded that the magazine "not only cracked the code of the new culture but also engineered the genome for the modern magazine."[57] Its irreverent, attention-grabbing style was, in a way, an idiosyncratic sideshow to the 1960s. *Esquire* did not seem to take the events and symbols of the decade seriously. One of its cover photographs had the sullen black face of heavyweight boxing champion Sonny Liston wearing a big red Santa Claus cap—for the ad-heavy Christmas issue. One depicted Andy Warhol drowning in a giant Campbell Soup can, and another had U.S. Army Lieutenant William Calley of My Lai massacre notoriety posing with Vietnamese children—in uniform and smiling, having been paid twenty thousand dollars by *Esquire* to cooperate. Yet the magazine's irreverence and detachment made it the perfect expression of the decade's cool. "[W]e offered to our readers in our better moments the promise of outright laughter," wrote editor Harold Hayes in his introduction to *Smiling Through the Apocalypse,* an anthology of articles from his years at *Esquire.* "[B]y the end of the sixties the best we could provide was a bleak grin."[58] Its droll yet frenetic style—a combination of jazzy cool, moral outrage, and slapstick—proved the right touch.

The important modern magazines in New York often reflected the personalities of editors or publishers who came from small-town, heartland America, where many of their readers remained. Such magazine sachems were not Ivy Leaguers to the manner born, like those in Henry Luce's Time-Life offices. They were born-again sophisticates, big-city converts whose provincial origins survived as eccentricities that rubbed off on their magazines. Harold Ross, founder and editor of the *New Yorker,* is a legendary example, a self-educated yokel from Colorado who created the most urbane magazine ever. The *Saturday Evening Post* was dominated for most of its final sixty years by George Horace Lorimer, a preacher's son from Louisville and Chicago, and Ben Hibbs, of Pretty Prairie, Kansas.[59] George Leonard said that *Look* was "tinged more with cornstalk and Spanish moss than ivy."[60] *Esquire*'s Harold Thomas Pace Hayes (1926–89) was a son of the South, but whatever qualities he brought to New York as an outlander might just as well be ascribed to any provincial American background. Other than a gentle North Carolina accent, he did not project a particularly southern identity. But his editorial style—quick, decisive, offbeat—betrayed the chastening distance he had traversed from his birthplace in Elkin, North Carolina, to the coveted corner office on the fourth floor of 488 Madison Avenue.[61]

Hayes spent half his childhood in coal country, in West Virginia, then moved to Winston-Salem, North Carolina, when he was eleven years old. His mother urged high culture and gentility on her three children, while his father, a fundamentalist Southern Baptist preacher, imposed strictures that left the boy with a "moral hangover." Hayes graduated without distinction from Wake Forest College and, between two stints in the military, covered politics in the Atlanta bureau of United Press International. Through a friend, he secured an interview in New York with *Esquire* editor Arnold Gingrich, who sent him to a new magazine, *Picture Week*. Hayes was put in charge. After two years with little confidence, he tried something bold—laying out a year-end issue that featured the worst of the previous twelve months instead of the highlights. It got him and his staff fired. But it won Hayes a job at *Esquire* by displaying his knack for finding entertainment in the kind of lampooning that would create *Esquire*'s Dubious Achievement Awards. From 1957 to 1961, Hayes competed in a vicious editorial free-for-all with other young Turks at *Esquire,* an arrangement Gingrich designed to draw out their youthful creativity even if it drew blood. Hayes's chief rival was Clay Felker, a brilliant idea-generator from St. Louis and a Duke University graduate. Hayes felt intimidated. He went off to Harvard for nine months as a Nieman Fellow, and then returned to the brutal competition. Felker and Hayes contributed what *Vanity Fair* would later call outsider perspectives, "built on smart writing, strong reporting, provocative visuals, and bringing a new sensibility to old subjects." Hayes, in 1961, finally won the fight to become managing editor. In the process, he had become a tough, suave editor, buffing away all vestiges of the naive, insecure boy from the sticks. When writers clashed with Hayes, it sometimes left permanent scars in the relationship. His talent was in choosing writers, giving them a snappy idea, and then letting them work on their own.[62]

Hayes consolidated his power and built his own staff. As associate editors he hired John Berent, who would later author a gothic-nonfiction book about Savannah, Georgia, called *Midnight in the Garden of Good and Evil,* and Bob Sherrill, not the southern journalist of that name who wrote *Gothic Politics in the Deep South* but a "hillbilly" college classmate of Hayes's from North Carolina. Felker left for the *New York Herald-Tribune,* where he would contribute as much as anyone to New Journalism by editing its Sunday magazine, *New York.* Hayes specialized in being able to pick an ordinary news story and flip it sideways by giving it an oddball point of view or assigning a literary figure to cover it. In 1960, he sent the then-novelist Norman Mailer to cover the Democratic convention. To cover the Democratic convention in 1968, he sent the hipster-writer William Burroughs and the French writer-provocateur Jean Genet. Hayes was responsible for Gay Talese's artful profiles and Michael Herr's novelistic dispatches from Vietnam. But perhaps Hayes's greatest contribution to journalism was getting into *Esquire* the work of a fellow southerner, Tom Wolfe. Hayes had to share Wolfe with rival Felker, for the young journalist of the white custom-tailored suits was on the staff at the *Herald-Tribune* with Felker. But New York newspaper workers were on strike for nearly four months in 1963, and Wolfe and Hayes got along well. So Hayes gave Wolfe most of the assignments that would become *The Kandy-Kolored Tangerine-Flake Streamline Baby,* the 1963 collection that shook the boundaries of both journalism and literature.[63]

Tom Wolfe (1931–), ever since that splashy start, has been a writing phenomenon of almost unmatched staying power. He delivered up literary triumphs to color every decade—not only two collections of his typographically frisky magazine articles and a book on hippie-maestro Ken Kesey, from the 1960s, but a distinctive new take on every decade that followed. He published four more collections, a couple of extended articles-turned-books that skewered modern painting and modern architecture, a nonfiction epic on the space program that became the hit movie *The Right Stuff,* and three fat best-selling novels. His name and sporty image became high-value commodities. Wolfe's eye for the surface-and-status details of American culture authorized him to define that culture. His labels for the era stuck like cotton candy. The 1970s became the "me decade," and the entire fin de siècle of the late twentieth century became the "purple decades," the color of greed as depicted in Wolfe's triumphant 1987 novel *The Bonfire of the Vanities.* Other phrases of Wolfe's also stuck. The white liberal fawning over testy black-power figures became "radical chic," and the leveraging that black activists discovered in shouting down the functionaries of President Johnson's Great Society became "mau-mauing the flak-catchers."

Underneath all this fame flexed some serious muscle power. Wolfe, who had been a daily news reporter at the *Springfield (Massachusetts) Union* (1956–59) and the *Washington Post* (1959–62) before hitting New York, was always a diligent, note-taking reporter. He gathered information not aggressively, but obsessively, even more so when he turned to novel writing. "Reporting is the heart of everything," he told the ASNE in 1990.[64] Furthermore, he was always an artist, thinking out problems of craft, design, and aesthetics. He is a sketch artist, too, his caricatures having some-times run with his articles and in one-man shows in New York. But his finest art is his writing. Literary scholars find his work shimmering with allusions to forebears from eighteenth- and nineteenth-century literature, such as echoes of Edgar Allan Poe's "The Descent into the Maelstrom" in the stream-of-consciousness scene of Kesey hiding from the law in Mexico while stricken with paranoia. Wolfe gathered his material from interviews to say what was happening inside Kesey's crazed point of view, but there is legitimate opportunity for professors like John Hellmann to apply their English department diagnostics: "Far from being the 'realist' he calls himself, Wolfe is an assertively self-reflexive ex-perimentalist who, through pattern and style, transforms as he re-ports, responds as he represents."[65] Finally, Wolfe is intellectually driven, always connecting up and deepening his lifelong interests in a variety of subjects from American history to neuroscience to sociology—but not American politics, which he finds boring. "Tom's great strength is his intellect," says a friend since college, Bill Hoffman, a distinguished Virginia fiction writer.[66]

Granting Wolfe all that—his resourceful reporting, art, and lib-eral learning—there remains plenty of room for theories about his originality. The mannered nature of Wolfe's work, and of Wolfe himself, invites further explanation. Many writers have tossed hypotheses into print. First, what's the deal with all those high-collared shirts, white suits, and spat-effect shoes? A *Vanity Fair* profile in 1990 suggested the late-Victorian costume signaled his abhorrence of modernism in the arts. Was it protective armor? Un-derneath the show-off pose seemed to be a quiet, gentle, private man—friendly but guarded. His aggression was nested somewhere deep. A two-part satire of the *New Yorker* that Wolfe published in

1965, abusing its beloved editor William Shaw (who refused to co-operate with the article and sought clumsily to have it killed), infuriated New York's literary elite. Wolfe seemed to enjoy the battle. He says he likes being different.[67] He hates being humiliated. "I never forget, I never forgive," he told an interviewer in 1966. He loves his adopted city, New York—loves window-shopping and party going, knowing names and how much his neighbors paid for their East Side cooperative apartments. Yet he has remained aloof. The city scene does not touch him, his friend Gay Talese says. "He doesn't *want* it to touch him." Wolfe was single until he was forty-seven, when he married Sheila Berger, a graphic artist who had been at *Esquire* and then at Willie Morris's *Harper's* as art director.[68] What was the meaning of his loud literary style, flaring with capitalization and punctuation marks and the lingo of his subjects? Was he celebrating or satirizing? Did he love his characters or loathe them? Was he a secret conservative, a moralist? He remained evasive, merry eyed. His great theme was status hierarchy, the absurd but implacable play of money, class, and power in social settings. But where did he fit into this status hierarchy? Who was this thin, observant figure who once claimed he needed to look at himself in the mirror first thing each morning?

One of the dominant theories, the key that several writers have offered to such questions, is that Wolfe is a white Protestant southerner-in-exile. "Very much the Southerner who feels distance," Talese says. A "Southern conservative of a very sophisticated kind," says the novelist Robert Stone.[69] Indeed, Wolfe is from Richmond, Virginia, where he graduated from the elite Episcopal prep school St. Christopher's. His undergraduate education was at Washington and Lee University, in western Virginia, a traditional liberal arts college that had been for sons of the modern

South's gentry ever since Robert E. Lee presided over the campus after the Civil War. But writers who have followed this analysis of Wolfe note that he was not born to this lofty social stratum. His parents came from the mountains of western Virginia, with a foreshortened ancestry that (to Tom Wolfe's chagrin) could not be tied even to that similarly scruffy frontier line that bore the earlier Thomas Wolfe farther down the Blue Ridge, in North Carolina. For Thomas Kennerly Wolfe Sr., the writer's father, the upward path in the status hierarchy was education. He earned a Ph.D. from Cornell University in agricultural science, taught at Virginia Polytechnic Institute, and edited a farm journal called the *Southern Planter,* the same magazine that had published Edmund Ruffin's proslavery articles a century earlier. The editing job brought the elder Wolfe and his family to Richmond. So, the theory goes, the bright, young, athletic lad, "T. K. Jr.," always felt the chill of being an outsider, a hillbilly, but he was so aggressively smart that he out-aristocrated his peers. He dressed well—in a photograph of his class at St. Christopher's, he is the only boy among twenty-three in coat and tie, which is a dark suit and light tie. And he pursued the bohemian path of being a writer, which had fine aristocratic potential harking back to Poe's role as a Richmond editor. He wrote a sports column for the prep school newspaper, "In the Bullpen," and in college he wrote psychological short stories and helped launch the literary periodical *Shenandoah.* He joined Phi Kappa Sigma fraternity at Washington and Lee but refused to drink, a healthful-diet pattern he maintained all his life. Like his father, he went north for a Ph.D.—in American studies at Yale. His father had suits tailored in Richmond, light-colored ones in the summer. The son found a tailor in Washington while he was at the *Post* and began bedecking himself like a southern Savile Row dandy. In New York, he turned his father's mild vanity into a conscious act, an affront, adding hats and wearing white year-round. "Never underestimate how much of your childhood is sewn into the lining of your garments when you go to New York," he once said.[70]

Whatever status anxiety or striving may have affected Wolfe in Virginia, he turned it to good use as a literary journalist. Once he moved to New York, the destination of so many southern literary aspirants since Poe, his outsider perspective was transformed. No longer hillbilly arriviste to Richmond society, he viewed all of American culture from the perspective of a kind of amused nineteenth-century southern gentleman on his grand tour. Like the southern character Basil Ransom in Henry James's novel *The Bostonians,* he held subversive notions of virtually everything he witnessed. But instead of pontificating or moralizing, he satirized. He parodied what he covered, and he had fun at it. The southern mind's reputed disdain for abstraction became, in Wolfe, a disdain for liberal pieties, literary fashion, and all *isms.* The southerner's supposed commitment to the concrete became his reporter's sharp eye for the surface of things. His early New Journalism celebrated the same youthful, rule-breaking energy George Leonard embraced—the 1960s!—but with secret moral reservations.[71] Wolfe's figures of manly independence and personal honor were usually southerners: the moonshine runner and NASCAR hero Junior Johnson and the test pilot Chuck Yeager. In his novels, southern protagonists at least know the moral truth of the premodern age: ex-football hero, Atlanta developer, and Turpmtine Plantation owner Charlie Croker in *A Man in Full* stands (and falls) for real manhood while small-town North Carolina star student Charlotte Simmons is battered by moral issues invisible to her peers at Dupont University in *I Am Charlotte Simmons.* Even the young investment banker who represents greed and pride run amok in

The Bonfire of the Vanities has a Tennessee grandfather and hillbilly name, McCoy, to whisper life's lessons to him.[72]

So the South provided Wolfe with the moral point of view implicit in his satire. But more than that, the old southern romance of the gentleman writer supplied Wolfe with an outsider's detachment, an education that encouraged him to ransack eighteenth- and nineteenth-century European traditions, and the right to fuse literary techniques with journalism. The melding of fiction and journalism that was necessary for meaningful coverage of the 1960s was not too difficult for southerners schooled in family stories and a complicated American history. Those whose talent brought them to the hot magazines of New York smuggled their perspectives into journalism as if in the false bottom of a suitcase.

EIGHT

ASSIMILATION AND ITS DISCONTENTS

Newspapers were born free, as one wit said in a twist on Jean-Jacques Rousseau, "yet everywhere they are in chains."[1] The second-largest newspaper chain in the country, Knight Ridder, was a merger of two companies that had each been born relatively free, generations earlier, under the control of the Knight brothers in Ohio and the Ridder family in New York. Both companies went public in 1969, in a Faustian bargain to secure capital at the risk of stockholder demands, and they merged in 1974. Daily newspapers that the Knights had bought in the South over the years were among the region's best, in terms of community influence, Pulitzer Prizes, and the honorable old standards of independent public-interest journalism. These included the *Charlotte Observer,* the *Columbia State,* the *Columbus (Georgia) Ledger-Enquirer,* the *Macon (Georgia) Telegraph,* the *Lexington (Kentucky) Herald-Leader,* the *Miami Herald,* the *Tallahassee Democrat,* and the *Fort Worth Star-Telegram.* But by 2005, despite relatively high profits, investors in Knight Ridder were demanding higher value on their stock. Suddenly, editors and reporters at thirty-two metro newspapers with distinct local histories and distinguished local missions were reading reports in the trade journals announcing that their owner was selling out. In June 2006, the properties sold for $4.5 billion plus assumption of $2 billion in debt to the smaller California-based McClatchy chain. The buyer kept twenty of the papers in faster-growing markets and offered to sell twelve, like properties on a Monopoly game board.[2]

The problems that caused Knight Ridder to vanish overnight ran deeper than its newsrooms, though the cuts it had recently made in some of its news staffs were the equivalent of throwing furniture into the fireplace to stay warm. And the problems ran deeper than the boardroom, though Knight Ridder's single class of stock gave its investors more bully power than most other newspaper families permitted. More broadly, the problems reflected trends that were vexing every metropolitan daily. Loyal readers were growing old. Young readers demanded free information online or simply did not pick up the newspaper habit of their parents. Advertising—including classified advertising—was leaching out to the Internet and other niche-market vehicles, such as direct mail. The "press" no longer meant a printing press; the mass media for news were no longer as "mass" as they had been. Not that the news business had ever been without cutthroat competition and crushing expenses in labor, pulp newsprint, and new machinery. But at least a coherent economic model, in the abstract, had hovered over what might be called the golden age of metro dailies from the 1920s through the 1980s. Big department stores wanted to reach everybody with the kind of sales information that fit better on a newspaper page than on television. So their advertising departments, along with other local and national advertisers, and plain folks wanting to use classified ads, turned over mountains of cash to support good journalism. It was a unique quirk in the capitalist system—so much money being transferred to strong, independent newspapers with no strings attached. But that commercial model, which was always under strain, underwent serious breakdown in the age of the Internet. The search for a new economic model seemed desperate. The daily news, in fact, had more readers than ever and more reader engagement, through the interactive nature of the Internet. But making money off these new readers would prove a fragmented, frantic, piecemeal job.[3]

Navigating the new media market was rough going in the larger metropolises of the American South in the years around the new millennium. Newspapers that once covered entire states and beyond shut down their satellite bureaus and pulled back to the metro areas. The *Miami Herald,* the flagship of Knight Ridder, was losing circulation as it struggled to cover a city of contradictions. As the sociologist John Shelton Reed points out, there is nothing "Southern" about Florida south of Daytona, but Miami is not even "Florida" in that cultural sense.[4] It is a city of colorful postmodern buildings, mob-style and drug-trade corruption, ethnic enclaves tied to agendas in New York and Cuba, and some of the poorest black neighborhoods in America, where the deadly Liberty City riot broke out in 1980. The *Herald's* difficulties seemed to hit a new low on July 27, 2005, when a once-respected black politician, embarrassed by corruption-investigation exposure in a weekly paper, shot himself dead in the lobby of the *Herald's* building and the editors responded, controversially, by firing an investigative reporter for having secretly tape-recorded a recent interview with the politician, against *Herald* policy.[5] The *Dallas Morning News,* which had achieved a high national reputation around the time its afternoon rival the *Dallas Times Herald* folded in 1991, made a series of bad investments in electronic media and an overstatement of circulation, all of which was quite costly. Between 2004 and 2006, to recoup some of its loses, the Dallas-based parent Belo Corporation cut 30 percent of the *Morning News* staff through layoffs and buyouts.[6]

At the *Atlanta Journal-Constitution* in 2007, after cuts of about 19 percent of the staff, a strange new organizational chart was blueprinted over the anxious reporters, editors, photographers, and artists. Instead of traditional department heads, such as sports, features, or business editors, the *Journal-Constitution* created two groups, Print and Digital, that were to concentrate entirely on presenting, not making, "content." Meanwhile, the more traditional roles of reporter and editor were further separated into another two groups—content providers—one group charged with getting fast-breaking, consumer-oriented news and information, and the other assigned to report and write in-depth or surprising enterprise stories. The Digital side was geared toward the elusive young online reader, which left the Print side to produce a somewhat traditional newspaper for what editor Julia Wallace called the "settled adults." Instead of fretting about circulation having dropped some 28 percent since a peak in the early 1990s, which should not have been happening in one of the fastest-growing metro areas in the country, the company could look at its newspaper as an elite product, with a more educated, higher-income reader. For a brief period, at least, the Web seemed to act as a sponge to dab away the superficial, leaving a more readable newspaper featuring articles that explained, exposed, or crafted narratives.[7]

Big-city newspapers are not just businesses but civic institutions. So the forces shaking up newsrooms also tested the degree to which citizens still depended on their last remaining local daily. In Virginia, with about 190 years of genteel history running in its veins, the *Richmond Times-Dispatch* seemed particularly stodgy in the age of new media. It was the surviving flagship paper of a Richmond newspaper dynasty, four generations of the Bryan family. Staffers tended to stay put, and editors came from within. In this, the Bryan newspapers reflected the culture of the settled white families of old Richmond. The newspapers had supported massive resistance to desegregation, and long after it embraced diversity, the *Times-Dispatch* retained its resistance to change. But the Bryan properties had grown into a large multimedia chain, Media General, with newspapers and television stations throughout the South and a commitment to "converged" new media. The company struggled to change its newsroom culture to reach a young, digital-savvy audience, but the results of its efforts remained uncertain.

In New Orleans, the apocalyptic rampage of Hurricane Katrina in late August 2005 thrust the 169-year-old *Times-Picayune* into a money-losing, public-service role of heroic dimensions. Staffers stalked the deadly flood on bicycles, in kayaks, from delivery trucks, and on foot. They sweated and cussed in a stifling, dark newsroom surrounded by rising waters, until they were forced to leave for ad-hoc newsrooms that operated out of town for six weeks. A house became the New Orleans "bureau" from which half a dozen photographers, reporters, and the columnist Chris Rose (who would later write about his own posttraumatic depression) bore witness and helped the desperate. They told of death, and of humanity, as when one reporter followed a Good Samaritan around in a skiff as he saved lives in Slidell.[8] With no way to print or distribute the paper, the Web site NOLA.com carried facsimiles of the paper's layout with color photographs, reports, and such giant headlines as HITTING BOTTOM and GROUND ZERO. The Web site was getting thirty million hits a day and letting the world know what was happening. The company that owned the paper, Advance Publications, was privately controlled by the Newhouse family, so it did not need to answer to investors when it resolved to take the loses.

But the devastation to New Orleans, especially the long-term loss of readers and advertisers, put the newspaper into the same ragged uncertainty as the city itself.[9] The newspaper aggressively covered the aftermath, demanding federal records daily, keeping the story on the front page for a year, and beyond. It won a Pulitzer Prize for its Katrina coverage. The *Times-Picayune* identified with the city's recovery and healing. Did this passion compromise its independence? "If being concerned about the very existence of your town is advocacy, then I plead guilty," editor Jim Amoss told a national media reporter. "When your very livelihood, and city, and community, and everything that's familiar to you is at stake and, in many cases, destroyed, it changes how you view the reporting of the news. You still have the same journalistic standards that are applied to stories, but every topic has an urgency."[10]

The great corporate and digital tremors that were rearranging metro newsrooms around the South, of course, could be felt everywhere from Los Angeles to Boston. What was noteworthy about the effect in the South was precisely that it was no different, that the bland, modern newsrooms of Birmingham, Nashville, Jacksonville, and so on, showed no sign at all of the distinctive, violent, and colorful history the southern press might claim. The region's newsrooms were as racially integrated as any, if not more so. Although the Newspaper Guild never made inroads in the South, the reporters and editors of the region were as well paid and well trained as any others. Many were from elsewhere anyway, following the profession's career ladders up a complex hierarchy having to do with newspaper reputation and size but nothing to do with geography. Reporters and editors believe in the importance of community, as a value, but it is an abstraction with as little sense of place or history as the policies of the giant newspaper chains that owned these media properties.

A more important perspective requires pulling back to see the entire landscape of corporate culture in the South, not only the news business. The decorously muffled environment of modern newsrooms in southern cities mirrored a deep transformation in all areas of the region's social, political, and economic life. Since World War II, but more dramatically since the civil rights era of the 1960s, a cosmopolitan, modern, fully American ethos had taken control. The causes and scope of this change do not need to be elaborated here because they have been described and analyzed at length by scholars from a number of academic disciplines. A good survey can be found in Numan V. Bartley's *The New South, 1945–1980,* the eleventh and concluding volume of the magisterial series *A History of the South.* Central air-conditioning and the bulldozer cleared the way. Then came the suburban cul-de-sacs, plastic-trimmed shopping malls, and infinitely replicated outlets of national syndicates. This assimilation into the American mold was rapid and resistless, across lands formerly wasted by the old cash crops of tobacco and cotton. The children of farm-borne poverty, black and white, had migrated to cities near and far. Wealthier white careerists and retirees moved in from the chilly latitudes, reducing the proportion of blacks in the political calculation even as the Voting Rights Act of 1965 secured pockets of black political power. The textile mills gave way to glass-clad office parks, silicon-chip amusements, and instant strip malls. Southern governors and their business partners persuaded public school administrators to standardize classrooms, whose pupils were still the lowest-scoring test-takers in the nation from long neglect. (The South's growth policy of cheap labor through the 1930s had discouraged investment in public education. The Southern Regional Education Board has attempted to reverse this since 1949.) A rising white middle class, augmented by corporate migrants happy to be in such a pleasant climate, created a conservative Republican Party that replaced the old conservative Democratic Party in the white South. Only two things were different about this Republican inversion: black southerners were at least empowered to vote in a minority bloc, as Democrats this time, and the U.S. Supreme Court had broken up the exclusive one-race party primary (in the 1944 case *Smith v. Allwright*) and the distorted representation, such as Georgia's county-unit system, that had given too much power in state assemblies to the wool-hat boys of rural county seats (in the 1962 case *Baker v. Carr*).[11]

The transmutation reached deep into the very soul of the South. Bartley put it this way: "By 1960 an impersonal and bureaucratic world based on formal contracts, legal procedures, and money transactions was approaching maturity. Even though wide diversity existed within white-collar ranks, the 'new middle class' relentlessly undermined the paternal foundations of the old social order. The sense of roots, place, and stability that had for so long been central to the southern value system retreated before new ideological currents emanating from the metropolitan areas."[12] In the modern literary South, the cosmopolitan dogma of autonomous man brought a queasy feeling of loss. For Walker Percy, a doctor-turned-novelist with roots in the Old South, viewing a modern or futuristic South from the perspective of an alienated native son produced a comic art of displacement. As an artist, he preferred this to what he called "total placement" in the South. "Total placement for a writer would be to live in a place like Charleston or Mobile, where one's family has lived for two hundred years," he wrote in 1980, explaining why he lived in suburban Covington, Louisiana. "A pleasant enough prospect, you might suppose, but not for a writer—or not for this writer. Such places are haunted. Ancestors perch on your shoulder while you write."[13]

For a southern literary journalist like Marshall Frady, the problem with a "domesticated" South was simply dullness. Gone was that tragic, baleful land capable of the lyrical and the brutish, replaced by a South "etherized . . . subtly rendered pastless, memoryless, blank," victim of a "cultural lobotomy," its racial sins trivialized into "the inconclusive grumpiness of everywhere else."[14]

Still, the vapors of a traditional South lingered in the folkways of family and church, especially in the smaller towns that were not overtaken by extruded suburbs or drained of their brightest high school graduates because of shriveling local prospects. The sociologist John Shelton Reed, who was Howard Odum's intellectual heir at the University of North Carolina at Chapel Hill, was only one of dozens of academics who continued to make a living as "professional southerners," as they jokingly called themselves, scholars at university-based centers dedicated to studying the South after its prematurely reported demise. Reed, aside from his research with social survey data, moonlighted as a witty columnist celebrating and satirizing the South, and teasing its critics. Such essays were collected and expanded into books with cleverly ambiguous titles such as *Whistling Dixie, Kicking Back, 1001 Things Everyone Should Know About the South* (with his wife, Dale Volberg Reed), and *Minding the South.* In a souvenir program explaining the South to international visitors to the 1996 Centennial Olympic Games in Atlanta, Reed noted that one does not find "the South" in what southerners do from nine to five on weekdays but outside of work. In those personal hours, one finds the manners, religious practices, cooking, sports, and music that still defined the subculture created by two hundred years of borrowing between blacks and Protestants of British descent. One of the many paradoxes of that culture, writes Reed, is that decades before it was largely assimilated into the American norm, it seeded itself nationally through clusters of southern migrants from coast to coast, "among Michigan auto workers, Southern blacks in Chicago and Harlem, or the children and grandchildren of Okies in California."[15] The Nashville-based writer John Egerton in 1974 described this as "the Southernization of America," and the *New York Times* Atlanta bureau chief Peter Applebome confirmed the phenomenon more than two decades later in his book *Dixie Rising.*[16]

If a distinct regional culture was missing from the big-city newsrooms of the modern South, it still flavored the smaller old newspapers. Such papers were often dull, craven, and compromised by the local powers that be. But initiation into even the shabbiest journalism offered a number of working-class or dirt-poor southern youths a personal liberation from the South's puckered rural culture and social hypocrisies. Several memoirs describe this pathway for sons of what has been called the rough South.

In the bleakest years of the Depression, Karl Fleming (1927–) was raised in a Methodist orphanage in Raleigh because his mother, who had left school in third grade and suffered two bad marriages with sorry men, felt her son would get a better upbringing there. In the navy at the end of World War II, Fleming devoured books written by the usual provocateurs beloved of aspiring southern reporters—Thomas Wolfe and H. L. Mencken. Mencken, in particular, became his hero, giving voice "to my growing doubts about religion, obedience to authority, and conformity." He dropped out of college to begin working at the *Wilson (North Carolina) Daily Times* for $30 a week as a reporter because "come to think of it my main heroes had been reporters—Dickens, Twain, Crane, Bierce, Mencken, and Hemingway." Slowly, from 1948 through 1958, he learned to write and to see through the surface of the southern social order, including the commercial interests of his publishers, with skeptical eyes. He disliked the newspapers where he worked, in Wilson, then Durham, then Asheville, but he loved the romance of being a tough-minded, life-sniffing reporter. After hours, he would stay up all night in a hotel room with his more educated colleagues at the *Durham Herald* drinking, playing poker, and talking about literature. Covering the trial of a black man who was executed in the gas chamber for attempted rape of a white woman sickened Fleming, as did the brutal picture of the South's unequal laws pointed out by the corrupt cop who drove the cub reporter around Wilson to show him, cynically, how things really were. The Asheville papers were full of puff pieces to flatter the business community, Fleming writes in his memoir, but he found inspiration in *A Treasury of Great Reporting.* Then came two lucky breaks—a job at the *Atlanta Journal-Constitution Sunday Magazine,* for which he had done some freelancing in Asheville, and a job covering the South for *Newsweek* out of the Atlanta bureau. Fleming would become one of the most celebrated national reporters of the civil rights movement, having the physique and face of a tough FBI agent and a tendency to be in the middle of violence from both black protesters and white rednecks. He was teargassed and just missed by bullets at Ole Miss in 1962. But he escaped serious harm until he transferred to the Los Angeles bureau of *Newsweek* and was beaten and almost killed by black rioters in Watts on May 17, 1966. Fleming had been an angry man most of his life, an outsider, as he put it. He thought it was racism he hated, but his boiling anger was more than that. "I hated bullies," he writes. "That's what it was. Perhaps I had an instinctive sense of fair play, but it was bullying that I had recoiled at and rebelled against."[17]

Another southerner from a scrappy, blue-collar background, Paul Hemphill (1936–), also discovered journalism as a form of rebellion against the Negrophobia of his upbringing. In a 1993 memoir, *Leaving Birmingham: Notes of a Native Son,* Hemphill recalled how the "nigger" talk of his own working-class people turned meaner around 1950 as President Harry Truman and the nation began to awaken to the plight of southern blacks. The Hemphills were in the lower middle class of Birmingham, poor compared to the "big mules" who ran the steel mills but comfortable enough to hire a black cleaning lady named Louvenia. His hard-drinking, truck-driving daddy began dragging every dinner-table topic into the mud of politics and race in ways that made the teenager nervous. At Auburn University, he was sports editor of the student paper, the *Plainsman,* where a columnist from Atlanta named Anne Rivers was fired for urging tolerance in the attempted integration of the University of Alabama in 1957. (Anne Rivers Siddons, as she became, later wrote for *Atlanta* magazine and turned to producing more than a dozen successful novels largely set in a coming-of-age modern South. Other Auburn alumnae who became notable southern journalists were Rheta Grimsley Johnson, a syndicated columnist for the papers in Memphis and Atlanta, and the *Atlanta Constitution* editorial page editor Cynthia Tucker.) Hemphill, who had briefly played minor-league baseball, hired on as a sportswriter at the *Birmingham News.* It was one of the city's two chain-owned rival newspapers that were allowed enough independence to bury or slant any news that smacked of the underlying racial reality of Birmingham. That reality was a paranoia, among blacks and whites, stimulated by a thuggish police commissioner named Eugene "Bull" Connor and enforced, as in Russia or South Africa, "by the whip, the razor, the gun, the bomb, the torch, the club, the knife, the mob, the police and many branches of the state's apparatus," as a fierce *New York Times* feature on Birmingham put it in 1960.[18] But the *News* and the *Post-Herald,* like the white city fathers, saw no evil except the "lies" and subversion of outside agitators, including the national press. So Hemphill claims that he was oblivious that Sunday afternoon of Mother's Day, 1961, in the *News* sports department, while "trying to create some literature out of a high-jump competition," when white mobs were beating freedom riders a few blocks away and one bus of this civil rights caravan still smoked from a bomb blast outside Anniston, Alabama. His final break with Birmingham came in the summer of 1962, after his deployment with the Alabama Air National Guard in France, when Hemphill visited his family and felt they had become near strangers to him in their rabid bigotry. He took a job as sports editor of the *Augusta (Georgia) Chronicle,* and found that "inbred, smelly, provincial" city just as racist as Birmingham but too small to be noticed by the national press or civil rights movement.[19] Hemphill, who had been educating himself as a writer by studying Ernest Hemingway, William Faulkner, John Dos Passos, and Irwin Shaw, discovered the *New York Herald-Tribune* of Red Smith, Jimmy Breslin, and Tom Wolfe. His managing editor in Augusta, although an old-fashioned newsman, encouraged Hemphill to experiment with this new style in his sports columns. He finally got a chance to be a southern-style Breslin in Atlanta, writing a metro column for an upstart *Atlanta Times,* which conservative Republican investors had launched to attack the monopoly they felt was giving Ralph McGill his "liberal" platform at the *Atlanta Constitution.* But that paper folded in August 1965, after only fourteen months, and Hemphill jumped to the *Atlanta Journal,* where he would write six columns a week for five years. "This, for me," he wrote, "was the journalism school they hadn't had at Auburn when I was there, my personal boot camp, where I could learn all of the basics: finding ideas, interviewing, composing the story, and then writing it under daily pressure. Strippers, hookers, athletes, troubadours, politicians, drunks, Klansmen, priests, pilots, plumbers, route salesmen, socialites—all were my people." Hemphill won a Nieman Fellowship at Harvard and went on to write fiction and nonfiction books about southern culture and his own life. Among these was a book on Nashville country music and an illuminating account, with Mayor Ivan Allen Jr., of how conservative business interests created Atlanta's liberal image on race and thereby made it the commercial, transportation, and media center of the South.[20]

Anger and class resentment fill the memoir of a much younger journalist from Alabama, Rick Bragg (1959–). His *All Over but the Shoutin'* tells of growing up in poverty and meanness, in a South that seems to belong to an earlier era of history than the 1960s. Still, this is his South, a rough land where poor white men worked in pulpwood yards or blast-furnace heat, where his mama picked boles of thin cotton and his drunkard daddy was "the kind of slim and lethal Southern man who would react with murderous fury when insulted." Bragg's anger, though, is not directed at his kinfolk, whom he seems to love out of some combination of sentimentality and guilt, or at the ragged landscape, which he describes with a touch that renders it beautiful. Rather, it is the privileged class, from the power brokers of Birmingham to college-educated Yankees, that weighs down the giant chip on his shoulder. He bristled at power and class, as he perceived them. They were things his mama never had and that he was determined to get. He set out for revenge with a single course in feature writing at a nearby state university. Soon, he was learning the craft as a sportswriter, the way so many other notable southern journalists first discovered how to do their storytelling in print—Ralph McGill, Tom Wicker, Lewis Grizzard Jr., Fleming, and Hemphill. But Bragg's ticket was feature writing, with which he ascended from the lowly to the highest points of journalistic status: from the Jacksonville State University student paper *Chanticleer,* to the *Talladega* (Alabama) Daily Home, the *Birmingham News,* the *Anniston Star,* the *St. Petersburg (Florida) Times,* and finally the crown, the *New York Times.* When he won a Pulitzer Prize in 1996 for his feature stories in the *Times* out of the South, he called it vindication and flew up to get the award in New York with his mama, her first flight ever. "It was like fights in the playground when I was a boy, when you take one last blind swing, wipe the dirt out of your eyes, and realize that the other boys you were fighting, biting and gouging have left the field of honor to you, and run for the teacher."[21]

Howell Raines (1943–) followed a path somewhat like Bragg's and Hemphill's, in terms of class and geography and newspaper work, all the way to the very summit of American journalism: three of the most coveted posts at the *New York Times*—Washington bureau chief (1988–93), editorial-page editor (1993–2001), and executive editor (2001–3). Raines's family came from hardscrabble hill-country stock to the steel-mill labor of Birmingham, but they stayed sober, worked hard in the lumber business, and accumulated wealth. His father became rich enough, at least, to pamper Howell, point him toward college, and hire a black housemaid. Unlike the sad homes that Hemphill and Bragg recalled, the Raines home did not permit the word *nigger.* The family had the same underdog mentality of hill people but with humanitarian instincts. In such a household, young Howell was given the rare gift of honest talk from the young family maid, Grady Williams Hutchinson, about race and what it was like being black in Birmingham. In a 1991 magazine feature that won a Pulitzer Prize, "Grady's Gift," Raines wrote about reconnecting with Grady forty years later and telling her how important their seven years together had been to him. She had inspired his proudest work, an oral history of the civil rights movement titled *My Soul Is Rested.*[22] And she had pointed him on the right road. "Every white Southerner must choose between two psychic roads—the road of racism or the road of brotherhood," he wrote. "Friends, families, even lovers have parted at that forking, sometimes forever, for it presents a choice that is clouded by confused emotions, inner conflicts and powerful social forces."[23]

The South in the last quarter of the twentieth century evened up the score and, in a way, beat the rest of the country at its own game. Far from being the nation's number-one economic problem or a problem at all, the South looked like a winner. Oil industry dollars brought a boom in Texas and Louisiana while the oil shocks of 1973 and 1979 battered the auto industry in Detroit and drove up the cost of staying warm in northern winters. The nomination of one-term Georgia governor Jimmy Carter as the Democratic Party's candidate for president in 1976 prompted *Time* magazine to publish a seventy-page special edition in September, "The New South Today: Carter Country and Beyond." The publisher noted that many of the seventy or so staffers who spent weeks on the project were from families in the South for generations, having come to New York for journalistic work. "Southerners never really leave," said Washington correspondent and Winston-Salem native Bonnie Angelo. "There's always a cranny of their psyche that cherishes the soft-edged South." Even the agonizing history of race in Dixie was seen as a plus, an experience that supposedly gave the South lessons the North still needed to learn and something in common with a multicultural world at large. But as Atlanta bureau correspondent Jack E. White observed from a black southern perspective: "Without unrelenting pressure from blacks and the Federal Government, white Southerners would never have changed. Southern behavior has changed, but the hearts, for the most part, are probably just the same."[24] Although the old "New South" of cheap raw materials and cheap nonunion labor had developed the region as a virtual colonial territory of northern capital, the new New South could boast of smart university-spawned high-tech industries. A black middle class in-migration or return was beginning to reverse the long drop in the percentage of black residents. Southern music—which, after all, was the only real American music—was in the air.

The change in newspapers was also notable. The South had long been a land of great newspaper editors—Ashmore, McGill, Hodding Carter Jr.—but "second-rate newspapers," the special-issue *Time* said. By 1976, newspapers seemed better than ever, paying their best reporters enough "to halt the traditional northward migration." *Time* identified what it considered the top five of "Dixie's Best Dailies": the *Charlotte Observer,* the *Memphis Commercial-Appeal,* the *Dallas Times Herald,* the *Miami Herald,* and the *St. Petersburg Times.* It also recognized the "cheeky" *Texas Monthly,* which since 1973 had been riding the state's oil boom with smart, irreverent coverage of contemporary Texas politics, business, and lifestyle.[25]

One still felt a lingering sense of southern newspapers as colonial properties of northern chains. More than a generation earlier, the Knight brothers had swooped down from Ohio, Governor James Cox from Ohio, S. I. Newhouse from New York, Paul and Nelson Poynter, father and son, from Indiana. But the problem was not so much Yankee owners as it was the power of free-market investors from anywhere and everywhere. Nelson Poynter (1903–78), who had inherited the *St. Petersburg Times* from his father, worried about the power of stockholders to control the future of his "sacred trust." He charged his lawyers with devising a legal mechanism to protect the newspaper's public-interest journalism from dilution by profiteering. He wanted a scheme that would endure in perpetuity. Other proud patriarchs of family-run newspapers like the Binghams in Louisville or the Sulzburgers at the *New York Times* depended on descendants protecting the patrimony. But Poynter said he had not met his great-grandchildren, and he might not like them. It took the attorneys nearly a decade. to construct a shield against corporate raiders, inheritance taxes, or stockholder greed. They created a nonprofit journalism-education foundation, later called the Poynter Institute for Media Studies, which would hold all the stock of the for-profit *St. Petersburg Times* and allied properties, such as *Congressional Quarterly* and *Florida Trend* magazine. The chairman on the educational institute would also be president of the Times company. Gene Patterson, who was editor of the newspaper when Poynter died in 1978, succeeded as chairman of the institute's board under the terms of Poynter's will. He also ran the newspaper, set his own salary, and appointed his successor for that joint position.[26] The threat of a buyout arose in 1988 from an outsider who had acquired stock from Poynter's nieces, but this was settled at a high cost and the newspaper finally achieved Poynter's dream of total protection. The *St. Petersburg Times* would continue to be an economically sound and highly regarded newspaper—cogently edited but with style, artful in design but not garish. It was the best career path in the South for writers on their way to the *New York Times* like Raines, Bragg, Dudley Clendenin, and Eleanor Randolph, and a good home for prize-winning writers of long-form journalism such as Tom French. The Poynter Institute, which built a plush facility on Tampa Bay in 1985, flourished as the heart of a professional-development movement in newsrooms and as a popular Web site for journalism tips and insider news.[27]

Another case of a southern newspaper wrapping itself in the protective armor of a foundation is the so-called Tupelo miracle.

The Tupelo miracle is a more southern story than Poynter's legalistic defense of editorial independence, for the newspaper in Tupelo, Mississippi, was a vehicle for regional values—Protestant religious faith, industrial development, and human growth. George McLean (1904–83), the longtime publisher of the *Northeast Mississippi Daily Journal* (formerly the *Tupelo Journal*), was the son of a lawyer, planter, and judge of the traditional Delta gentry. McLean's devout Presbyterian outlook and his graduate-level education at Boston University, University of Chicago, and Stanford University nurtured a liberality of spirit unusual for Mississippi. James W. Silver, a liberal Ole Miss professor who was driven out of the state by the forces he described in his 1964 classic *Mississippi: The Closed Society,* called McLean's paper "a genuine community leader."[28] Tupelo, where Elvis Presley was born and raised, anchored a corner of the state—the northeast—that differed in essential ways from the rest of the "closed society." It had virtually no natural resources that could be exploited, save the development of its citizens. Also, four-fifths of the population was white, a far greater percentage than the rest of the state, and these whites were more similar to Appalachian hill farmers in origin. During the Depression, McLean had lost his teaching job at a college in Memphis, probably in retaliation for his trying to organize farmworkers on Arkansas plantations. He dabbled in journalism, then with family money bought the failing *Tupelo Journal* in 1936 with the notion that it would be his means for Christian service and ministry.[29] (His motto, "A locally-owned newspaper dedicated to the service of God and mankind," remained on the masthead permanently.) McLean, as his paper prospered and made him wealthy, donated money and editorial columns to the goal of civic, industrial, and rural development. He saw all three as harmonically linked. In 1948, he led the founding of a Rural Community Development

Program, which boldly included blacks and whites while delicately maintaining customary segregation. The slow success of such community-interest efforts drew national attention, always featuring the quiet, square-jawed McLean as the dynamo behind it all. Hodding Carter Jr., in a 1951 article praising Tupelo in the *Saturday Evening Post,* credited McLean's rural development program with "the amazingly far-reaching integration of agriculture and civic objectives which in its three years of existence has been copied by at least twenty other towns and cities from Louisiana to West Virginia."[30] McLean created another nonprofit foundation to which he gave away his newspaper in 1973—Christian Research Education Action Technical Enterprises, or CREATE. He thus secured the *Daily Journal* as a locally controlled public trust. "We regard the increasing concentration of ownership of newspapers, radio, and television stations in the hands of a few big chains as potentially very dangerous to freedom of information in this country," McLean wrote at the time. "Another serious problem with increasing outside control of the media is that the 'bottom line,' that is the desire for more and more profits, will take the place of service to readers, listeners, or advertisers."[31]

McLean's missionary zeal seemed a curious mix of values, hard to place on a political scale running from conservative to progressive. He tended to avoid controversy, a caution he may have acquired early on when his support for striking garment workers in Mississippi in 1937 brought retaliation that almost put his newspaper out of business. He became a pragmatist, preferring action to rhetoric, and local initiative to government intervention. His uncritical boosterism seemed to be a local version of the New South creed of promoting economic growth and agricultural diversification above all else. He supported the status quo in race relations, believing that goodwill and better jobs would solve the problem of inequality. He downplayed race news to keep attention on his main project, economic uplift for all. To McLean, "extremists" and "outside agitators" led both sides of the historic fight over civil rights in Mississippi—the white backlash against the federal courts and the action of civil rights workers. The violence of the white riots around James Meredith's attempt to integrate Ole Miss in 1962 horrified McLean, pushing him to a more "liberal" position in support of reason, nonviolence, and the rule of law. McLean finally came to support integration as inevitable only after he saw that white resistance threatened to ruin the public schools. Perhaps the most hard-to-categorize element of McLean's journalism was his Christianity. His faith was explicit and traditional but not like the moralistic religious right that Donald E. Wildmon and his American Family Association would later represent in Tupelo. McLean believed in progress that was measured not by money or power but by making "better" men and women. "Men are God's methods," McLean preached.[32]

The successful amalgam of progrowth, Protestant, and sunny pragmatism embodied in McLean's *Daily Journal* was hardly typical of the South, or anywhere else. But it was in some ways a southern foreshadowing of the civic or public journalism movement of the 1990s. Newspapers that embraced public journalism reached out to their readers through town-hall meetings, surveys, or citizen-run forums in the newspaper. Frustrated by horse-race political campaigns and sterile government policies, and especially by ineffective news coverage that failed to engage citizens or solve their problems, these newspapers sought to embrace a "public agenda." To critics, this violated standards of objectivity, noninvolvement in the news, and skepticism. The movement came under fire from the large, powerful newspapers such as the *New York Times* and *Washington Post*. The movement was debated by scholars, both supporters and critics, for it evoked what passes for excitement among intellectuals—controversies like the communitarian debate and the Walter Lippmann–John Dewey disagreements in the 1920s over the role of the ignorant masses in a democracy. One scholar noted that public journalism remained a peripheral phenomenon associated with smaller cities such as Charlotte, Wichita, Kansas, and Columbus, Georgia, rather than the big cities that defined public life in America. In these smaller cities, one found a closer, or less evolved, relationship between actual neighborhoods and the idea of a mass public. This contributed to what critics called a blind spot in public journalism. The movement tended to value the "people" part of democracy but not democracy's mature political institutions such as unions, interest groups, parties, or protest movements. This may help explain why public journalism occurred mainly in the Sunbelt South, with its smaller cities and suspicion of government and political organizations.[33] Some of the early experiments in public journalism were a 1987 project of the *Columbus Ledger-Enquirer* called "United Beyond 2000," the *Charlotte Observer*'s "Citizen's Agenda" for covering elections in 1992, and the *Norfolk Virginian-Pilot*'s "public life teams" that replaced political beats in the 1990s. A number of public journalism newspapers in the South were in the Knight Ridder chain, promoted largely by the company's president in Miami, James K. Batten. Batten, a genteel Virginian educated at Davidson and Princeton, had outlined in 1971, a year before he became executive editor of the *Charlotte Observer,* an important change that would occur in the tone of American newspapers. Assigned as a kind of tryout to write a critique of that paper's traditional emphasis on government and politics, Batten called for a friendlier, more polished style— less of an "us-versus-them" siege mentality, more useful tips on local events, and more stories about ordinary people and unsung heroes representing the average reader.[34] Cole C. Campbell, a former reporter and editor at the papers in Chapel Hill, Raleigh, and Greensboro, became one of the leading pioneers of public journalism as editor of the *Virginian-Pilot* in Norfolk. He described the movement as an experiment in a tradition of journalism that he called "conversation-keeping." Journalism, he said, was more than fact-finding, which at best took the form of muckraking and investigative journalism, and more than that other side of journalism, storytelling. Conversation-keeping was a third element, and one that Campbell argued needed reinvigorating "if we don't want to further debase democracy."[35]

The public journalism movement seemed to die around 2002 as quickly as it had emerged, replaced by an older term with less academic packaging, *community journalism*. As the larger newspapers struggled with cutbacks and corporate restructuring, community journalism came to be the name for a more stable form of newspapering in smaller communities. The *Anniston (Alabama) Star,* a midsize daily famous as a training ground for ambitious young Ivy Leaguers taking a turn in the Deep South, offered itself in partnership with the University of Alabama as a learning laboratory for community journalism. Having the newspaper operate with a university journalism department, like a teaching hospital with a med school, was unprecedented for the press. The first ten Knight Community Journalism Fellows, given full scholarships plus stipends, began their twelve-month master's degree program in the fall of 2006. The *Star* had survived as one of the last two locally owned newspapers left in Alabama. Associated with the Ayers family for three generations, the paper had long been an independent, feisty "attorney for the most defenseless," as Colonel Harry Ayers, publisher from 1910 until his death in 1964, had called it. His son, publisher H. Brandt Ayers, was determined that an impersonal media chain would not gobble up the *Star* and smaller papers the family also owned. In 2002, he formed the nonprofit Ayers Family Institute for Community Journalism. He and a sister created wills that would transfer ownership to the foundation after they die. They could have sold the *Star* for more than $50 million but instead donated $750,000 for the educational program. (The John S. and James L. Knight Foundation in Miami supplied another $1.5 million.) The program's educational mission would protect the *Star* from inheritance taxes and allow total control by the institute, like the Poynter Institute and the *St. Petersburg Times.*

"Brandy" Ayers had made a career of writing about the persistence of southern history in the region's culture and politics. He was a founding member of the L. C. Q. Lamar Society, a group of progressive southerners from the 1960s who took the society's name from a Confederate-turned-conciliator. Ayers's comment to an academic conference on the South following the Republican sweep of the region in 2004 was typical of his undying hope for a liberal revival in the region: "The South's hard and tragic history has given us a wise and tolerant heart." Likewise, he felt that the *Star*'s control by a foundation and its new role as a classroom could offer something of immense value to the metropolitan newspapers of the nation. What it came down to was a love of place. "We really do care about this one little patch of earth more than any other," Ayers told the *Birmingham News.*[36] Yet it was a small patch on a South whose character had been murdered, as Rick Bragg put it, "by generic subdivisions and generic fast-food restaurants."[37]

NINE

CONCLUSION

A poet looks for images to capture an idea or feeling. So the poet James Dickey summoned up the image of a pure spirit flying over the South in a wide circle, from the New World's first city of St. Augustine in Florida across the Gulf Coast to Texas, up through Arkansas and Kentucky to Virginia, and down the Atlantic coast. "I endow you with the power to fly," he wrote in a hefty coffee-table book from 1974 called *Jericho: The South Beheld*. The book featured watercolor paintings by the southern artist Herbert Shuptrine and Dickey's voluptuous word-pictures of the South's land, people, and sheer existence. Holding up the image of a gull or buzzard or hummingbird, he asked the reader "to give up your body and to hover, to sweep, to enter into the veer of the land and rivers, to zigzag over the landscape of people, to live the trembling Web of custom and family."[1]

To survey what we call the southern press today requires a similar flight of swoops and hovers. You learn almost nothing keeping your feet on the ground, except that the present-day publishing and newspaper industries of the region are like most other industries of the South, or anywhere—anxious, changing, unhistorical, and digitizing. To draw out meaningful connections between our story of the southern press and any future prospects requires some historical imagination and a literary ear. If there is any heart or soul left in the southern press, it draws on its past and its personalities. Let us review those from the air, aloft in time, and see how they connect to the now and the possible.

We began with the southerner's tendency to gaze backward with long farewells. The region was also tenacious about not letting go of the past. But when it was time to move on, the southern way was to do so loquaciously, with a backward gaze. Writers before and after the Civil War staked their literary careers on ideas that were passing, or long gone: a golden-age planter society (the novelists William Gilmore Simms and Thomas Nelson Page), a feudal agricultural economy (the proslavery essayists Edmund Ruffin and George Fitzhugh), and codes of honor (the Virginia editors George Bagby and John Moncure Daniel). George Washington Cable, before his brave and moral stand for racial justice drove him to Massachusetts, was beloved in the South (and North) for his elegiac depictions of old Creole days. The daily news of crime and scandal, characteristic of the penny press in northern cities, was less engaging in the slower-paced South. Poe wrote entirely out of his imagination and esoteric learning. Augustus Baldwin Longstreet and Joel Chandler Harris, as newspapermen in Georgia, wrote their memorable stories based on recollections of times gone by. Even the more news-savvy editor Henry Grady, famous as a crusader for industrialization, built his career around beautifully written pictures of the preindustrial South (including what he claimed was a stable and harmonious system of white supremacy). Moving ahead to the so-called liberal editors of the mid-twentieth century, Harry Ashmore's *Epitaph for Dixie* is only one of a half dozen books worth rereading today for their lyrical accounts of a South thought to be disappearing. Hodding Carter Jr., Jonathan Daniels, Virginius Dabney, Ralph McGill, and Gene Patterson all wrote their pleas for gradual progress on race (a carefully mixed message) embedded within rich memories from their youths and affection for southern history. Their best-known conservative counterparts, such as James J. Kilpatrick and John Temple Graves II, wrote from the same sensibility for an opposite goal— holding firm against change. To be a great southern editor in those times meant to be an amateur poet or historian.

Today, history in the popular press of the South is often reduced to columns on the Civil War that still appear regularly in the back pages of some newspapers.[2] On Virginia public radio, a professor from the Virginia Center for Civil War Studies broadcast a series on the war with weekly commentaries for fourteen years through 2007.[3] Interest in the Civil War in the South has not diminished, but the perspective has broadened over time. An American Civil War Center opened in Richmond in 2006 advertising that it would present three perspectives—that of the Confederacy, the Union, and blacks.[4] Books on local history and American history are almost as popular as southern cookbooks in the three hundred or so bookstores of the Southern Independent Booksellers Alliance. Civil War reenactors gather in increasing numbers on historic battlefields of the South to sweat out old conflicts wearing historically correct woolen uniforms of butternut, gray, and blue. These Civil War buffs have their political and controversial branch in what has been called the neo-Confederate movement, epitomized by ultraconservative South Carolina–based *Southern Partisan* magazine. The magazine, which considers General Stonewall Jackson a better man than Abraham Lincoln, gave the legislatures of Virginia and North Carolina its Scalawag Award for their "cowardly and self-righteous" resolutions in 2007 apologizing for slavery. (Maryland and Alabama also apologized for slavery with similar resolutions.)[5] The neo-Confederate movement suffers from a highly selective historical memory. The more recent sectional conflict following *Brown v. Board of Education* seems to vanish into a huge gap of amnesia. In that furious decade from 1954 to 1963, the white massive resistance movement, which overwhelmed white liberals and moderates, appropriated the old Confederate battle flag as a symbol. The rebel flag wagged defiantly over crowds at the football stadium at Ole Miss, became a license plate on the front bumpers of hot rods, and by an act of the state legislature in 1956 was added to Georgia's official flag. Several decades later, the link between that symbol and massive resistance, and further back, its connection to slavery, prompted black-led protests and boycotts against public displays of the flag, such as the one atop the state capitol of South Carolina. Although the white Civil War buffs continued to insist, perhaps sincerely, that they were honoring heritage without bigotry, the impasse seemed to cool down as the rebel flag lost most of its state support. Resistance had been privatized and coded almost to the point of irrelevancy.[6]

Meanwhile, the civil rights movement and the broader history of the black struggle in the South began to be recognized across the region as another worthy heritage. This newer historical consciousness was fed by a growing bibliography of books by southern journalist-historians such as Jack Bass, who published important biographies of post–World War II southern federal judges and politicians, and Taylor Branch, whose authoritative three-part biography of Martin Luther King Jr. was completed in 2007. Since the 1990s, especially, newspapers of the region have devoted resources to publishing high-quality investigative projects on racial conflict in the twentieth-century South. The motivation behind such projects seemed to be partly atonement for past sins of noncoverage. "It has come to the editor's attention," said an editor's note accompanying a 2004 front-page story on long-ago civil rights protests in Lexington, Kentucky, "that the *Herald-Leader* neglected to cover the civil rights movement. We regret the omission."[7] The *Jackson (Mississippi) Clarion-Ledger* in 1990 aired its own dirty laundry in an eight-page package based on documents, finally unsealed by court order, of the state-funded Sovereignty Commission. The commission, beginning in 1956, had secretly waged a propaganda war against *Brown v. Board* and black civil rights leaders by planting articles, altering stories prior to publication, or censoring news, all with the secret cooperation of local newspaper editors, including those at the *Clarion-Ledger*.[8] Jerry Mitchell, the reporter on the exposé, continued to investigate long-dormant cases of the murders of civil rights workers in Mississippi. His success was given glancing recognition in the 1996 movie *The Ghosts of Mississippi,* on the trial that finally brought a conviction of Byron De La Beckwith for the murder of Medgar Evers thirty-one years earlier. In 2004, a former *Birmingham News* photo intern, Alexander Cohn, discovered five thousand photographs from the civil rights years buried in a cardboard box at the newspaper. Few had been published at the time, apparently because they made Birmingham look bad. The newspaper published an eight-page section in 2006, called "Unseen. Unforgotten," displaying more than thirty of these photographs for the first time.[9] Newspapers of all sizes dug up stories of local lynching and terrorism that drove blacks out of their communities decades before the civil rights movement.[10] Another type of newspaper project on race focused on everyday relationships between blacks and whites in the post–civil rights era and unearthed the brutal reality of pre–civil rights race relations. The *New Orleans Times-Picayune,* for example, spent most of a year in

1993 digging into the city's racial history and the views of some one thousand readers who phoned in statements about race. The series, "Together Apart: The Myth of Race," ran on 105 full pages over twenty-seven days throughout the year. It exhumed much bitter history, including the newspaper's own refusal before the 1970s to hire black reporters or cover black citizens who were not committing crimes. Many readers said the series was emotionally draining for them, and not particularly healing.[11] It was not necessarily soothing to have "A Conversation on Race," as President Bill Clinton called his yearlong series of town-hall forums in 1998 to communicate honestly in a new racial environment.

Like the Civil War, which was fought almost entirely on southern soil, the civil rights movement has its historical sites scattered throughout the old Confederacy. These began to be dignified with monuments and museums, such as the National Civil Rights Museum, which opened in 1991 within the former Lorraine Motel, where King was assassinated in Memphis, and the Birmingham Civil Rights Institute, which opened in 1992. Schoolchildren visited these sites and bus tours followed the Civil Rights Freedom Trail from Virginia to Louisiana. A 1998 book that traces the history of the movement geographically, *Weary Feet, Rested Souls,* lists 384 surviving sites that may be visited, such as Ebenezer Baptist Church in Atlanta and Aaron Henry's drugstore in Clarksdale, Mississippi.[12] In January 2007, about one hundred students from four colleges and universities in Nashville, riding in four buses with veterans of the freedom rides of 1961, retraced the path of that bloody crusade.[13] Later that summer, a class from the University of Richmond spent nineteen days on a bus tour of civil rights sites in eight southern states. A black female student from Maryland ran into her cousin in Selma, a city she was looking forward to seeing because she had family roots there and kinfolk who marched to Montgomery in 1965. A white female student from a Boston suburb wrote in her journal, "The more I learn on this trip, the more I realize how ignorant I am about this time in American history."[14]

Meanwhile, it was time for political journalists to revisit another strand of southern history that had been lost in the fog of sectional and racial conflicts. This was the old history of the white "cracker" whom W. J. Cash had sought to explain. To Cash, the poor white was a pathetic character, a class victim of the planter and mill baron. A more flattering portrait has come recently from an unlikely source. This is the novelist, ex-marine, and former Republican secretary of the navy who turned Democrat in opposition to President Bush's war in Iraq, U.S. Senator Jim Webb of Virginia. Webb brought out his first nonfiction book in 2004, *Born Fighting,* on the history of the Scots-Irish and their influence on America. He writes that the book was the result of "decades of research and thought." Although Webb covers a millennium of battles and migrations, he also puts himself into the saga. He feels a deep connection with the people of the mountains as he drives "through history" on Interstate 81 down the western valleys of Virginia into Tennessee. In a neglected cemetery near Natural Bridge, Virginia, he muses over the grave of his great-great-great-great-great-grandfather Thomas Lackey, born in Ulster, Northern Ireland, in 1732 and descended from the MacGregor clan in Scotland. Webb quotes from an eleven-page handwritten note his Granny Doyle produced for him long ago recounting from memory the wanderings of their lineage, which had brought her branch of the family from Virginia to Tennessee to Mississippi and finally to Arkansas.[15]

Waves of immigrants bearing Scottish heritage poured into the American colonies between 1715 and 1775, most of them moving restlessly inland, into the mountain frontier, and southward, away from the settled English culture of the Atlantic coast. As Scots, they carried in their makeup a long history of border skirmishes, religious independence, and hardscrabble cottage life. The Scots, as Webb describes them, were a mix of the lost tribes of northern Europe, the Picts and Scotti, the Britons and Angles, wild warriors pushed into the cold wastes beyond Hadrian's Wall and outside the civilized sway of Rome, Normandy, and London. Their loyalties, by ancient custom, were to family and clan, not to abstractions like king or nation. They were tolerant of differences, having no deep racial identity, but intolerant of insult to their personal dignity. The power of the English ruling class was particularly galling to their sense of family honor and justice, although many alliances of convenience had been struck with English rulers. In the seventeenth century, for example, many lowland Scots left for Ulster, in North Ireland, with the encouragement of English monarchs. For a century, these Scottish wayfarers endured hardship, religious persecution, and betrayal in Ireland, writing in blood their motto of "No surrender" when under siege. They became even more battle hardened and less modern than their cousins back in Scotland, for they missed out on the changes that eighteenth-century industrial progress and the Scottish Enlightenment brought to the homeland. It was these more primitive and unsettled hybrid people, the Scots-Irish, who immigrated to America in the greatest numbers (as high as four hundred thousand before the American Revolution). They scattered and mixed all over America, leaving their imprint on the heartland and rural culture without clinging to a particular European "hyphenated" identity. They were simply Americans. Their values became the values of the working-class South, the South of country music, NASCAR, churchgoing, hunting, drinking, fighting, and joining the armed services (and dying, in Vietnam, for example) in disproportionate numbers.[16]

Webb's history of the Scots-Irish—earlier historians called them "Scotch-Irish," but Webb believes that sounds too much like a whiskey—has a political aim. He seeks to show another side of the redneck or cracker not only as victim, the way W. J. Cash depicted him, but also inheritor of a proud and ancient culture, dedicated to family, God, and freedom. Webb recasts the stereotype of redneck bigotry in terms of Scottish loyalties, before clan degenerated to Klan and before the Cross of St. Andrews became the Confederate battle flag on the back of pickup trucks. The Scottish system of extended kinship was not interested in a person's ethnic identity, he says, so much as in that person's loyalty. "An individualistic society based on loyal service reaches to the person rather than to his or her ethnicity, although it certainly is capable of opposing an enemy on racial or national grounds if it is threatened."[17]

Webb interprets southern history as a series of tensions that re-enact the conflicts experienced by the Scots in olden days, mostly at the hands of feudal English lords. The slave-based plantation society, like the Anglo-Norman nobility that intermarried with Scottish leaders in the Middle Ages, corrupted a class of Anglo-Saxon southerner with a false sense of entitlement demeaning to ordinary whites as well as blacks, Webb says. He sees the arrogance of the planter class surviving even today. The American Civil War becomes, in Webb's view, a clash between an English-style mercantile North and a Celtic South. "The Northern army was most often run like a business, solving a problem. The Southern army was run like a family, confronting a human crisis." It was size, not style, that won, for the South fought with amazing success against overwhelming odds "because it was so wildly and recklessly Celtic." Reconstruction, to the descendants of Scotland in the South, seemed an echo of the English invasions or attempts to impose Anglican conformity in Ulster, according to Webb.[18]

For a politician-historian to project Scottish tribal identity back into the South of today is tricky, for those bloodlines are not so neatly national. Even among the eighteenth-century Scots in America, the lines were not very clear. The Highlanders who came into the Carolinas by way of southern ports like Wilmington, North Carolina, after losing the battle of Culloden in 1746, including William Faulkner's ancestors, had backed a Catholic claimant to the English throne, Bonnie Prince Charlie. They were getting early practice at a lost cause, and many fought for the Crown in the American Revolution.[19] As Webb admits, southerners like him may be obsessed with family stories and genealogy but not with ethnic identity. Patriotism for them is more a passion than a doctrine. Loyalty to a flag or party comes from the heart, not the mind. It can shift sides, as it did in Scotland and Ulster many times.

The emotional traits and moral values that Webb identifies can explain the success of the Republican Party in winning over the white South since the 1970s. The southern strategy since Richard Nixon's 1968 campaign played on racial fears (most southern whites of that era having as little personal contact with middle-class blacks as had northern whites) and a host of cultural and moral values.[20] But the same cultural and moral values, minus the racial code words, could pull the white South back into the Democratic fold, if the national Democratic Party remembers how to speak with a southern accent, honestly, about guns and God. Such a prospect could point toward that old quixotic dream of a southern heartland populism making progressive demands of big government and big business.

This cannot be easy, in a majority white South where negative use of the words *liberal* and *taxes* lifted Newt Gingrich of Atlanta's suburbs to Speaker of the House in the Republican revolution in 1994, and in 2002 turned out of office Democratic senator Max

Cleland of Georgia, a seasoned politician who had lost both legs and an arm serving in Vietnam.[21] In 2004, the Democratic presidential candidate John Kerry, also a decorated veteran of Vietnam, announced he would not campaign in the South, giving up to George W. Bush the 164 electoral votes packed in a solid red-state South. But while the Republican Party seemed to have control over the "values" voter of the white South, frustrating many liberal editorial boards of southern newspapers, the victories in Virginia of Democrats Mark Warner for governor in 2002, and Jim Webb for U.S. Senate and Tim Kaine for governor in 2006, seemed to point to a winning strategy. Two Democratic consultants for both Warner and Webb, reminiscent of James "Ragin' Cajun" Carville for candidate Bill Clinton in 1992, drew on their down-home roots. Steve Jarding and Dave "Mudcat" Saunders deployed a born-fighting spirit in blasting what they call the "Metropolitan Opera Wing" of the Democratic Party as lustily as they attacked "smug and elitist" Republicans like Bush and Vice President Dick Cheney.[22]

Jarding, Saunders, and others, such as the Texas political consultant Raymond Strother and the former Georgia congressman Ben "Cooter" Jones, are architects of a resurgent Democratic South of white "bubbas." Jarding and Saunders explained their strategy in *Foxes in the Henhouse: How the Republicans Stole the South and the Heartland, and What the Democrats Must Do to Run 'Em Out.*[23] Their recommendations for Democratic campaigns boil down to this: fight back hard and talk to people where they live. Democratic candidates should relate to people they call "bubbas," who vote, as opposed to "rednecks," who don't. Their labels seem arbitrary and interchangeable, but the point is that many of the descendants of the Scots-Irish in the South are decent folks who like to hunt, watch college football, drink, and go to church, but are not mean, bigoted, stupid, irresponsible, or otherwise embodiments of a type even Jarding and Saunders say is real—the "redneck." Their strategy worked in 2002 for Mark Warner, even though he was a Harvard-educated, Connecticut-raised multimillionaire. Warner won the trust of the NASCAR crowd, a rowdy multitude known for consumer-brand loyalty, by sponsoring in the short-track circuit an F-150 truck with an Ernie Elliot engine.[24] He appeared with bluegrass legend Ralph Stanley and the Clinch Mountain Boys, and he had a bluegrass campaign song that, as *Newsweek* put it, "stuck to your brain like pine tar." The song, which Jarding and Saunders wrote to the tune of a Dillards classic about moonshining, ended with the lines, "War-ner, vote in this election / To keep our children home."[25] The consultants introduced Warner to the popular southern pastime of hunting, disarming the cynical press by admitting upfront that Warner "didn't know shit" about what he was doing. But Jarding and Saunders did. They knew to make it clear that Warner was not going to take anybody's guns and was going to improve wildlife habitat and keep the air and water clean. They avoided the tree-hugger term *environment*. Mark Warner won the election, becoming the first Democratic governor elected in Virginia in more than a decade, even though the state was "trending Republican faster than almost any state in the union."[26] Warner also won overwhelmingly in his run for U.S. Senate in 2008, and Virginia's thirteen electoral votes went for the Democratic presidential candidate, Obama, for the first time since 1964.

The Republican sweep of the white South, paradoxically, smothered a distinctive conservatism that moral philosopher Richard Weaver had delineated in his book *The Southern Tradition at Bay*. This tradition, according to Weaver, holds on to the premodern values of honor, chivalry, faith, and good manners. The Republican embrace of free-market capitalism was an unacknowledged abandonment of these older values. Eugene Genovese, a controversial historian whose neo-Marxist (and lapsed Catholic) perspective gradually drew him to an odd, conditional sympathy with antebellum southern conservatism, points out this contradiction in modern Republican orthodoxy. He argues that free-market individualism, with its love of wealth and tax cuts, corrodes every fiber of traditional family values. Ronald Reagan and both Bushes found allies among southern conservatives because of their fight against socialism and big government, he says. But southern conservatives understood what Reagan and both Bushes did not, according to Genovese: "Capitalism has historically been the greatest solvent of traditional social relations." The free market, in fact, is classical liberalism. Family, faith, and moral values were the South's other lost cause against this powerful force.[27]

Vaguely echoing Jefferson and the conservative Fugitive-Agrarians of the 1930s, Jarding and Saunders consider rural life the historic and social incubator of traditional moral values. And yet the very ground of rural and small-town life has nearly vanished because of Republican policies, they write. The only growth industries of the rural South are prisons and casinos. Rural school systems are in decline, along with job opportunities and salaries, leaving little "to keep our children home." They were outraged that John Kerry and other northeastern liberal Democrats deluded themselves into thinking they could ignore the South. Defined as the eleven states of the former Confederacy plus Delaware, Maryland, Kentucky, Arkansas, and Oklahoma, the South will become more important in the future, growing from 32 percent of the U.S. population in 2004 to 40 percent in 2030. "The truth is, voters in southern and rural regions of our country have been devastated by Republican policies," they write. "These voters are yours, Democrats. Go get them."[28]

The land that Dickey's poetic bird swoops over has a powerful hold on southerners, and southern writers know how to express that tug of nature. George Washington Cable and Walter Hines Page proclaimed their love of the South's earth and people even as they left, permanently, for the North's safe havens. Later, the call of the North to expatriate editors and writers was purely mercantile. But in retirement or on weekends, they found ways to return to the South of their memories. For example, John Shaw Billings II, the second in command at Henry Luce's Time-Life-Fortune magazine headquarters in New York, dreamed of reclaiming the plantation house in Beech Island, South Carolina, where he had been born in 1898. Billings, whose great-great-grandfather Senator James Henry "Cotton Is King" Hammond built that house, came into possession of the Hammond family estate in 1935. With his wife's help, he restored Redcliffe with the idea of becoming "a Southern landowner in the grand sense." Cartons of his ancestors' letters in the attic included those of a Maria Bryan of Mount Zion, Georgia, letters full of the keen eye and sensibility of a Jane Austen. After each day of editing the world's news in the early 1950s, Billings would retreat to his Fifth Avenue penthouse to pore over these letters, "which were so much more interesting."[29] Turner Catledge, the Mississippi-raised journalist who rose to be vice president of the *New York Times,* retired in 1970 with his wife to a mansion in the Garden District of New Orleans where he lived until his death in 1983.[30] Atlanta native John Huey, formerly the southern bureau chief for the *Wall Street Journal,* moved to New York to be the executive editor of *Fortune* and then the editorial director of Time Inc. in 2003. Unhappy with a New York lifestyle, he moved with his family to Wadmalaw Island, near Charleston, South Carolina, from where he commuted to New York in a corporate jet for his workweek.

The path home was roundabout for some. Willie Morris, after his fall from *Harper's* in 1971 and bleak years of freelancing and bar sitting in Long Island, returned to Mississippi in 1980. Happily remarried and writing books, Morris held court in Oxford with students from Ole Miss, fellow writers, and visiting admirers until his death in 1999.[31] William A. Emerson stayed around New York writing books and growing a stout beard for several years after the *Saturday Evening Post* collapsed around him in 1969. In 1975, he moved to Columbia, South Carolina, to teach journalism at the state university, and in 1986 back to Atlanta to stay. The pull of Dixie, and of Atlanta in particular, was evident enough in a piece Emerson wrote for *Georgia* magazine in 1972. "There's no way to explain why you spend your life leaving places, but the bitch goddess success speaks directly to the original sin in man," Emerson wrote. "The poet is as greedy as the salesman." Leaving Atlanta for an opportunity in New York, one feels at the last minute as if he were on the doomed Children's Crusade, he wrote. "All of us who left had our secret plans, we just weren't aware of a larger design. 'We'll be back,' we said. 'We're just going to get a little fame and glory and Yankee money.' Actually, those children in the Crusade weren't going to Jerusalem, they were being kidnapped and sent to Saudi Arabia as slaves to work in the sand mines. Better to stay with the old red clay at home."[32]

For ambitious journalists, staying at home with the old red clay or the marshlands (lushly described by the novelist Pat Conroy) or the foggy mountains (as McGill knew them and as documented in the *Foxfire* books) or the postmodern corporate cityscapes (Atlanta or Charlotte) is still a challenge.[33] If American-style journalism was slow to come to the South in the nineteenth century because of the lack of dense-packed cities, in the twenty-first century the region's daily press suffers from too much growth of huge, border-less megalopolises. It is now possible to be stuck any weekday in rush-hour traffic midway between Atlanta and Chattanooga, or between Richmond and Washington, D.C., and to be in a zone where nobody reads a local metropolitan paper. A study by Virginia Tech's Metropolitan Institute in 2005 identified ten "mega-politan" clusters that are increasingly defining the nation, and four are in the South: the I-35 Corridor, from Kansas City down to San Antonio; the Gulf Coast from Mobile down to Brownsville, Texas; the Peninsula, from Orlando and Tampa down to Miami; and the Piedmont, from Birmingham up through Atlanta and Charlotte to Raleigh. Additionally, Richmond is in a fifth megapolitan ter-ritory stretching up the Atlantic coast to Maine. Even the smallest of these super cities contains, or will by 2040, more than ten mil-lion souls.[34] Yet newspapers no longer form a center of gravity for such population blobs, the way they did for cities in the past. Fifty years ago, every household subscribed to at least one newspaper on average.[35] Now it is only one of every two households. In 2005, the percentage of American newspaper readers fell to 60 percent, down from 67 percent seven years earlier. Circulation seemed to be in free fall with the dissipation of news and advertising to the Internet, where readership was growing fast. Changes in the in-dustry seemed so rapid and radical, it was hard to tell whether the future looked bright or bleak. *Epochal* was the word, "as momen-tous as the invention of television or the telegraph, perhaps on the order of the printing press itself," said the report "State of the News Media, 2007."[36]

Meanwhile, magazines in the contemporary South were find-ing more commercial support than had been available in Poe's day, but the underlying questions remained the same as in the 1830s: can the South support its own distinctive periodicals, and by what literary or journalistic standards are they to be judged? John Shelton Reed, the South-loving sociologist, appreciates any magazine that attempts to show the South's distinctiveness, from the glossy *Southern Bride* to the prize-winning social-justice advocacy magazine *Southern Exposure.*[37] "Month after month, year after year," Reed writes, "the very titles even of such humdrum trade magazines as the *Southern Sociologist* and the *Southern Funeral Director* say that the South exists, that there's something different (and usually at least by implication better) about it."[38]

Successful regional magazines always project a myth about the land and its people, and no region is better at manufacturing myths than the South.[39] A monthly magazine called *Southern,* launched in Little Rock in 1986, laid claim to the new myth that many southerners like Reed were seeking. It was a synthesis, replacing the former myths of the romantic South and the mercantile South. Linton Weeks, the founding editor, rejected both of these, the Old South of "status quo at any price" and the New South of "change at any price," for a droll alternative of "good bourbon at any price."[40] *Southern* acknowledged the South's sins and flaws but appreciated its good people, food, music, and writing. Its motto was "The South, the whole South, and nothing but the South." It published new writers as well as some of the best-known journalists and novelists from the region, including the humorist Roy Blount Jr., the food and history aficionado John Egerton, and the iconoclastic feminist "Southern belle" Florence King. In 1989, the Birmingham-based Southern Progress bought *Southern* (and its quarter million subscribers) to replace it with a metropolitan-oriented *Southpoint*. The inventor and editor of *Southpoint* was John Huey of Atlanta. He wanted a magazine that eschewed all myths in favor of the "real" South that he had covered for the *Wall Street Journal,* a magazine that featured good

journalism by national standards, without navel-gazing to "understand" the South. "At the heart of the magazine," Huey wrote in
the premiere issue, "is the belief that today's South is big enough,
smart enough, rich enough, and secure enough to enjoy looking at itself through an unclouded lens."[41] Reed disliked what
he thought was the implied message of *Southpoint*—that the hip,
young urban dwellers of today's South need not be embarrassed
about where they lived—and correctly predicted that it would
not find an eager readership.[42] The search for an original southern
magazine formula continues, with offbeat concept titles such as
Oxford American ("The Southern Magazine of Good Writing"),
relocated and relaunched several times, and *Garden and Gun* ("21st
Century Southern America"), launched in 2007 by the heir of
the Manigault dynasty, Charleston's newspaper publishers since the
1890s, with a quirky name meant to imply something about the
outdoors, food, and southern snob appeal.

Americans who happen to live in the South today get their news
and information in every multimedia flavor. Printing plants and
distribution warehouses off interstate junctions download *USA
Today,* the *New York Times,* and the *Wall Street Journal* by satellite,
allowing plastic-bagged copies to be flung into suburban drive-
ways of subscribers every morning. Metro newspapers compete
with these national newspapers while defending their dominance
on other battlefronts—running twenty-four-hour Internet pages
and competing with free city weeklies, slick city magazines, and
hyperlocal suburban newspapers. Coffee tables in trophy homes
and second homes exhibit the lifestyle magazines of Southern
Progress, now a Time Warner subsidiary. The working poor have
less and less discretionary time for news, unless it is on cable television. "Local, local, local," say the news consultants, reinforcing the
gut instincts of editors.

Yet to be truly local and to find truly local readers requires a certain kind of rooted or renegade journalist, something the South may have produced in earlier times but not much today. Al Scardino believed he could produce good aggressive journalism when he came back to his hometown of Savannah in his late twenties to start the *Georgia Gazette,* a small weekly, in 1978. The topics that the local dailies had skirted, such as the gap between rich and poor and the cozy deals between government and business around the conservative old city, seemed clear and like low-hanging fruit, ripe for picking. But developing a muckraking newspaper with a dozen staffers left the *Gazette* in debt most of the time, despite its winning the contract to publish official city and county legal ads. The paper won a Pulitzer Prize in 1984 for its editorials but did not survive for long after that, and Scardino moved on to write for the *New York Times.*[43] Another option for fearless local journalism is to go low budget, such as the monthly that Doug Harwood launched, writes, edits, and hand delivers in Rockbridge County, Virginia. The *Rockbridge Advocate* ("Independent as a Hog on Ice") runs local public-record data, comments, and embarrassments without stinting, and it has an eccentric affection for local characters and history going back to antebellum news. But it has no love of the Internet. Its teasing Web site says the online page contains little that is in this fine little news magazine: "Why give away what we sell?"[44] Local community journalism in the South might develop new forms that draw more on a southern sense of community than on whatever sense of journalism the South owns. A good community newspaper, according to a Chapel Hill journalism professor who wrote a textbook on the subject, should be the community's bulletin board, refrigerator door, mirror, scrapbook, history book, chat room, and voice. This is not necessarily a profitable idea in communities as small as Carrboro, North Carolina (population seventeen thousand). So under the market model, Carrboro would never get its own newspaper, says Jock Lauderer, the community-journalism professor. But under a different model, a weekly newspaper and Web site called the *Carrboro Citizen* was launched in March 2007. Lauderer, who lives in Carrboro, admits that this is a financially risky proposition. He proposed a public-radio model, urging local citizens and businesses to support the newspaper not only as readers but also as underwriters. The editor, Kirk Ross, was thinking of a retro-journalism model. Although it has a Web site, ninety-nine out of a hundred local people surveyed said they wanted a paper that they could hold in their hands. Carrboro, a hip, progressive settlement near the University of North Carolina at Chapel Hill, is seeking a family-friendly, sustainable localism. "If you are familiar with the slow food movement," Ross said, "we're trying to start the slow news movement. . . . We're going back to basics, we're not trying to do the unusual."[45]

Hope springs eternal. A new localism for news reporting, a kind of slow journalism for the slow-town, home-cooking myth of the South, might take root. A new Mencken, boisterous and brilliant, could emerge to shake things up. New coalitions could revive a Democratic Party majority in the post–civil rights South, giving the region's press a healthier politics to cover and a story that national elites might take seriously.

But experience says, "No way." The fact is, the South has not enjoyed anything like the cultural or literary rebirth Walker Percy saw as a great possibility after the old bugbear of white supremacy was put to rest.[46] The South has made nothing of its racial reconciliation except money. The region still serves, occasionally, as a vicarious Punch-and-Judy show for the nation's anxieties about race, as when network news teams and protesters mobbed Jena, Louisiana, in 2007 over school-yard meanness that brought unfair criminal penalties for the black men involved.[47] But whatever deeper wisdom the South may have gained from its hard history, if any, such wisdom flickers today not in a movement or a regional press, but in what T. S. Eliot called the "individual talent." Certain journalists with southern connections have a distinct awareness of history's complexity, and of the difference between sociological abstractions and actual people living in the web of custom and family.

Some of these southern émigrés are influencing American journalism from atop institutions. Nicholas Lemann and Walter Isaacson, both from New Orleans, are respectively the dean of Columbia School of Journalism and director of the Aspen Institute. (Lemann, a former *Texas Monthly* editor, writes about the media for national magazines, and Isaacson has been managing editor of *Time,* head of CNN, and a biographer of Benjamin Franklin, Henry Kissinger, and Albert Einstein.) Bill Kovach, a native of East Tennessee who was editor of the *Atlanta Journal-Constitution* from 1986 to 1988, was curator of the Nieman Foundation for a year, and then became founding director of the Coalition for Concerned Journalists, an advocacy group trying to defend journalistic standards against commercial encroachment.[48] Rea S. Hederman Sr., who in the early 1980s transformed the *Jackson (Mississippi) Clarion-Ledger* from the racist laughingstock it was under his Hederman elders to a respectable prize-winning daily, has been publisher of the liberal *New York Review of Books* since 1984. And Alex S. Jones, whose family has run the daily paper in Greeneville, Tennessee, for three generations, covered the media for the *New York Times,* with his wife Susan Tifft cowrote books on the newspaper families behind the *Times* and in Louisville, and became head of Harvard's Shorenstein Center on the Press, Politics and Public Policy.

Other such journalists retain a southerner's awareness of evangelical Christianity as a way of life and not necessarily as a political label or sign of stupidity. Chattanooga native Jon Meacham, who became the managing editor of *Newsweek* at age twenty-nine and editor eight years later in 2006, was the campus paper editor and salutatorian at Oxford-style Sewanee: The University of the South, in Tennessee. Meacham edited an anthology of nonfiction writing from the civil rights era in the South (*Voices in Our Blood: America's Best on the Civil Rights Movement,* 2001) and wrote a history of American civil religion (*American Gospel: God, the Founding Fathers and the Making of a Nation,* 2006). Meacham, an active Episcopalian, seems to have an intellectual interest in Christianity that shows in the amount of coverage *Newsweek* has given religion under his editorship, including a cover story he wrote on Billy Graham.[49] Likewise, two staffers at the *New Yorker* with southern roots, Lawrence Wright and Peter J. Boyer, have been unusually attuned to religious dimensions of American news and culture. Boyer, whose mother was a radio evangelist from Mississippi, wrote a touchingly sympathetic *New Yorker* profile of a faith healer named the Reverend Charles Jessup of Gulfport who raised gamecocks, fell afoul of the law over the millions he made as a radio faith healer, and was Boyer's childhood hero. "In the world of my youth, which was populated by itinerant prophets, preachers, and mystics, J. Charles Jessup occupied his own exalted realm," Boyer wrote. "[H]e was said to have been the role model for both Oral Roberts and Elvis Presley, and even now, after everything that happened, I believe he was."[50]

Finally, the tradition of the southern press comes down to the individual, for underneath it all is the notion that journalism is a disguised opportunity to be a professional writer or a training

ground for fiction. To become a writer means to acquire the sha-
man's status, the secret skill of the storyteller, the magic power of
persuasion, self-expression, and emotional release. This is not the
prevailing or correct motivation for an American journalist. Journalists are supposed to be idealists who serve the common good by
exposing corruption, keeping citizens informed, and being "the
tocsin" for policies of equality and justice, as Raleigh publisher
Josephus Daniels put it in his will. But choosing that career in
the South was, historically, tinged with the romance of writing as
much as with democratic idealism. "To write for a newspaper was
a move in the direction of a career in letters," notes Louis D. Rubin Jr., who began by working for news organizations in Virginia
in the 1940s and 1950s but then became an English professor—and
eminent scholar of southern literature. Rubin's reminiscence of
his work in the daily press, *An Honorable Estate,* recalls an earlier
time, before aspiring playwrights, novelists, and poets could opt for
creative-writing programs and university appointments. Between
about 1875 and 1950, he says, the pathway to a literary vocation was
news reporting, if one "wasn't independently wealthy." Although
Rubin does not ascribe this situation to the South in particular, it
holds true for most of the key figures of the southern press.[51]

To the extent that journalism in the South was different, it
was a more personal vocation, more related to literary expression,
and it often ran in families. Father-son pairs of editors crop up
often: Thomas Ritchie Sr. and Jr., Robert Barnwell Rhett Sr. and
Jr., John Temple Graves I and II, Grover C. Hall Sr. and Jr., Hodding Carter Jr. and III, and three generations of Howell editors in
Atlanta and Bryan publishers in Richmond. It seems significant
that the sons often have an ambiguous relationship with the fathers, using journalism both to emulate the tradition and to ex-
pose the myths of the fathers. Thomas Sancton Sr. and Jr. of New

Orleans are a good illustration. The father attacked segregation as fiercely as any other white southern liberal, like Lillian Smith, for progressive northern publications. He became an editor at the *New Republic* and the *Nation* in the 1940s, moving back to the Deep South in 1949 to work for the *New Orleans Item*. He published novels in 1956 and in 1960. His son, Thomas Sancton Jr., the Paris bureau chief of *Time,* recently published a passionate memoir about his love of the old black Dixieland jazz his father introduced him to but also about the tensions between father and son.[52] Love-hate tensions abound, as well, in the memoir that *Newsweek* writer Christopher Dickey, also a former Paris bureau chief, wrote about his father, not a journalist but the poet James Dickey. The son's confessional book, *Summer of Deliverance,* bitterly arraigns the poet for his infidelities and drunkenness but also finds much to love in the man and his poetry. The book seeks to demythologize the son's experience of the family, as southern journalists like Karl Fleming and Paul Hemphill clenched the hard facts of news reporting to demythologize their experience of growing up in the South.[53]

Here is the deepest riddle of a journalistic tradition that braids literary aspirations with the realism of facts. James Dickey the poet lived the life of the imaginative artist and became the flamboyant object of gossips and scolds. A biographer, Henry Hart, was so appalled at the amount of mendacity he found in Dickey's life that Hart posited lying as the central metaphor for the biography, *James Dickey: The World as a Lie.* Bronwen Dickey, a half sister of Christopher who is thirty years younger and a fine nonfiction writer, objects that Hart failed to see that her father, like any great poet, "subordinated clinical facts to spiritual truths." Poetry, she writes, is the inverse of journalism. "Journalists present a sequence of facts about a given situation and allow their reader to interpret their own meaning. Poets begin with meaning, and facts are only incidental to their poetic purpose."[54] Bronwen Dickey is looking at too narrow a definition of journalism, for there is a wayward spirit of American journalism that also begins with meaning, feeling, and the human story. This side of the craft, for good and ill, found a nourishing environment in the hothouse land that was long considered a different part of America. It is no longer so different. But the tradition abides that insists on the human and peculiar details of the story, which are always at odds with the social data of the universal.[55]

CHAPTER ONE

1. Douglas Southall Freeman, *Robert E. Lee* (New York: Scribner's and Sons, 1934), 1:104. W. J. Cash, in *The Mind of the South* (New York: Alfred A. Knopf, 1941), referred to "the cardboard medievalism of the Scotch novels" (62) as the most perfect expression of this type of nostalgia.

2. Henry W. Grady, *The New South: Writings and Speeches of Henry Grady* (Savannah, Ga.: Beehive Press, 1971), 6–7.

3. Francis W. Dawson, *Reminiscences of Confederate Service: 1861–1865* (Baton Rouge: Louisiana State University Press, 1980); Henry Watterson, *"Marse Henry": An Autobiography* (New York: George H. Doran Co., 1919). Richard M. Weaver notes that Grady spent most of his remaining years "defending the social creed of antebellum civilization" and that Watterson's repudiation of sectionalism was hedged with a pride in old Kentucky's provincialism and originality. Weaver, *The Southern Tradition at Bay: A History of Postbellum Thought* (New Rochelle, N.Y.: Arlington House, 1968), 343, 380–81.

4. C. Vann Woodward, *The Burden of Southern History* (Baton Rouge: Louisiana State University Press, 1960), 168; Richard M. Weaver, "The South and the American Union," in *The Lasting South: Fourteen Southerners Look at Their Home,* ed. Louis D. Rubin Jr. and James J. Kilpatrick (Chicago: Henry Regnery Co., 1957), 46–68.

5. Ferald J. Bryan, *Henry Grady or Tom Watson? The Rhetorical Struggle for the New South, 1880–1890* (Macon, Ga.: Mercer University Press, 1994), 24–31; Francis P. Gaines, *Southern Oratory: A Study in Idealism* (Tuscaloosa: University of Alabama Press, 1945), 11–13.

6. Waldo W. Braden, *The Oral Tradition in the South* (Baton Rouge: Louisiana State University Press, 1983), 26–28.

7. Reed Sarratt, *The Ordeal of Desegregation* (New York: Harper and

Row, 1966), 57–59, 155–60; James T. Patterson, *Brown v. Board of Education* (Oxford: Oxford University Press, 2001), 65–69, 101–13.

8. Harry Ashmore, *Hearts and Minds* (Cabin John, Md.: Seven Locks Press, 1988), 259.

9. Harrison E. Salisbury, *Without Fear or Favor: The* New York Times *and Its Times* (New York: Times Books, 1980), 352–53; Benjamin Fine, "The Little Rock Story," *The Education Beat* (Fall 1957): 360–61.

10. Gene Roberts and Hank Klibanoff, *The Race Beat* (New York: Alfred A. Knopf, 2006), 176–80.

11. Ashmore, *Hearts and Minds,* 276.

12. http://www.pulitzer.org/awards/1958.

13. "Dilemma in Dixie," *Time,* February 20, 1956, 76–81.

14. Sarratt, *Ordeal,* 253.

15. James McBride Dabbs, *Civil Rights in Recent Southern Fiction* (Atlanta: Southern Regional Council, 1969), vii. Fred Hobson, in an essay on Dabbs, puts him in the tradition of the liberal writers George Washington Cable, W. J. Cash, and Lillian Smith but ties him like no other liberal to an opposing conservative tradition that saw divine Providence in the South's history. Hobson, *The Silencing of Emily Mullen and Other Essays* (Baton Rouge: Louisiana State University Press, 2005), 82.

16. Nathania K. Sawyer, "Harry S. Ashmore: On the Way to Everywhere," paper presented in the History Division, Association for Education in Journalism and Mass Communication (AEJMC), Washington D.C., August 5, 2001. Ashmore also became editor of *Encyclopaedia Britannica.*

17. Jonathan Daniels, *A Southerner Discovers the South* (New York: Macmillan Co., 1938).

18. Michael O'Brien, *Rethinking the South: Essays in Intellectual History* (Baltimore: Johns Hopkins University, Press 1988), 183–88.

19. Ashmore, *Hearts and Minds,* 86.

20. John T. Kneebone, *Southern Liberal Journalists and the Issue of Race, 1920–1944* (Chapel Hill: University of North Carolina Press, 1985), 223.

21. "Two Custodians of Dixie's Conscience," *Charlotte (North Carolina) News,* January 18, 1958.

22. Edmund Wilson, *Patriotic Gore: Studies in the Literature of the American Civil War* (New York: Oxford University Press, 1962), xi, 379.

23. Sawyer, "Harry S. Ashmore," 23.

24. Orville Prescott, "Books of the Times," *New York Times,* January 13, 1958, 27.

25. Sawyer, "Harry S. Ashmore," 6.

26. Harry Ashmore, *Epitaph for Dixie* (New York: W. W. Norton and Co., 1958), 51.

27. Ibid., 101.

28. Ibid., 45, 59, 60–61.

29. Jack Temple Kirby, *Media-Made Dixie: The South in the American Imagination* (Baton Rouge: Louisiana State University Press, 1978), 44–52.

30. Anne Edwards, *The Road to Tara* (New York: Tichnor and Fields, 1983), 3–5.

31. Joseph L. Morrison, *W. J. Cash: Southern Prophet* (New York: Alfred A. Knopf, 1967), 68–69, 89–92.

32. Ashmore, *Hearts and Minds,* 215.

33. Ashmore, *Epitaph,* 179.

34. Lillian Smith, *Killers of the Dream* (New York: W. W. Norton, 1949), 66, 89–91, 109–33.

35. Anne C. Loveland, *Lillian Smith: A Southerner Confronting the South* (Baton Rouge: Louisiana State University Press, 1986), 23.

36. Ibid., 268n6.

37. Ibid., 191.

38. Margaret Rose Gladney, introduction to the 1994 edition of *Killers of the Dream,* available online at http://www.misslilscamp.com/biography.html.

39. Smith, *Killers,* 65.

40. Loveland, *Lillian Smith,* 46, citing *Atlanta Constitution,* November 24, 1949.

41. "Liberals Are Criticized for Their Silence on Human Rights," *New York Times,* April 4, 1948, E8.

42. Loveland, *Lillian Smith,* 141.

43. Gladney, http://www.misslilscamp.com/biography.html.

44. Smith, *Killers,* 17.

45. Ibid., 221.

46. Ibid., 218, 228.

47. Smith to Mozell Hill, editor of *Phylon,* March 11, 1957, Loveland, *Lillian Smith,* 162.

48. Smith to Paul Tillich, November (?), 1960, ibid., 213.

49. Ralph McGill, *The South and the Southerner* (Boston: Little, Brown, 1963), 225.

50. Ralph McGill, "My First Boss," *Atlantic Monthly* 203, no. 2 (February 1959): 69.

51. McGill, *The South and the Southerner,* 34.

52. Ibid., 103.

53. Ibid., 104.

54. Ibid., 79.

55. Ibid., 90–91.

56. Barbara Barksdale Clowse, *Ralph McGill: A Biography* (Macon, Ga.: Mercer University Press, 1998), 148.

57. Harold Martin, *Ralph McGill, Reporter* (Boston: Atlantic Monthly Press, 1973), 43.

58. McGill, *The South and the Southerner,* 217.

59. Clowse, *Ralph McGill,* 138.

60. Ibid., 132.

61. Ibid., 78, 79.

62. Ibid., 133, 152, 159.

63. Ibid., 49.

64. Leonard Ray Teel, "Ralph McGill," New Georgia Encyclopedia, http://www.georgiaencyclopedia.org/nge/Article.jsp?id=h-2769 &hl=y.

65. Clowse, *Ralph McGill,* 193.

66. Ibid., 117.

67. Ibid., 50.

68. Ibid., 103.

69. Ibid., 218.

70. Taylor Branch, *Parting the Waters* (New York: Simon and Schuster, 1988), 747.

71. Claude Sitton, "A Man's Own Story," April 14, 1963, *New York Times,* 342.

72. Rick Bragg, *All Over but the Shoutin'* (New York: Vintage Books, 1998), 23. Note: "full mechanization of cotton harvesting ... was all but complete by 1960" (81). Gavin Wright, "Persisting Dixie: The South as an Economic Region," in *The American South in the Twentieth Century* (Athens: University of Georgia Press, 2005), 77–90.

73. Bragg, *All Over,* xi–xii.

74. Rick Bragg, *Somebody Told Me: The Newspaper Stories of Rick Bragg* (Tuscaloosa: University of Alabama Press, 2000), 1–2.

CHAPTER TWO

1. David K. Jackson, *Poe and the* Southern Literary Messenger (Richmond, Va.: Dietze Printing Co., 1934), vi, 3–4.

2. Michael Allen, *Poe and the British Magazine Tradition* (New York: Oxford University Press, 1969), 38; Poe to Charles Anthon, undated [October ?] 1844, Edgar Allan Poe, *The Letters of Edgar Allan Poe,* ed. John Ward Ostrom, vol. 1 (Cambridge, Mass.: Harvard University Press, 1948), 270. Poe overlooks his one novel, *The Narrative of Arthur Gordon Pym of Nantucket,* originally a hoax he tried to sell as a travelogue by "Pym."

3. Jeffrey Meyers, *Edgar Allan Poe: His Life and Legacy* (New York: Charles Scribner's Sons, 1992), 108.

4. John S. Wise, *End of an Era* (Boston: Houghton, Mifflin and Co., 1899), 92.

5. Sam G. Riley, *Magazines of the American South* (New York: Greenwood Press, 1986), 287.

6. Robert D. Jacobs, *Poe: Journalist and Critic* (Baton Rouge: Louisiana State University Press, 1969), 63.

7. Riley, *Magazines,* 258–61, 106–7. See also essays on Legaré (217–20) and Simms (275–92) in *Dictionary of Literary Biography,* vol. 73 (Detroit: Gale Research Co., 1988).

8. Edgar Allan Poe, "Graham's Magazine," in *Broadway Journal,* March 1, 1845, in *Collected Works of Edgar Allan Poe* (New York: Gordian Press, 1986), 3:25.

9. Allen, *Poe,* 58, 102–3.

10. Michael O'Brien, *Conjectures of Order: Intellectual Life and the*

American South, 1810–1860, 2 vols. (Chapel Hill: University of North Carolina Press, 2004), 1:100–106.

11. Riley, *Magazines,* 234.

12. It should be noted, however, that the Jeffersonian principles among southern planters were increasingly attenuated to the single issue of states' rights, as the northern antislavery movement claimed the Jeffersonian principles of equality and personal liberty. W. G. Bean, "Anti-Jeffersonianism in the Ante-Bellum South," *North Carolina Historical Review* 12, no. 2 (April 1935): 103–25.

13. Merrill D. Peterson, *Thomas Jefferson and the New Nation* (London: Oxford, 1970), 113–24. In query 19 of Jefferson's *Notes on the State of Virginia,* ed. William Peden (Chapel Hill: University of North Carolina, 1982), 164–65, he penned what would become holy writ for the agrarian vision of later southern writers: "Those who labour in the earth are the chosen people of God, if he ever had a chosen people, whose breasts he has made his peculiar deposit for substantial and genuine virtue."

14. Ibid., 48–68. See also Thomas E. Watson, *Life and Times of Thomas Jefferson* (New York: D. Appleton and Co., 1903) 165–76. Watson, a populist reformer and demagogue of Georgia's stormiest political decades, edited *Watson's Jeffersonian Weekly.* His chapter on Jefferson in Virginia romanticizes the medieval inheritance of Europe and credits Jefferson with fighting the privileges that limited such patrimony to a greedy elite.

15. Frank Luther Mott, *Jefferson and the Press* (Baton Rouge: Louisiana State University Press, 1943), 51–53; Dumas Malone, *Jefferson the President: First Term, 1801–1805,* vol. 4, *Jefferson and His Time* (Boston: Little, Brown, 1970), 212–18. Whether Jefferson secretly fathered any children with his slave Sally Hemings has reappeared as a modern-day controversy, with DNA evidence leaving open the possibility. But the original source of the published charge, Callender, remains a scorned figure in American journalism, for example, in Mott, *Jefferson and the Press,* and in Virginius Dabney, *The Jefferson Scandals: A Rebuttal* (New York: Dodd, Mead and Co., 1981), 6–15.

16. O'Brien, *Conjectures of Order,* 563.

17. Meyers, *Edgar Allan Poe,* 21–22; Dumas Malone, *The Sage of*

Monticello, vol. 6, *Jefferson and His Time* (Boston: Little, Brown, 1970), 464–68.

18. "Editor's Table," *Russell's Magazine,* vol. 3, no. 4 (1858): 370.

19. Kenneth Silverman, *Edgar A. Poe: Mournful and Never-Ending Remembrance* (New York: HarperCollins, 1991), 1, 12; Meyers, *Edgar Allan Poe,* 6.

20. Silverman, *Edgar A. Poe,* 28; Meyers, *Edgar Allan Poe,* 20.

21. Henrick Hertzberg, "Journals of Opinion: An Historical Sketch," *Gannett Center Journal* (Spring 1989): 62.

22. Silverman, *Edgar A. Poe,* 18; Meyers, *Edgar Allan Poe,* 13.

23. Meyers, *Edgar Allan Poe,* 13.

24. Ibid., 23–24.

25. Silverman, *Edgar A. Poe,* 64–67.

26. Poe to Sarah Helen Whitman, October 18, 1848, quoted in Jacobs, *Poe,* 9.

27. Edward Davidson, *Poe: A Critical Study* (Cambridge, Mass.: Harvard University Press, 1957), 208; Henry Calridge, "Edgar Allan Poe," in *Companion to the Literature and Culture of the American South,* ed. Richard J. Gray and Owen Robinson (Malden, Mass.: Blackwell Publishers, 2004), 356.

28. Jacobs, *Poe,* 3–19. This opening section of *Poe: Journalist and Critic* focuses on the writer's southern influences, prejudices, and pretensions.

29. Michael Schudson, *Discovering the News: A Social History of American Newspapers* (New York: Basic Books, 1978), provides a useful discussion of the connections between Jacksonian democracy and the penny press in this period.

30. Stuart Levine and Linda Levine, eds., *The Short Fiction of Edgar Allan Poe* (Indianapolis: Bobbs-Merrill, 1976), 588–96.

31. See, e.g., Poe's short story "Mystification," in ibid., 460.

32. Levine and Levine, *Short Fiction,* 454.

33. Edmund Wilson, *Patriotic Gore: Studies in the Literature of the American Civil War* (New York: Oxford University Press, 1962), 638.

34. Ibid., 142–44, 174–75.

35. *New York Herald,* quoted in Schudson, *Discovering the News,* 54.

36. From *Life on the Mississippi,* quoted in Wilson, *Patriotic Gore,* 444–45.

37. Poe to Henry Wadsworth Longfellow, June 22, 1841, *Letters,* 168.

38. Poe, "Review of *Twice-Told Tales,*" *Graham's Magazine,* May 1842, in *Edgar Allan Poe: Essays and Reviews,* ed. G. R. Thompson (New York: Library of America, 1984), 572.

39. Jacobs, *Poe,* 3–4.

40. Regarding journalistic hoaxes, Poe's short story in the June 1835 *Southern Literary Messenger* titled "Hans Pfaal—A Tale" may have inspired the famous moon hoax that ran in the *New York Sun* three weeks later. Poe called his science-fiction tale a "sketchy triffle" compared to the "downright earnest" hoax by *Sun* editor Richard Adams Locke, a fabrication that convinced a multitude of readers and gullible editors that a powerful new telescope had spied flying creatures on the moon. Nine years later, Poe showed his own skill in the genre by writing a newslike account of a made-up transatlantic balloon flight, which filled an extra of the *New York Sun* on April 13, 1844. "The rush for the 'sole paper which had the news' was something beyond even the prodigious," Poe boasted. Levine and Levine, *Short Fiction,* 613.

41. Jacobs, *Poe,* 68–69, 123.

42. Meyers, *Edgar Allan Poe,* 82–83.

43. Jackson, *Poe,* 61.

44. Meyers, *Edgar Allan Poe,* 74–75; Allen, *Poe,* 47–50, 61–68.

45. Allen, *Poe,* 40–42.

46. Jackson, *Poe,* 40–41.

47. Jacobs, *Poe,* 126.

48. Allen, *Poe,* 69–70.

49. Ibid., 157. Poe apparently exaggerated. Calridge, in his 2004 essay in *Companion,* says that the circulation was only 3,500 when Poe left (358).

50. Edmund Wilson, *The Shock of Recognition* (New York: Doubleday, Doran and Co., 1943), 82.

51. Jacobs, *Poe,* 249.

52. Sidney P. Moss, *Poe's Literary Battles: The Critic in the Context of His Literary Milieu* (Durham, N.C.: Duke University Press, 1963), 3–4.

53. Review of poems of Drake and Halleck, *Southern Literary Messenger,* April 1836, in Thompson, ed., *Edgar Allan Poe,* 506.

54. Jackson, *Poe,* 21.

55. Ibid., 32

56. Meyers, *Edgar Allan Poe,* 73–74.

57. Jacobs, *Poe,* 86.

58. Poe to Thomas W. White, April 30, 1835, *Letters,* 57–58.

59. Jacobs, *Poe,* 98–99.

60. Ibid., 94.

61. Riley, *Magazines,* 235.

62. *Southern Literary Messenger,* March 1836, in Thompson, ed., *Edgar Allan Poe,* 779.

63. Jacobs, *Poe,* 84.

64. Jackson, *Poe,* 105.

65. Ibid., 110.

66. Ibid., 115.

67. Moss, *Poe's Literary Battles,* 38–82.

68. Review of Lambert A. Wilmer's "Quacks of Helicon," *Graham's Magazine,* August 1841, in Thompson, ed., *Edgar Allan Poe,* 1007.

69. "Marginalia," *Southern Literary Messenger,* April 1849, in Thompson, ed., *Edgar Allan Poe,* 1439–40. William P. Trent, in contrast, argued that Simms was a victim not of northern condescension but of the backwardness of southern culture in education and appreciation of its native talent. Trent, *William Gilmore Simms* (Boston: Houghton, Mifflin and Co., 1892), 246–47, 319–20.

CHAPTER THREE

1. Frank Luther Mott, *American Journalism, A History: 1690–1960,* 3rd ed. (New York: Macmillan Co., 1962), 167–80.

2. J. Cutler Andrews, *The South Reports the Civil War* (Pittsburgh, Pa.: University of Pittsburgh Press, 1970), 56–58; Ford Risley, "The Confederate Press Association: A Revolutionary Experience in Southern Journalism?" paper presented in the History Division, AEJMC, Phoenix, August 11, 2000.

3. Michael O'Brien, *Conjectures of Order: Intellectual Life and the American South, 1810–1860,* 2 vols. (Chapel Hill: University of North Carolina Press, 2004), 1:359.

4. Carl R. Osthaus, *Partisans of the Southern Press: Editorial Spokesmen of the Nineteenth Century* (Lexington: University Press of Kentucky, 1994), 10; John D. Allen, "Journalism in the South," in *Culture in the South,* ed. W. T. Couch (Chapel Hill: University of North Carolina Press, 1935), 136.

5. Gavin Wright notes that at the height of immigration to the United States, in 1910, fewer than 2 percent of the people in the South were foreign born. Wright, "Persisting Dixie: The South as an Economic Region," in *The American South in the Twentieth Century,* ed. Craig S. Pascoe, Karen Trahan, and Andy Ambrose (Athens: University of Georgia Press, 2005), 79.

6. Osthaus, *Partisans,* 9–11.

7. W. J. Cash, "Of Time and Frontiers," in *The Mind of the South* (New York: Alfred A. Knopf, 1941), 3–28. See also Daniel Joseph Singal, "Cavalier Myth and Victorian Culture," in *The War Within: From Victorian to Modernist Thought in the South, 1919–1945* (Chapel Hill: University of North Carolina Press, 1982), 11–33; and Michael O'Brien, *Rethinking the South* (Baltimore: Johns Hopkins University Press, 1988), esp. chapter 8, "A Private Passion: W. J. Cash," 179–89.

8. Frederick Law Olmsted, *The Cotton Kingdom: A Traveller's Observations on Cotton and Slavery in the American Slave States,* ed. Arthur M. Schlesinger (New York: Alfred A. Knopf, 1953), xvi, 17–18.

9. Osthaus, *Partisans,* 8–9.

10. David Rachels, introduction to *Augustus Baldwin Longstreet's Georgia Scenes Completed,* ed. David Rachels (Athens: University of Georgia Press, 1998), xxxiii.

11. The first nineteen of these were published by Longstreet's own press in 1835 in a book titled *Georgia Scenes, Characters, Incidents, Etc. in the First Half Century of the Republic.* A second collection published by his nephew Fritz Longstreet in 1912 was titled *Stories with a Moral Humourous and Descriptive of Southern Life a Century Ago,* which contained the story of the Gnatville editor under the changed title "The Village Editor."

12. Wade, a descendant of Georgia planters who would become the founding editor of the *Georgia Review* in 1947, originally wrote his biography of Longstreet as a dissertation at Columbia University under

William P. Trent. Trent was the founding editor of the *Sewanee Review* starting in 1892.

13. John Donald Wade, *Augustus Baldwin Longstreet: A Study in the Development of Culture in the South* (New York: Macmillan Co., 1924), 4.

14. Ibid., 17, 53–54.

15. Rachels, introduction to *Georgia Scenes,* xv; Wade, *Augustus Baldwin Longstreet,* 9–11.

16. Wade, *Augustus Baldwin Longstreet,* 16, 17.

17. Ibid., 18.

18. Ibid., 23–47; Rachels, introduction to *Georgia Scenes,* xvii.

19. Wade, *Augustus Baldwin Longstreet,* 1; see also E. Kate Stewart, "Augustus Baldwin Longstreet," *Dictionary of Literary Biography* (Detroit: Gale Research Co., 1988), 74:243–48.

20. Rachels, introduction to *Georgia Scenes,* xxi.

21. Quoted in Wade, *Augustus Baldwin Longstreet,* 117.

22. Ibid., 98, 117.

23. Ibid., 132–33.

24. The first seven sketches originally ran in the *Milledgeville (Georgia) Southern Recorder,* a weekly newspaper, beginning October 30, 1833, and then were reprinted in the *State Rights Sentinel* in early 1834. Rachels, introduction to *Georgia Scenes,* 267–68.

25. Wade, *Augustus Baldwin Longstreet,* 134–38.

26. Rachels, introduction to *Georgia Scenes,* xxxiv–xlii.

27. Ibid., xxxiii.

28. Ibid., xxxii–xxxiii.

29. Augustus Baldwin Longstreet, *Letters on the Epistle of Paul to Philemon, or the Connection of Apostolic Christianity with Slavery* (Charleston: n.p., 1845), 7, cited in Wade, *Augustus Baldwin Longstreet,* 280–82.

30. Wade, *Augustus Baldwin Longstreet,* 283–84.

31. Ibid., 285–87.

32. Longstreet, "Georgia Theatrics" and "The Dance," in Rachels, introduction to *Georgia Scenes,* 4–13.

33. Richard Gray, *Writing the South: Ideas of an American Region* (Cambridge, U.K.: Cambridge University Press, 1986), 62–74; Rachels, introduction to *Georgia Scenes,* xlix.

34. Longstreet felt that the public totally missed the point in believing

that his book was primarily for humor and entertainment. He wrote that his aim was "to supply a chasm in history which has always been overlooked—the manners, customs, amusements, wit, dialect, as they appear in all grades of society to an ear and eye witness of them." Original date and source unknown but quoted in O. P. Fitzgerald, *Judge Longstreet: A Life Sketch* (Nashville, Tenn.: Methodist Episcopal Church, South, 1891), 164–66, cited in Rachels, introduction to *Georgia Scenes,* xlviii–xlix.

35. Longstreet, "Preface," in Rachels, introduction to *Georgia Scenes,* 3.

36. Wade, *Augustus Baldwin Longstreet,* 155; *Southern Literary Journal,* 152.

37. *Southern Literary Messenger,* March 1836, 287.

38. Edwin Mims, *The Advancing South: Stories of Progress and Reaction* (New York: Doubleday, Page and Co., 1926), 130.

39. Longstreet, "The Gnatville Gem," in Rachels, introduction to *Georgia Scenes,* 227–35.

40. Ibid., 235.

41. Ibid., 236–42.

42. Osthaus, *Partisans,* 1–11.

43. Amy Reynolds and Debra Reddin van Tuyll, *The Greenwood Library of American War Reporting,* ed. David Copeland (Westport, Conn.: Greenwood Press, 2005), 3:298. Van Tuyll notes that vast sweeps of the South had no newspaper, and on the eve of the Civil War the swampland hamlets of south Georgia had no papers.

44. Osthaus, *Partisans,* 71.

45. Mott, *American Journalism,* 203.

46. Osthaus, *Partisans,* 8.

47. Ibid., 5.

48. Leland Krauth, "Mark Twain Fights Sam Clemens' Duel," *Mississippi Quarterly* 33, no. 2 (1980): 141–53.

49. Mark Twain, *The Complete Short Stories of Mark Twain,* ed. Charles Neider (Garden City, N.Y.: Hanover House, 1957), 27–32.

50. F. N. Boney, "Rivers of Ink, A Stream of Blood: The Tragic Career of John Hampden Pleasants," *Virginia Cavalcade* (Summer 1968): 33–39.

51. Ritchie Sr. in a letter to son William, February 27, 1847, in Barbara Griffin, "Thomas Ritchie and the Code Duello," *The Virginia Magazine of History and Biography* 92 (January 1984): 71–95.

52. Ritchie Sr. in a letter to daughter Isabella Harrison, January 22, 1843, ibid., 87.

53. Robert S. Scott in a letter to Ritchie Sr., March 3, 1846, ibid., 95.

54. Frederick Hudson, *Journalism in the United States from 1690 to 1872* (1873; repr., New York: Haskell House Publishers, 1968), 271–72. Virginia passed an antidueling bill in 1810, but this rarely resulted in prosecution, nor did it seem to slow the practice. A. W. Patterson, *The Code Duello, with Special Reference to the State of Virginia* (Richmond: n.p., 1927), 80, cited in Griffin, "Thomas Ritchie," 76n11.

55. Virginius Dabney, *Pistols and Pointed Pens: The Dueling Editors of Old Virginia* (Chapel Hill: University of North Carolina Press, 1987), 40–46, and Mott, *American Journalism,* 366.

56. J. H. Whitty, *Evening Journal,* January 19, 1909, cited in Dabney, *Pistols and Pointed Pens,* 40–46; see also Kenneth Silverman, *Edgar A. Poe: Mournful and Never-Ending Remembrance* (New York: HarperCollins, 1991), 352.

57. Robert C. Post, "The Social Foundations of Defamation Law: Reputation and the Constitution," *California Law Review* 74, no. 3 (May 1986): 693–717.

58. Jack K. Williams, *Dueling in the Old South* (College Station: Texas A&M Press, 1980), 53; Lafcadio Hearn, *Historical Sketch Book and Guide to New Orleans and Environs* (New York: Will H. Coleman, 1885), 181–87; and *The Maury River Atlas: Nineteenth-Century Inland Navigations of the Virginias* (Lexington: Virginia Canals and Navigations Society, 1991), 14.

59. John Lyde Wilson, *The Code of Honor, or Rules for the Government of Principals and Seconds in Duelling* (Charleston: n.p., 1838), reprinted in Williams's *Dueling in the Old South.* Other available manuals on dueling were John McDonald Taylor's *Twenty-six Commandments of the Duelling Code,* Joseph Hamilton's *The Only Approved Guide Through All the Stages of a Quarrel,* and Henry Ware's *The Law of Honor.* Williams, *Dueling in the Old South,* 41.

60. Frederick Marryat, *A Diary in America with Remarks on Its Institution* (New York: Alfred A. Knopf, 1962), 161.

61. Letter to George Roberts, confidential, editor of *Roberts' Semi-Monthly Magazine,* in *Letters of William Gilmore Simms,* ed. Mary C. Simms

Oliphant et al. (1952; repr., Columbia: University of South Carolina Press, 1982), 2:243.

62. Lambert A. Wilmer, *Our Press Gang; or, A Complete Exposition of the Corruptions and Crimes of the American Newspapers* (1859; repr., New York: Arno Press, 1970), 11–12.

63. Clement Eaton, *Freedom of Thought in the Old South* (Durham, N.C.: Duke University Press, 1940), 163; John Hope Franklin, *The Militant South, 1800–1861* (Cambridge, Mass.: Harvard University Press, 1956), 55.

64. Hudson, *Journalism in the United States,* 763–64; Williams, *Dueling in the Old South,* 72–73.

65. Sharon Joyce Gates and Catherine C. Mitchell, "Research Notes— Adolph Ochs: Learning What's Fit to Print," *American Journalism* 8, no. 4 (Fall 1991): 228–29.

66. Gerald W. Johnson, *An Honorable Titan: A Biographical Sketch of Adolph S. Ochs* (New York: Harper and Row, 1946), 22–26.

67. E. Culpepper Clark, *Francis Warrington Dawson and the Politics of Restoration: South Carolina, 1874–1889* (Tuscaloosa: University of Alabama Press, 1980), 64–66, 105–8, 215–17, 224.

68. Dabney, *Pistols and Pointed Pens,* 174.

69. Lewis Pinckney Jones, *Stormy Petrel: N. G. Gonzales and His State* (Columbia: University of South Carolina Press, 1973), 293–308. The progressive magazine editor Walter Hines Page, a self-exiled southerner working in New York, foresaw in the Tillman acquittal the emergence of racist demagogues in the twentieth-century South: "An aristocracy in a democracy means a group of a few privileged persons; outside this group, the bully; behind the bully an ignorant populace that will elect the bully to office, will hold him in honor and will acquit him of crime." Page, "The Matter with South Carolina," *World's Work* 5, no. 5 (March 1903): 3153.

70. Ralph McGill, *The South and the Southerner* (Boston: Little, Brown, 1963), 90–91.

71. Hodding Carter III, "The Difficult Isolation Courage Can Bring," *Nieman Reports,* Summer 2006, 90–91.

72. Thomas Nelson Page, Preface, *The Old Virginia Gentleman and Other Sketches,* by George W. Bagby (New York: Charles Scribner's Sons, 1911), vi–vii.

73. Douglas Southall Freeman, introduction to Bagby, *Old Virginia Gentleman,* xxiv.

74. Bagby, *Old Virginia Gentleman,* 100.

75. Bagby to Ellen Turner, May 4, 1860, Bagby-Turner Papers, MSS 4750, Special Collections, University of Virginia.

76. Michael O'Brien, a scholar of southern intellectual history, argues that the tradition of writing anonymously or under a pen name should not be seen as evidence that writing was considered vulgar in the South. "To write was respectable. *Only* to write was less so. To advertise was vulgar, and the prefix of one's name to an essay was a form of self-aggrandizement. In a society whose authors did not usually depend upon payments for words, it was not only vulgar, it was superfluous." *Rethinking the South: Essays in Intellectual History* (Baltimore: Johns Hopkins University Press, 1988), 22.

77. John Moncure, "John M. Daniel: The Editor of *The Examiner,*" *Sewanee Review* 15, no. 3 (July 1907): 258.

78. Bishop Oscar Penn Fitzgerald, "John M. Daniel and Some of His Contemporaries," *South Atlantic Quarterly* 4, no. 1 (1905): 13.

79. Walter M. Brasch, *Brer Rabbit, Uncle Remus, and the "Cornfield Journalist"* (Macon, Ga.: Mercer University Press, 2000), 276–81.

80. Ibid., 289.

81. Paul M. Cousins, *Joel Chandler Harris: A Biography* (Baton Rouge: Louisiana State University Press, 1968), 135; Francis Pendleton Gaines, *The Southern Plantation: A Study in the Development and the Accuracy of a Tradition* (New York: Columbia University Press, 1925), 75; John Herbert Nelson, *The Negro Character in American Literature* (Lawrence, Kansas: Department of Journalism Press, 1926), 107, 108.

82. Brasch, *Brer Rabbit,* xvii.

83. Cousins, *Joel Chandler Harris,* 178.

84. Ibid., 19–23.

85. Ibid., 30–31, 34–49, 64.

86. Joel Chandler Harris, *The Countryman,* February 13, 1866, ibid., 65.

87. Ibid., 71–72.

88. Ibid., 71–81.

89. Ibid., 92–106.

90. Ibid., 108–10.

91. Harris, "Literature in the South," ibid., 109–10.

92. Clark, *Francis Warrington Dawson,* 138–41. Raymond B. Nixon, in his biography of Grady, suggested that a negative review of Grady's speech from the Charleston paper perhaps reflected "a touch of envy" from the less recognized Dawson. Clark goes further. "Compared with the general reaction [to Grady's speech], the criticism raised by the Charleston *News and Courier* seemed personal, vindictive, and churlish. The motive was likely jealousy, along with pique at imagined slights, and Dawson felt them with childlike intensity." Nixon, *Henry W. Grady: Spokesman of the New South* (New York: Alfred A. Knopf, 1943), 251.

93. Joel Chandler Harris, *Life of Henry W. Grady, Including His Writings and Speeches* (New York: Cassell Publishing Co., 1890), 16.

94. Nixon, *Henry W. Grady,* 189–91, 264–68, 315–16.

95. Ibid., 194–97, 277.

96. Harris, *Life of Henry W. Grady,* 11.

97. Nixon, *Henry W. Grady,* 54–63.

98. Ibid., 64.

99. J. W. Lee, "H. W. Grady," *Arena* 2 (June 1890): 9–23, quoted in Russell Franklin Terrell, *A Study of the Early Journalistic Writings of Henry W. Grady* (Nashville, Tenn.: Peabody College, 1927), 9.

100. Terrell, *Study,* 3.

101. Nixon, *Henry W. Grady,* 133–34.

102. Henry W. Grady, "Florida," *Atlanta Constitution,* December 8, 1876, in Terrell, *Study,* 138.

103. Simon J. Bronner, ed., *Lafcadio Hearn's America: Ethnographic Sketches and Editorials* (Lexington: University Press of Kentucky, 2002), 16–20.

104. Charles W. Coleman, "The Recent Movement in Southern Literature," *Harper's New Monthly Magazine* 74, no. 444 (May 1887): 855.

105. Lafcadio Hearn, "The Scenes of Cable's Romances," *Century Magazine,* November 1883, 40–47, reprinted in Arlin Turner, ed., *Critical Essays on George W. Cable* (Boston: G. K. Hall and Co., 1980), 53.

106. S. Frederick Starr, ed., *Inventing New Orleans: Writings of Lafcadio Hearn* (Jackson: University of Mississippi Press, 2001), xiii, 3.

107. Bronner, *Lafcadio Hearn's America,* 31–33.

CHAPTER FOUR

1. The term *fire-eater* was probably derived from Missouri senator Thomas Hart Benton's description of South Carolina senator John C. Calhoun as a firebrand.

2. Gavin Wright, *The Political Economy of the Cotton South: Households, Markets and Wealth in the Nineteenth Century* (New York: W. W. Norton, 1978), 10–42.

3. Carl R. Osthaus, *Partisans of the Southern Press: Editorial Spokesmen of the Nineteenth Century* (Lexington: University Press of Kentucky, 1994), 78.

4. William Gilmore Simms to Nathaniel Beverly Tucker, April 7, 1851, quoted in Osthaus, *Partisans,* 79.

5. *De Bow's Review,* June 1857, 583–93, in *The Cause of the South: Selections from De Bow's Review 1846–1867,* by Paul F. Paskoff and Daniel J. Wilson (Baton Rouge: Louisiana State University Press, 1982), 209. Ruffin also frequently contributed to one of the longest-published agricultural magazines in the nation, the Richmond-based *Southern Planter,* including a major proslavery series, "Slavery and Free Labor Defined and Compared" *Southern Planter* (19, no. 12:723–41 [1858]; 20, no. 1:1–10 [1859]). Betty L. Mitchell, *Edmund Ruffin: A Biography* (Bloomington: Indiana University Press, 1981), 34–44.

6. Debra Reddin van Tuyll, introduction to section on the South in *The Civil War, North and South,* vol. 3, *The Greenwood Library of American War Reporting,* ed. David Copeland (Westport, Conn.: Greenwood Press, 2005), 295.

7. Sam G. Riley, *Magazines of the American South* (New York: Greenwood Press, 1986), 236–37.

8. Paul F. Paskoff and Daniel J. Wilson, "J. D. B. De Bow and the *Commercial Review,*" introduction to Paskoff and Wilson, *Cause of the South,* 1–9.

9. George Fitzhugh, "Cui Bono?—The Negro Vote," *De Bow's Review* 4 (October 1867): 289–92, in Paskoff and Wilson, *Cause of the South,* 299.

10. Clement Eaton, *Freedom of Thought in the Old South* (Durham, N.C.: Duke University Press, 1940), vii.

11. Michael O'Brien, *Rethinking the South: Essays in Intellectual History* (Baltimore: Johns Hopkins University Press, 1988), 34–35, 22.

12. W. J. Cash, *The Mind of the South* (New York: Alfred A. Knopf, 1941), 135.

13. Hinton Rowan Helper, *The Impending Crisis of the South: How to Meet It* (New York: Burdick Brothers, 1857); and *Nojoque: A Question for a Continent* (New York: G.W. Carlton and Co., 1867).

14. Edmund Wilson, *Patriotic Gore: Studies in the Literature of the American Civil War* (New York: Oxford University Press, 1962), 364–79.

15. V. O. Key Jr. and Alexander Heard, *Southern Politics in State and Nation* (New York: Alfred A. Knopf, 1949), 664.

16. Bruce Clayton, *W. J. Cash: A Life* (Baton Rouge: Louisiana State University Press, 1991), 184–89.

17. Cable to his wife, January 16, 1885, in Arlin Turner, ed., *Mark Twain and George W. Cable: The Record of a Literary Friendship* (East Lansing: Michigan State University Press, 1960), 83.

18. Louis D. Rubin Jr., *George W. Cable: The Life and Times of a Southern Heretic* (New York: Pegasus, 1969), 185–86.

19. W. E. B. DuBois, *The Souls of Black Folk* (New York: Dover Publications, 1994), 11.

20. Louis Harlan, *Booker T. Washington: The Making of a Black Leader, 1856–1901* (New York: Oxford University Press, 1972), 220.

21. David L. Lewis, *W. E. B. DuBois: Biography of a Race, 1868–1919* (New York: Henry Holt, 1993), 288–91, 343–85, 386–407, 408–27.

22. Joel Williamson, *The Crucible of Race: Black-White Relations in the American South Since Emancipation* (New York: Oxford University Press, 1984), 79–139, 414–59.

23. Historians have blamed the four daily newspapers in Atlanta for fomenting the riot of 1906, which resulted in about two dozen blacks being killed and thousands fleeing the city. The *Atlanta Constitution,* whose editor Clark Howell was running for governor, had been battling its rival the *Atlanta Journal,* which supported the other leading candidate, Hoke Smith, former owner of the *Journal.* The main issue was whether blacks should be further disenfranchised (Smith's position) or whether blacks in Georgia were already powerless enough without additional laws (Howell's position). Meanwhile, two upstart Atlanta papers, the

new Hearst-owned *Georgian* and the *Evening News,* reported in the lurid style of yellow journalism a series of alleged sexual attacks against white women by black "brutes" and "half clad Negroes," most of which were wild distortions or false rumors. The two established newspapers were more restrained but also reported the alleged attacks. After the *News* declared it was time for men to "act," mobs of whites began attacking blacks throughout downtown. Jim Auchmutey, "Deadline: How Atlanta's Newspapers Helped Incite the 1906 Race Riot," *Atlanta Journal-Constitution,* September 17, 2006, B1, B3.

24. Williamson, *Crucible of Race,* 79–85, 85–88, 93–100, 111–19, 414–15, 449–58.

25. Rubin, *George W. Cable,* 25, 31, 128.

26. See "Creole" (426–27), "*Plessy v. Ferguson,*" (828–29), in *Encyclopedia of Southern Culture,* ed. Charles R. Wilson and William Ferris (Chapel Hill: University of North Carolina Press, 1989).

27. Rubin, *George W. Cable,* 34; Turner, *Mark Twain and George W. Cable,* xii.

28. George W. Cable, "My Politics," in *The Negro Question: A Selection of Writings on Civil Rights in the South by George W. Cable,* ed. Arlin Turner (Garden City, N.Y.: Doubleday and Co., 1958), 10.

29. George W. Cable, *Old Creole Days: A Story of Creole Life* (Gretna, La.: Pelican Publishing Co., 2001), 184.

30. Cable, "Sieur George," in *Old Creole Days,* 260.

31. Charles DeKay, "Cable's 'Old Creole Days,'" *Scribner's Monthly Magazine,* July 1879, 473.

32. Rubin, *George W. Cable,* 59.

33. Ibid., 78.

34. Cable, "Segregation in the Schools," in *Negro Question,* 28–32.

35. Cable, "My Politics," 15.

36. Ibid., 19.

37. Rubin, *George W. Cable,* 109.

38. Douglas A. Blackmon, a *Wall Street Journal* reporter, investigated the history of the convict-labor-leasing system as it evolved in the Deep South through the 1930s. Blackmon, *Slavery by Another Name* (New York: Doubleday, 2008).

39. Cable, "My Politics," 18; Rubin, *George W. Cable,* 110–11.

40. Cable, "My Politics," 19.

41. Ibid., 20.

42. Rubin, *George W. Cable,* 111.

43. Cable, "The Freedman's Case in Equity," in *Negro Question,* 74–75.

44. Ibid., 58.

45. Cable, "My Politics," 22. Cable is quoting a paragraph from his speech in Alabama, of which no copy survives. See Rubin, *George W. Cable,* 158.

46. Grady, "In Plain Black and White," *Century,* April 1885, reprinted in Joel Chandler Harris, *Life of Henry W. Grady, Including His Writings and Speeches* (New York: Cassell Publishing Co., 1890), 287.

47. Rubin, *George W. Cable,* 159.

48. Cable, "The Silent South," in *Negro Question,* 86–87.

49. Rubin, *George W. Cable,* 147.

50. Ibid., 68–69.

51. Ibid., 105.

52. Ibid., 126.

53. Ibid., 128.

54. *Boston Herald Supplement,* November 28, 1883, cited in Rubin, *George W. Cable,* 131.

55. Cable to Boyesen, January 3, 1878, quoted in Rubin, *George W. Cable,* 70.

56. Rubin, *George W. Cable,* 263.

57. Ibid., 179.

58. Ibid., 178–79.

59. Alice Hall Petry, "Native Outsider: George Washington Cable," *Literary New Orleans: Essays and Meditations,* ed. Richard S. Kennedy (Baton Rouge: Louisiana State University Press, 1992), 6.

60. Rubin, *George W. Cable,* 275.

61. John Milton Cooper, *Walter Hines Page: The Southerner as American, 1855–1918* (Chapel Hill: University of North Carolina Press, 1977), 73, 147, 212.

62. Ibid., 146.

63. Walter Hines Page, "The Hookworm and Civilization," *World's Work,* September 1912, 504–18, cited in Cooper, *Walter Hines Page,* 228.

64. Cooper, *Walter Hines Page,* 108, 396.

65. Ibid., 112, 116.

66. Ibid., 42.

67. Ibid., 47, 55.

68. Walter Hines Page, "The Southern Educational Problem," *International Review,* October 1881, in Cooper, *Walter Hines Page,* 58–60.

69. Cooper, *Walter Hines Page,* 60.

70. Ibid., 8.

71. Ibid., 7–9.

72. Ibid., 41.

73. Ibid., 43–45.

74. Ibid., 75.

75. Ibid., 78–79.

76. Ibid., 75.

77. Ibid., 43.

78. Ibid., 43–44.

79. Ibid., 80, from the so-called mummy letter, *Raleigh State Chronicle,* February 1, 1886.

80. Frank Luther Mott, *A History of American Magazines: 1885–1905* (Cambridge, Mass.: Harvard University Press, 1957), 8–9, 511–16.

81. Page ran several articles about lynching in the South, which was also the subject of the only signed article he wrote for the magazine, "The Last Hold of the Southern Bully," *Forum,* November 1893, 303–4.

82. Cooper, *Walter Hines Page,* 102.

83. Walter Hines Page, "An Intimate View of Publishing," *World's Work,* September 1902, 2562–63.

84. Cooper, *Walter Hines Page,* 126.

85. Walter Hines Page, *The Southerner: A Novel* (New York: Doubleday, Page and Co., 1909).

86. Cooper, *Walter Hines Page,* 217–18.

87. Ibid., 184–85.

88. Ibid., 105.

89. Lewis H. Blair, *A Southern Prophecy,* introduction by C. Vann Woodward (1889; repr., Boston: Little, Brown, 1964), xlv, 15–19.

90. Cooper, *Walter Hines Page,* 168–69. Dixon, who had been in a progressive-reform club with Page that advocated a North Carolina technical college in the 1880s, published four novels with Doubleday, Page

and Company: *The Leopard's Spots* (1902), *The One Woman* (1903), *The Clansman* (1905), and *The Traitor* (1907). *The Clansman* became the basis for the historic D. W. Griffith film *The Birth of a Nation* (1915).

91. Ibid., 146.

92. Ibid., 216–17.

93. C. Vann Woodward, introduction to *A Southern Prophecy,* by Lewis H. Blair, xii.

94. Page to Robert C. Ogden, December 17, 1903, in Cooper, *Walter Hines Page,* 213.

CHAPTER FIVE

1. Alistair Cooke calls him the prince of journalists in his introduction to *The Vintage Mencken* (New York: Vintage Books, 1956), vii. Mencken was more famously called the "Sage of Baltimore" and the "Bad Boy of Baltimore." See also "H. L. Mencken," *Dictionary of Literary Biography,* vol. 29, *American Newspaper Journalists, 1926–1950* (Farmington Hills, Mich.: Gale Group, 1984), 223–40.

2. Fred C. Hobson, *Serpent in Eden: H. L. Mencken and the South* (Chapel Hill: University of North Carolina Press, 1974), 147.

3. H. L. Mencken, "The Sahara of the Bozart," in *Prejudices—Second Series* (New York: Alfred A. Knopf, 1920), 136–37.

4. Fred Hobson, *Mencken: A Life* (New York: Random House, 1994), 269–70.

5. Gerald W. Johnson, foreword to Hobson, *Serpent in Eden,* x.

6. "The Literature of a Moral Republic," *Smart Set,* August 1913, 153, quoted in Hobson, *Serpent in Eden,* 21.

7. Cooke, *Vintage Mencken,* 198.

8. Originally in *Smart Set,* August 1921, 139.

9. Hobson, *Serpent in Eden,* 27–28.

10. Henry Timrod, "Literature in the South," in *The Literary South,* ed., Louis D. Rubin Jr. (New York: John Wiley and Sons, 1979), 209.

11. Joel Chandler Harris, "Literature in the South," in Paul M. Cousins, *Joel Chandler Harris: A Biography* (Baton Rouge: Louisiana State University Press, 1968), 109–10.

12. Louis D. Rubin Jr., *George W. Cable: The Life and Times of a Southern Heretic* (New York: Pegasus, 1969), 66–67.

13. Southern Publication Society, *The South in the Building of the Nation: A History of the Southern States Designed to Record the South's Part in the Making of the American Nation; to Portray the Character and Genius, to Chronicle the Achievements and Progress and to Illustrate the Life and Traditions of the Southern People* (Richmond, Va.: Southern Publication Society, 1909).

14. Edwin A. Alderman and Joel Chandler Harris, eds., *The Library of Southern Literature*, vols. 1–17 (Atlanta: Martin and Hoyt Co., 1909–23).

15. Hobson, *Serpent in Eden*, 14.

16. Ibid., 13.

17. Ibid., 59–60, 261–63, 355–56.

18. Hobson, *Mencken*, 497–99.

19. H. L. Mencken, "Journalism in American," in *Prejudices—Sixth Series* (New York: Alfred A. Knopf, 1927), 31–37.

20. H. L. Mencken, "The South Begins to Mutter," *Smart Set*, August 1921, 138.

21. The first of nine verses by James Ryder Randall (1839–1908), a Maryland native who worked for several southern newspapers, finally as editor and correspondent with the *Augusta (Georgia) Chronicle*.

22. Bruce Clayton, *The Savage Ideal: Intolerance and Intellectual Leadership in the South, 1890–1914* (Baltimore: Johns Hopkins University Press, 1972), 44–45.

23. H. L. Mencken, "The Calamity of Appomattox," in Cooke, *Vintage Mencken*, 198.

24. H. L. Mencken, "Holy Writ," *Smart Set*, October 1923, 144, quoted in Hobson, *Serpent in Eden*, 62.

25. Elizabeth S. Scott, "'In Fame, Not Specie,'" *Virginia Cavalcade* (Winter 1978): 128–43; Mencken to Emily Clark, May 1921, in Emily Clark, *Innocence Abroad* (New York: Alfred A. Knopf, 1931), 112.

26. Hobson, *Serpent in Eden*, 33–39. The journal's title was taken from the title of a William Congreve comedy of 1693 and was explained in the first issue this way: "We mean to deal double, to show the other side, to throw open the back windows stuck in their sills from disuse." *Double Dealer* 1, no. 1 (January 1921): 3.

27. Hobson, *Serpent in Eden,* 31, 45–46.

28. Ibid., 37.

29. Ibid., 38–39, 52.

30. Clark, *Innocence Abroad,* 7.

31. Ibid., 5, 18

32. Hobson, *Serpent in Eden,* 44.

33. Edwin Mims, *The Advancing South: Stories of Progress and Reaction* (New York: Doubleday, Page and Co., 1926), 188–89.

34. Hobson, *Serpent in Eden,* 104.

35. Ibid., 38.

36. Ibid., 101.

37. Gerald W. Johnson, "Old Slick," in *South-Watching: Selected Essays by Gerald W. Johnson,* ed. Fred Hobson (Chapel Hill: University of North Carolina Press, 1983), 200–207.

38. Johnson, *South-Watching,* x.

39. Ibid., xi.

40. Ibid., xvi–xvii.

41. Gerald W. Johnson, "The Congo, Mr. Mencken," in *South-Watching,* 3–8. See also Cooke, *Vintage Mencken,* vi, xi.

42. William Manchester, *Disturber of the Peace: The Life of H. L. Mencken* (Amherst: University of Massachusetts Press, 1966), 124–25.

43. Mims, *Advancing South,* 172–81.

44. H. L. Mencken, "The South Looks Ahead," *American Mercury* 8 (August 1926): 508, quoted in Hobson, *Serpent in Eden,* 163–64.

45. John T. Kneebone, *Southern Liberal Journalists and the Issue of Race, 1920–1944* (Chapel Hill: University of North Carolina Press, 1985), 33.

46. Letter from Jaffé to Dabney, March 14, 1931, quoted in Marie M. Nitschke, "Virginius Dabney of Virginia: Portrait of a Southern Journalist in the Twentieth Century" (Ph.D. diss., Emory University, 1987), 59.

47. Virginius Dabney, *Liberalism in the South* (Chapel Hill: University of North Carolina Press, 1932), 268.

48. Daniel Joseph Singal, *The War Within: From Victorian to Modernist Thought in the South, 1919–1945* (Chapel Hill: University of North Carolina Press, 1982), 126–27.

49. Edwin McNeill Poteat Jr., "Religion," in *Culture in the South,* ed. W. T. Couch (Chapel Hill: University of North Carolina Press, 1935), 251.

50. Hobson, *Serpent in Eden,* 147.

51. Carl Bode, *Mencken* (Carbondale: Southern Illinois University Press, 1969), 264–65; Hobson, *Serpent in Eden,* 147–48. Bode points out that accounts vary as to how Darrow became involved in the case.

52. Marion Elizabeth Rodgers, *Mencken: The American Iconoclast* (Oxford, U.K.: Oxford University Press, 2005), 271–94; Manchester, *Disturber of the Peace,* 164.

53. Rodgers, *Mencken,* 271–78, 282, 288.

54. Ibid., 291.

55. Ibid., 292.

56. Hobson, *Serpent in Eden,* 104–5.

57. Rodgers, *Mencken,* 294.

58. Howard Odum, "The Duel to the Death," *Social Forces* 4, no. 1 (November 1925): 189–94.

59. Donald Davidson, *Southern Writers in the Modern World* (Athens: University of Georgia Press, 1958), 18.

60. Hobson, *Serpent in Eden,* 73–74.

61. Donald Davidson, "The Thankless Muse and Her Fugitive Poets," in *Southern Writers in the Modern World,* 30.

62. Louis D. Rubin Jr., ed., *I'll Take My Stand: The South and the Agrarian Tradition, by Twelve Southerners* (1930; repr., Baton Rouge: Louisiana State University Press, 1977).

63. Odum to Mencken, in Hobson, *Serpent in Eden,* 169.

64. Nitschke, "Virginius Dabney," 65.

65. H. L. Mencken, "Uprising in the Confederacy," *American Mercury* 22, no. 87 (March 1931): 379–81.

66. Gerald W. Johnson, "The South Faces Itself," *Virginia Quarterly Review* 7, no. 1 (January 1931): 157. James K. Vardaman (1861–1930), Mississippi governor and U.S. senator; Coleman Blease (1868–1942), South Carolina governor and U.S. senator; J. Thomas Heflin (1869–1951), Alabama congressman and U.S. senator; and Thomas E. Watson (1856–1922), Georgia populist candidate, publisher, and U.S. senator, were all known for their lavish oratory advancing white supremacy among poor whites.

67. The university press's editor, W. T. Couch, rejected a chapter on southern journalism written for the book by the Pulitzer Prize–winning editor of the *Asheville Citizen,* Robert Lathan. When Couch

asked Lathan to rewrite his chapter with specific examples of news being suppressed because of private business interests, Lathan was not willing to risk the criticism such an approach would bring him. Singal, *War Within,* 283–84.

68. Dabney in 1932 branded the *Atlanta Constitution* and *Charlotte Observer,* along with the *Louisville Courier-Journal,* as formerly liberal organs that had turned conservative, by which he meant lacking in criticism and new ideas. *Liberalism in the South,* 409. All three would be considered the most liberal southern papers in the 1960s.

69. John D. Allen, "Journalism in the South," in *Culture in the South,* ed. W. T. Couch (Chapel Hill: University of North Carolina Press, 1935), 134, 139.

70. Ibid., 132–34.

71. Ibid., 158.

72. Walter C. Johnson and Arthur T. Robb, *The South and Its Newspapers: The Story of the Southern Newspaper Publishers Association and Its Part in the South's Economic Revival, 1903–1953* (Chattanooga, Tenn.: Southern Newspaper Publishers Association, 1954), 140.

73. Ibid., 141–43; Allen, "Journalism in the South," 134.

74. John M. Barry, *Rising Tide: The Great Mississippi Flood of 1927 and How It Changed America* (New York: Simon and Schuster, 1997), 225–33.

75. "Books for the Hammock and Deck Chair," *Smart Set* 28 (June 1909): 155, quoted in Hobson, *Serpent in Eden,* 19.

76. Gerald W. Johnson, "Old Slick," in Johnson, *South-Watching,* 200.

CHAPTER SIX

1. Joseph L. Morrison, *W. J. Cash: Southern Prophet* (New York: Alfred A. Knopf, 1967), 7, 40–45, 55–56, 65. See also Bruce Clayton, *W. J. Cash: A Life* (Baton Rouge: Louisiana State University Press, 1991).

2. National Emergency Council, *Report on Economic Conditions in the South* (Washington, D.C.: U.S. Government Printing Office, 1938).

3. Morrison, *W. J. Cash,* 60.

4. Ibid., 168.

5. Ibid., 41, 59–60.

6. Morrison, *W. J. Cash,* 46; Clayton, *W. J. Cash,* 83.

7. Morrison, *W. J. Cash,* 45.

8. W. J. Cash, "Genesis of the Southern Cracker," *American Mercury* 55 (May 1935): 105–8.

9. W. J. Cash, *The Mind of the South* (New York: Alfred A. Knopf, 1941), 135.

10. Morrison, *W. J. Cash,* 52.

11. Ibid., 59, 66, 80–81.

12. Clayton, *W. J. Cash,* 162.

13. Ibid., 166–67.

14. Fred Hobson, "Booking Passage: W. J. Cash and a Southern Awakening," in *The Silencing of Emily Mullen and Other Essays* (Baton Rouge: Louisiana State University Press, 2005), 209.

15. Edwin M. Yoder Jr., in *The South Today: 100 Years After Appomattox,* ed. Willie Morris (New York: Harper and Row, 1965), 94, 98.

16. Michael O'Brien, "W. J. Cash, Hegel, and the South," *Journal of Southern History* 44, no. 3 (August 1978): 379.

17. The symposium papers were published in *W. J. Cash and the Minds of the South,* ed. Paul D. Escott (Baton Rouge: Louisiana State University Press, 1992).

18. The two-volume anthology compiled by Clayborne Carson, David Garrow, Bill Kovach, and Carol Polsgrove, *Reporting Civil Rights* (New York: Library of America, 2003), starts with journalism from 1941 to 1963.

19. Gene Roberts and Hank Klibanoff, *The Race Beat: The Press, the Civil Rights Struggle, and the Awakening of a Nation* (New York: Alfred A. Knopf, 2006), 12–23.

20. Ibid., 23.

21. John Edgerton, *Speak Now Against the Day* (New York: Alfred A. Knopf, 1994), 216.

22. John T. Kneebone, *Southern Liberal Journalists and the Issue of Race, 1920–1944* (Chapel Hill: University of North Carolina Press, 1985), 95.

23. The university president was Homer P. Rainey. Morrison, *W. J. Cash,* 121.

24. The speech was captured on the only tape recording known to exist of the writer's voice. An audio replication and the transcript are in

the Southern Historical Collection at the University of North Carolina at Chapel Hill.

25. Morrison, *W. J. Cash,* 127–35; Clayton, *W. J. Cash,* 185–89. Morrison and Clayton both weigh possible explanations for Cash's death and conclude that there was no foul play and that fatigue and the alien setting contributed to a crisis in Cash's mental and physical weaknesses, which led to suicide—but beyond that, it is impossible to assign a definite cause.

26. Gunnar Myrdal, *An American Dilemma: The Negro Problem and Modern Democracy,* with Richard Sterner and Arnold Rose (New York: Harper and Brothers, 1944). Two other influential books on the South published in the 1940s were Arthur F. Raper and Ira De A. Reid, *Sharecroppers All* (Chapel Hill: University of North Carolina Press, 1941), and V. O. Key and Alexander Heard, *Southern Politics in State and Nation* (New York: Alfred A. Knopf, 1949).

27. Cash, *The Mind of the South,* vii.

28. Harry Ashmore, *Hearts and Minds* (Cabin John, Md.: Seven Locks Press, 1988), 113–14.

29. Harry S. Ashmore, "Address Before Southern Governors' Conference at Hot Springs," November 12, 1951, Rare Book Collection, Southern Pamphlet Folio, University of North Carolina at Chapel Hill.

30. Ashmore, *Hearts and Minds,* 156.

31. Ibid., 204.

32. Patrick J. Gilpin, "Charles S. Johnson: An Intellectual Biography" (Ph.D. dissertation, Vanderbilt University, 1973), 203.

33. "The No. 1 Story," *Time,* January 17, 1955, 67; Maria Luisa Cisneros of *Time* to McKnight, February 16, 1955, in Race Relations Information Center (RRIC)/SERS, Amistad Research Center, Tulane University.

34. Morrison, *W. J. Cash,* 76–77.

35. Historians in the 1950s and 1960s often used the SERS as a fruitful archival collection but have not done so much since then. More than a million news clippings, articles, and documents collected by the SERS are accessible at more than one hundred university libraries in the indexed microfilm series Facts on Film. Also, the archives of the SERS itself, later called the Race Relations Information Center before closing

in 1975, are housed at the Amistad Research Center on the Tulane University campus, New Orleans.

36. Booker to Don Shoemaker, June 30, 1955, RRIC.

37. Doug Cumming, "Facing Facts, Facing South: The SERS and the Effort to Inform the South After *Brown v. Board,* 1954–1960" (Ph.D. diss., University of North Carolina at Chapel Hill, 2002), 209–11.

38. Ibid., 160, 206–8; Emilie Tavel, "Integration Seen Aid to All," *Christian Science Monitor,* November 18, 1954, 11. In a letter to Valien as she was let go, McKnight praised her work and did not mention Waring's objection to her Boston speech. Also, Valien was told for months that her future office at the SERS was under construction, but letters among board members suggest that they were worried that violating Nashville's segregation customs in an office would draw controversy.

39. Virginius Dabney, C.A. McKnight, and Q&A period, "How Is the Press Reporting School Desgregation?" *Problems of Journalism* (Washington, D.C.: ASNE, 1955), 79–94.

40. C.A. McKnight, "Troubled South: Search for a Middle Ground," *Collier's,* June 22, 1956, 25–31; letters from readers to McKnight, Box 5, RRIC.

41. Virginius Dabney, "Virginia's Peaceable, Honorable Stand," *Life,* September 22, 1958, 51–56; and *Across the Years: Memories of a Virginian* (Garden City, N.Y.: Doubleday, 1978), 234.

42. McKnight, "Troubled South," 25, 31.

43. Clayton, *W. J. Cash,* 130–31.

44. The person who called down Ayers is not identified in the ASNE proceedings, but letters between Ayers and Sarratt indicate that it was Sarratt. Sarratt Papers, Southern Historical Collection, University of North Carolina at Chapel Hill.

45. Reed Sarratt, *The Ordeal of Desegregation* (New York: Harper and Row, 1966).

46. Gwyneth Mellinger, "A Failed Crusade: Newsroom Integration and the Tokenization of John Sengstacke," paper presented at the AEJMC, San Francisco, August 5, 2006, 7–8, 13.

47. Gerald W. Johnson, *An Honorable Titan: A Biographical Study of Adolph S. Ochs* (New York: Harper and Brothers, 1946), 305–7.

48. Susan E. Tifft and Alex S. Jones, *The Trust: The Private and Powerful Family Behind the* New York Times (Boston: Little, Brown, 1999), 255, 426.

49. Harrison E. Salisbury, *A Time of Change: A Reporter's Tale of Our Time* (New York: Harper and Row, 1988), 44.

50. Harrison E. Salisbury, *Without Fear or Favor: The* New York Times *and Its Times* (New York: Times Books, 1980), 368.

51. Roberts and Klibanoff, *Race Beat,* 383. The photographer was Flip Schulke and the anecdote came from an interview with Schulke by one of the authors.

52. Fred Powledge, *Free at Last? The Civil Rights Movement and the People Who Made It* (Boston: Little, Brown, 1991), xx.

53. Roger Williams, "Newspapers in the South," *Columbia Journalism Review* 6 (Summer 1967): 26–35.

54. Roberts and Klibanoff, *Race Beat,* 82.

55. Calvin Trillin, "State Secrets," *New Yorker,* May 29, 1995, in *Voices in Our Blood: America's Best on the Civil Rights Movement,* ed. Jon Meacham (New York: Random House, 2001), 501.

56. Steven D. Classen, *Watching Jim Crow: The Struggles over Mississippi TV, 1955–1969* (Durham, N.C.: Duke University Press, 2004), 125–33.

57. Daniel Webster Hollis, *An Alabama Newspaper Tradition: Grover C. Hall and the Hall Family* (Tuscaloosa: University of Alabama Press, 1983), 29–31, 92–132.

58. Hall missed reading Cash's *Mind of the South* when it came out in 1941, the year of his father's death, but finally got around to reading it hurriedly as things heated up in 1956. Ibid., 103.

59. This is the conclusion of an early biographer of King in analyzing Hall's editorials on the boycott. Lawrence D. Reddick, *Crusader Without Violence: A Biography of Martin Luther King, Jr.* (New York: Harper and Brothers, 1959), 163–65. King, in his book about the boycott, *Stride Toward Freedom: The Montgomery Story* (New York: Harper and Brothers, 1959), wrote that he "could not help admiring this brilliant but complex man who claimed to be a supporter of segregation but could not stomach the excesses performed in its name" (176).

60. G. C. Hall, "The N.Y. Herald Tribune's Enlightenment," *Montgomery Advertiser,* February 26, 1956.

61. The series was also nominated for a Pulitzer Prize in 1957. *Montgomery Advertiser,* May 27, 1956. See also Doug Cumming, "Building Resentment: How the Alabama Press Prepared the Ground for *New York Times v. Sullivan," American Journalism* 22, no. 3 (Summer 2005): 7–32.

62. The ad ran March 29, 1960.

63. "Editorial," *Montgomery Advertiser,* April 7, 1960.

64. Anthony Lewis, *Make No Law: The Sullivan Case and the First Amendment* (New York: Random House, 1991), 35, and Bruce L. Ottley, John Bruce Lewis, and Younghee Jin Ottley, "*New York Times v. Sullivan:* A Retrospective Examination," *DePaul Law Review* 33 (Summer 1984): 741–81.

65. Cumming, "Building Resentment," 8, 24.

66. Judy Means Wagnon, "Grover C. Hall Jr.: Profile of a Writing Editor" (master's thesis, University of Alabama, 1975), 85–90.

67. The firing was never made public. However, an anonymous account of it in Earle Dunford, Richmond Times-Dispatch: *The Story of a Newspaper* (Richmond, Va.: Cadmus, 1995), 327–28, matches a version given to this writer by Kilpatrick in an e-mail on May 18, 2004.

68. Wagnon, "Grover C. Hall Jr.," 111–14; letter from McKnight to Hall, November 4, 1970, 114n82.

69. Ibid., 117.

70. Dunford, Richmond Times-Dispatch, 323.

71. Sarratt, *Ordeal,* 255.

72. Numan V. Bartley, *The New South, 1945–1980* (Baton Rouge: Louisiana State University Press, 1995), 188–89.

73. James J. Kilpatrick, *The Sovereign States: Notes of a Citizen of Virginia* (Chicago: H. Regnery Co., 1957), 222–23.

74. Ibid., ix.

75. See also Louis D. Rubin Jr. and James J. Kilpatrick, eds., *The Lasting South: Fourteen Southerners Look at Their Home* (Chicago: Henry Regnery Co., 1957). The theme of the book was that the South's identity was worth preserving even as times changed. A variety of viewpoints were expressed, but the conservative and pro-states'-rights tone of the whole was set by the essays of Richard Weaver, "The South and the American Union," and Kilpatrick, "Conservatism and the South."

76. Bartley, *New South,* 198.

77. James J. Kilpatrick, *The Southern Case for School Segregation* (New York: Crowell-Collier, 1962), 101.

78. James J. Kilpatrick, *The Foxes' Union: And Other Stretchers, Tall Tales, and Discursive Reminiscences of Happy Years in Scrabble, Virginia* (McLean, Va.: EPM Publications, 1977).

79. James J. Kilpatrick, *The Writer's Art* (Kansas City, Mo.: Andrews, McMeel and Parker, 1984).

80. James J. Kilpatrick, "My Journey from Racism," *Atlanta Journal-Constitution,* December 22, 2002, C-1, C-4.

81. Roberts and Klibanoff, *Race Beat,* 405–6.

82. Morton Sosna, *In Search of the Silent South* (New York: Columbia University Press, 1977), 174.

83. David Hackett Fischer, "Two Minds of the South: Ideas of Southern History in W. J. Cash and James McBride Dabbs," in *W. J. Cash and the Minds of the South,* ed. Paul D. Escott (Baton Rouge: Louisiana State University Press, 1992), 134–64.

84. James McBride Dabbs, *The Southern Heritage* (New York: Alfred A. Knopf, 1958), 211.

85. James McBride Dabbs, *Who Speaks for the South?* (New York: Funk and Wagnalls, 1964), 371.

86. Fred Hobson, *But Now I See: The White Southern Racial Conversion Narrative* (Baton Rouge: Louisiana State University Press, 1999), 1–17.

87. Pat Watters, *Down to Now: Reflections on the Southern Civil Rights Movement* (New York: Pantheon Books, 1971), 3.

88. Ibid., 20, 10–11.

CHAPTER SEVEN

1. Gay Talese, "Origins of a Nonfiction Writer," in *The Literature of Reality,* introduction by Barbara Lounsberry (New York: HarperCollins, 1996), 16–19.

2. Tom Wolfe, *The New Journalism* (New York: HarperCollins, 1973), 10–11. For a rich account of Talese's development, see Gay Talese, *A Writer's Life* (New York: Alfred A. Knopf, 2006), chap. 1.

3. Willie Morris, *North Toward Home* (New York: Houghton, Mifflin, 1967), 131, 138–39, 141.

4. Larry L. King, *In Search of Willie Morris: The Mercurial Life of a Legendary Writer and Editor* (New York: Public Affairs, 2006), xxii, 14.

5. Morris, *North Toward Home,* 184–85.

6. Willie Morris, *New York Days* (Boston: Little, Brown, 1993), 8.

7. See Michael Schudson, *Discovering the News: A Social History of American Newspapers* (New York: Basic Books, 1978), and James Carey, *Communication as Culture: Essays on Media and Society* (Boston: Unwin Hyman, 1989).

8. Willie Morris, *Yazoo: Integration in a Deep-Southern Town* (New York: Harper, 1971); *The Last of the Southern Girls* (New York: Alfred A. Knopf, 1973); *Taps: A Novel* (New York: Houghton Mifflin, 2001); *Always Stand in Against the Curve and Other Sports Stories* (Oxford, Miss.: Yoknapatawpha Press, 1983); *The Courting of Marcus Dupree* (New York: Doubleday, 1983); *After All, It's Only a Game* (Oxford: University Press of Mississippi, 1992); *Prayer for the Opening of the Little League Season* (New York: Harcourt Brace, 1995).

9. J. Speed Carroll, "Bright Boy from Yazoo," *New Republic* 157, no. 21 (1967): 32.

10. Jonathan Yardley, "How an Ambitious Son of Mississippi Rose and Fell in Manhattan Before Returning Home to Southern Comfort," *Washington Post Book World,* April 2, 2006, T-2.

11. Morris, *New York Days,* 9–10.

12. Ibid., 107–6.

13. Ibid., 103.

14. Ibid., 104.

15. Ibid., 111.

16. Robert Penn Warren, ed., *Faulkner: A Collection of Critical Essays* (Englewood Cliffs, N.J.: Prentice-Hall, 1966), 1.

17. Marshall Frady, "A Personal Preliminary," in *Southerners: A Journalist's Odyssey* (New York: New American Library, 1980), xxi, xxiv.

18. Alfred Sandlin Reid, *Furman University: Toward a New Identity, 1925–1975* (Durham, N.C.: Duke University Press, 1976), 176–77.

19. Frady, as a young *Newsweek* correspondent, was roughed up while

assisting an injured black girl during a civil rights march in St. Augustine, Florida, that a violent white mob attacked. *Newsweek,* July 6, 1964, 16, and quoted in Taylor Branch, *Pillar of Fire: America in the King Years, 1963–65* (New York: Touchstone, 1998), 378.

20. Frady, "Personal Preliminary," xxiv.

21. Morris, *New York Days,* 95–96; Frady, *Southerners,* xxiv. Frady's novelistic models for his Wallace biography were Robert Penn Warren, *All the King's Men* (New York: Harcourt Brace and Co., 1946), and William Faulkner, *The Hamlet* (New York: Random House, 1940) and *The Town* (New York: Random House: 1957).

22. Frady, *Southerners,* xxii.

23. Joseph B. Cumming Jr., "Books," *Atlanta* (August 1968): 102.

24. Hal Crowther, "Son of a Preacher Man," *Oxford American* (Winter 2005): 126.

25. Marshall Frady, *Billy Graham: A Parable of American Righteousness* (Boston: Little, Brown, 1979), vii.

26. Clayborne Carson, David Garrow, Bill Kovach, and Carol Polsgrove, comps., *Reporting Civil Rights* (New York: Library of America, 2003), 857.

27. David Halberstam, "Marshall Frady: A Son of the South," introduction to the reissued *Billy Graham* (New York: Simon and Schuster Paperbacks, 2006), xiv.

28. Morris, *New York Days,* 104.

29. Ibid., 95, 98.

30. Frady, *Southerners,* xxv.

31. Ibid., xxvi–xxvii.

32. Morris, *New York Days,* 97.

33. Crowther, "Son," 128.

34. Laurence Bergreen, *James Agee: A Life* (New York: Penguin, 1985), 12–17, 20–31.

35. Ibid., 74.

36. Ibid., 136–37. The sentence: "Near Knoxville the streams still fresh from mountains are linked and thence the master stream spreads the valley most richly southward, swims past Chattanooga and bends down into Alabama to roar like blown smoke through the floodgates of Wilson Dam, to slide becalmed along the crop-cleansed fields of Shiloh, to march

due north across the high diminished plains of Tennessee and through Kentucky spreading marshes toward the valley's end where finally, at the toes of Paducah, in one wide glassy golden swarm the water stoops forward and continuously dies into the Ohio."

37. Walker Evans, foreword to *Let Us Now Praise Famous Men,* by James Agee and Walker Evans (1941; repr., Boston: Houghton Mifflin, 1980), x.

38. Agee's film criticism, which the poet W. H. Auden in 1944 called "the most remarkable regular event in American journalism today" (Bergreen, *James Agee,* 274), is collected in *Agee on Film* (1941; repr., New York: McDowell, Obolensky, 1958); see also *James Agee: Selected Journalism,* ed. Paul Ashdown (Knoxville: University of Tennessee Press, 2005).

39. Richard Severo, "Joseph Mitchell, Chronicler of the Unsung and the Unconventional, Dies at 87," *New York Times,* May 25, 1996, 12; Joseph Mitchell, *My Ears Are Bent* (New York: Pantheon Books, 2001), 3–24.

40. Otto Friedrich, *Decline and Fall* (New York: Ballantine Books, 1970), 86.

41. Ibid., 187.

42. Morris, *New York Days,* 73.

43. Friedrich, *Decline and Fall,* 83.

44. Ibid., 230.

45. Ibid., 83–87.

46. See, generally, Friedrich, *Decline and Fall;* Morris, *New York Days;* George Leonard, *Walking on the Edge of the World* (New York: Houghton Mifflin, 1988).

47. Leonard, *Walking,* 17.

48. William Bradford Huie, a former *Birmingham Post* reporter who wrote several best-selling novels, had been editor of Mencken's *American Mercury* in the 1940s. Randy Sparkman, "The Murder of Emmett Till," *Slate,* June 21, 2005, http://slate.com/id/2120788/.

49. William Bradford Huie, "The Shocking Story of Approved Killing in Mississippi," *Look,* January 24, 1956, in Carson et al., comps., *Reporting Civil Rights,* 1:232–40.

50. Leonard, *Walking,* 84.

51. Ibid., 13.

52. Ibid., 277.

53. Ibid., 333.

54. Ibid., 336.

55. Ibid., 300.

56. John Shelton Reed, "Editing the South," in *Whistling Dixie: Dispatches from the South* (Columbia: University of Missouri Press, 1990), 67–79. For an insider history of the magazine, see John Logue and Gary McCalla, *Life at Southern Living: A Sort of Memoir* (Baton Rouge: Louisiana State University Press, 2000).

57. Frank Digiacomo, "The Esquire Decade," *Vanity Fair* 557, January 2007, 124–41.

58. Harold Hayes, introduction, *Smiling Through the Apocalypse: Esquire's History of the Sixties* (New York: McCall Publishing Co., 1969).

59. Friedrich, *Decline and Fall,* 7–14.

60. Leonard, *Walking,* 19.

61. Digiacomo, "Esquire Decade," 136–37.

62. Ibid., 134–39.

63. Ibid., 139–41.

64. ASNE, *ASNE Proceedings* (Washington, D.C.: ASNE, 1990), 201.

65. John Hellmann, *Fables of Fact: The New Journalism as New Fiction* (Champaign: University of Illinois Press, 1980), 125.

66. Toby Thompson, "The Evolution of Dandy Tom," *Vanity Fair,* October 1987, 118–27, 160–64, reprinted in Dorothy M. Scura, ed., *Conversations with Tom Wolfe* (Jackson: University of Mississippi Press, 1990), 218.

67. Scura, *Conversations,* 35, 95.

68. Thompson, in Scura, *Conversations,* 210, 214–16.

69. Ibid., 210, 214.

70. Scura, *Conversations,* 206.

71. Joe David Ballamy, introduction, in Tom Wolfe, *The Purple Decades: A Reader* (New York: Farrar, Straus and Giroux, 1982).

72. Tom Wolfe, *The Bonfire of the Vanities* (New York: Farrar, Straus and Giroux, 1987), 225–26.

CHAPTER EIGHT

1. Michael Kinsley, "Do Newspapers Have a Future?" *Time,* October 2, 2006, 75.

2. Richard Siklos, "Before Its Time, the Death of a Newspaper Chain," *New York Times,* March 19, 2006, Money and Business section, 3.

3. Mark Fitzgerald and Jennifer Saba, "Where Is the Bottom?" *Editor and Publisher,* October 2007, 22–28.

4. John Shelton Reed, *Minding the South* (Columbia: University of Missouri Press, 2003), 218–19.

5. Tom Austin, "Miami Noir," *Columbia Journalism Review* (January/February 2006): 28–37; Abby Goodnough, "After Politician's Suicide at Newspaper, Columnist Is Fired for Taping His Phone Call," *New York Times,* July 29, 2005, A10.

6. Craig Flournoy and Tracy Everback, "Damage Report," *Columbia Journalism Review,* July/August 2007, 33–37.

7. Carl Sessions Stepp, "Transforming the Architecture," *American Journalism Review,* October/November 2007, 15–21.

8. James Varney, "Rare Strokes of Luck Mark Rescue," August 31, 2005, http://www.NOLA.com.

9. Douglas McCollum, "Uncharted Waters," *Columbia Journalism Review,* November/December 2005, 28–34.

10. *Online NewsHour with Jim Lehrer,* March 27, 2006.

11. See Numan V. Bartley, *The New South, 1945–1980* (Baton Rouge: Louisiana State University Press, 1995).

12. Ibid., 266.

13. Walker Percy, "Why I Live Where I Live," *Esquire,* April 1980, 35–37.

14. Marshall Frady, *Southerners: A Journalist's Odyssey* (New York: New American Library, 1980), 283–84.

15. Reed, *Minding the South,* 7–8.

16. John Egerton, *The Americanization of Dixie* (New York: Harper's Magazine Press, 1974); Peter Applebome, *Dixie Rising: How the South Is Shaping American Values, Politics, and Culture* (New York: Times Books, 1996).

17. Karl Fleming, *Son of the Rough South: An Uncivil Memoir* (New York: Public Affairs, 2005), 28, 32, 51–53, 136, 139, 144–45.

18. Harrison Salisbury, "Fear and Hatred Grip Birmingham," *New York Times,* April 12, 1960, 1. Local and state officials filed a libel suit against the *Times* for the two-part feature but lost their case.

19. Augusta may have avoided attention for other reasons, besides being smaller than Birmingham. It integrated its movie theaters in 1962

to stop a pre-Masters Golf Tournament protest and to keep King from coming, as one observer recalled. James C. Cobb, "From the First New South to the Second," in *The American South in the Twentieth Century,* ed. Craig S. Pascoe et al. (Athens: University of Georgia Press), 6.

20. Paul Hemphill, *Leaving Birmingham* (New York: Viking, 1993), 62–63, 100–102, 116–19, 134–35, 176. Among Hemphill's books are *The Nashville Sound: Bright Lights and Country Music* (New York: Simon and Schuster, 1970) and *Mayor: Notes on the Sixties,* with Ivan Allen Jr. (New York: Simon and Schuster, 1971).

21. Rick Bragg, *All Over but the Shoutin'* (New York: Vintage Books, 1998), 7, 23, 141, 121, 297.

22. Howell Raines, *My Soul Is Rested: Movement Days in the Deep South Remembered* (New York: G. P. Putnam's Sons, 1977).

23. Howell Raines, "Grady's Gift," *New York Times Magazine,* December 1, 1991, reprinted in *Voices in Our Blood,* ed. Jon Meacham (New York: Random House, 2001), 517–28.

24. "Forum: What's New About the South?"; "Segregation Remembered," *Time,* September 27, 1976, 4–6, 48–49. A southerner who had moved to New York to become president of Union Theological Seminary, Donald W. Shriver Jr., wrote in *Time*'s New South issue that the South's obsession with the past—with saving what was good while casting off what was bad—connected it with most of the world's people and "the vital business of achieving a particular identity in a plural world" (4).

25. "Dixie's Best Dailies," "Cheeky TM," in ibid., 64–65.

26. Robert N. Pierce, *A Sacred Trust: Nelson Poynter and the* St. Petersburg Times (Gainesville: University of Florida Press, 1993), 349–78.

27. http://www.poynter.org.

28. James W. Silver, *Mississippi: The Closed Society* (New York: Harcourt, Brace and World, 1964), 297.

29. Laura Nan Fairley, "George McLean and the *Tupelo Journal,*" in *The Press and Race: Mississippi Journalists Confront the Movement,* ed. David R. Davies (Jackson: University Press of Mississippi, 2001), 140.

30. *Saturday Evening Post,* February 17, 1951, and *Wall Street Journal,* August 20, 1952, both quoted in Fairley, "George McLean," 145.

31. Danny Duncan Collum, "The Tupelo Miracle: How Faith and a Newspaper Transformed a Mississippi Community," *Sojourner's,* Oc-

tober 2004, http://www.sojo.net/index.cfm?action=magazine.article& issue=sojo410&article=041.

32. Fairley, "George McLean," 151–52, 155, 159, 169.

33. Theodore L. Glasser, ed., *The Idea of Public Journalism* (New York: Guilford Press, 1999), 129, 145, 164.

34. Jack Claiborne, *The* Charlotte Observer: *Its Times and Place, 1869–1986* (Chapel Hill: University of North Carolina Press, 1986), 265, 293.

35. Cole C. Campbell, "Foreword: Journalism as a Democratic Art," in *Idea of Public Journalism,* xxii–xxiv.

36. "UA, Newspaper Offer Master's Program," *Birmingham News,* September 22, 2004; H. Brandt Ayers, "Col. Harry Mell Ayers, Anniston, Alabama," in *The First 100 Years: Southern Newspaper Publishers Association,* ed. Reg Ivory (Birmingham, Ala.: SNPA, 2003), 106–7; H. Brandt Ayers, "Community Journalism Can Benefit Big Cities," *Charleston (West Virginia) Gazette,* October 26, 2003, P3C; Kendal Weaver, "New South Proponents Take Stock as GOP Redraws Political Map," Associated Press, November 21, 2004, *Lexis-Nexis Academic;* Thomas Spencer, "Anniston Star to Create Institute," *Birmingham News,* December 17, 2002.

37. Bragg, *All Over,* 5.

CHAPTER NINE

1. James Dickey and Herbert Shuptrine, *Jericho: The South Beheld* (Birmingham, Ala.: Oxmoor House, 1974), 15.

2. Ned Harrison, for example, writes a monthly column on the Civil War for the *Greensboro News and Record* that is reprinted in other papers.

3. http://www.civilwar.vt.edu/.

4. http://tredegar.org.

5. http://www.southernpartisan.net/2007/10/24/a-sorry-state/.

6. John Shelton Reed, "The Banner That Won't Stay Furled," in *Minding the South* (Columbia: University of Missouri Press, 2003), 201–17.

7. Barbara Bedway, "Late, but Not Lost," *Editor and Publisher,* August 2004, 5–6.

8. Mark Fitzgerald, "Newspaper Reveals Its Own Seamy Past," *Editor and Publisher,* February 17, 1990, 9–10.

9. Barnett Wright, "From Negatives to Positive," *Birmingham News,* February 26, 2006.

10. For example, Allison Brophy and Zann Miner, "The Lynching of Allie Thompson," a three-part series on the local lynching of a black man in 1918 in the *Culpeper (Virginia) Star-Exponent,* January 15–17, 2006, won first place for online coverage in the Associated Press Managing Editors Award that year. Also, the journalist Elliot Jaspin discovered by use of computer data analysis the long-forgotten terrorizing of blacks in nearly a dozen counties that underwent what he labeled "racial cleansing." His stories on these cases ran in many papers served by the Cox news service and were collected in *Buried in the Bitter Waters: The Hidden History of Racial Cleansing in America* (New York: Basic Books, 2007).

11. "Together Apart: The Myth of Race," a special report on race relations in the *Times-Picayune* in six installments, from May 9 to November 18, 1993.

12. Townsend Davis, *Weary Feet, Rested Souls: A Guided History of the Civil Rights Movement* (New York: W. W. Norton and Co., 1998).

13. Theo Emery, "On a Trip Through History, Students Join Freedom Rides," *New York Times,* January 29, 2007, A12.

14. Kellie Clark and Jill Eisenberg, "Road Trip to History," *Richmond,* Fall 2007, 22–27.

15. James Webb, *Born Fighting: How the Scots-Irish Shaped America* (New York: Broadway Books, 2004), 3, 123–26.

16. Ibid., 36, 116–17, 124, 129, 132.

17. Ibid., 38.

18. Ibid., 186, 214, 233.

19. Kevin Phillips, *Cousins' War: Religion, Politics, and the Triumph of Anglo-America* (New York: Basic Books, 1999), 201–7.

20. The political scientists Byron E. Shafer and Richard Johnston tested the widely accepted hypothesis that the Republican realignment in the white South was achieved by the manipulation of racial fears and moral values. Analyzing social data, they conclude that it was, instead, a case of dramatic class reversal as the rich, instead of voting Democratic as before, voted Republican and economic prosperity swelled the ranks of the rich. Desegregation, contrary to the popular theory, actually slowed

the shift to the Republican Party in areas where desegregation was more pronounced, they found. Shafer and Johnston, *The End of Southern Exceptionalism: Class, Race, and Partisan Change in the Postwar South* (Cambridge, Mass.: Harvard University Press, 2006).

21. Mary McGrory, "Dirty-Bomb Politics," *Washington Post,* June 20, 2002, 23, and Steve Jarding and Dave "Mudcat" Saunders, *Foxes in the Henhouse: How the Republicans Stole the South and the Heartland, and What Democrats Must Do to Run 'Em Out* (New York: Touchstone, 2006), 110, 121–22. By 2006, there were increasing signs that labeling southern Democrats "liberal" was not working for Republicans any longer. For example, the representative Charles H. Taylor (R-NC) held his seat for eight terms using that strategy when needed. But it did not work in 2006, when the North Carolina native and Democrat Heath Shuler, a former quarterback for the Washington Redskins, defeated Taylor.

22. Jarding and Saunders, *Foxes in the Henhouse,* 12, 35.

23. Ibid., 107, 111, 148–54, 166–68, 187.

24. Ibid., 83–85.

25. Ibid., 90–93.

26. Ibid., 111.

27. Richard M. Weaver, "The Heritage," in *The Southern Tradition at Bay: A History of Postbellum Thought,* ed. George Core and M. E. Bradford (New Rochelle, N.Y.: Arlington House, 1968), 47–111; Eugene D. Genovese, *The Southern Tradition: The Achievement and Limitations of an American Conservatism* (Cambridge, Mass.: Harvard University Press, 1994), 83.

28. Jarding and Saunders, *Foxes in the Henhouse,* 63, 113, 115.

29. Carol Blesser, ed., *Tokens of Affection: The Letters of a Planter's Daughter in the Old South* (Athens: University of Georgia Press, 1996), xi–xii.

30. Edward E. Adams, "Turner Catledge," *American National Biography,* 4:574–75.

31. Willie Morris, *Terrains of the Heart and Other Essays on Home* (Oxford, Miss.: Yoknapatawpha Press, 1981), and University of Mississippi Press, *Remembering Willie: A Collection of Tributes Memorializing Willie Morris, the Acclaimed Southern Author* (Jackson: University of Mississippi Press, 2000).

32. William A. Emerson Jr., "Atlanta, Georgia: As Pretty as a Fable out of Camelot," *Georgia* 16, no. 4, November 1972, 26–27.

33. For example, Pat Conroy, *Prince of Tides* (Boston: Houghton Mifflin, 1986), 1–6; Ralph McGill, *The South and the Southerner* (Boston: Little, Brown, 1963), 6–18; Eliot Wigginton, ed., *Foxfire* (Garden City, N.Y.: Doubleday and Co., 1972).

34. Haya El Nasser, "Population Boom Spawns Super Cities," *USA Today,* July 11, 2005, 6A.

35. Peter Burke and Asa Briggs, *A Social History of the Media: From Gutenberg to the Internet* (Malden, Mass.: Polity, 2005), 172.

36. See the Project for Excellence in Journalism, http://stateofthe media.org/2007/.

37. *Southern Exposure* was published quarterly by the Institute for Southern Studies, a nonprofit center in Durham, North Carolina, dedicated to social and economic change in the region.

38. John Shelton Reed, "Editing the South," in *Whistling Dixie: Dispatches from the South* (Columbia: University of Missouri Press, 1990), 67.

39. Stephen Smith, *Myth, Media, and the Southern Mind* (Fayetteville: University of Arkansas Press, 1985), 133–55.

40. Mark A. Newman, "A Great One Remembered . . . *Southern Magazine* (1986–1989)," *Folio* 32, no. 3, March 2003, 68.

41. John Huey, "What's the Point?" *Southpoint* 1, no. 1, October 1989, 1.

42. Reed, "Editing the South," 77. *Southpoint* folded in 1990 after nine issues.

43. Reginald Stuart, "Editorials Get Small Weekly a Big Honor," *New York Times,* April 19, 1984, A16.

44. http://rockbridgeadvocate.com/.

45. Jock Lauderer, "Why We Should Support Our Hometown Newspaper," *Carrboro Citizen,* May 24, 2007, http://www.carrborocitizen.com/main/2007/05/24/why-we-should-support-our-hometown-newspaper/#more-316; Kirk Ross, quoted in Public Journalism Network blog at http://pjnet.org/post/1615/.

46. Walker Percy, "Going Back to Georgia," Phinizy Lecture, Athens, Ga. 1978, in *Signposts in a Strange Land* (New York: Farrar, Straus and Giroux, 1991), 26–38.

47. Jacob Levenson, "Divining Dixie," *Columbia Journalism Review,* March/April 2004, 20–27; Warren Hayes, "Supporters from Across Nation Converge," *Town Talk,* September 20, 2007, 1, 1 of 110 stories this

Gannett daily in Alexandria, thirty-two miles from Jena, published over a twelve-month period and archived online at http://www.thetowntalk .com/apps/pbcs.dll/article?AID=/99999999/NEWS/70915030.

48. Tracy Thompson, "A Newsroom Hero—Journalist Bill Kovach," *Washington Monthly,* May 2000, 17–23.

49. Jon Meacham, "Pilgrim's Progress," *Newsweek,* August 14, 2006, 36.

50. Peter J. Boyer, "Miracle Man," *New Yorker,* April 12, 1999, 64–82.

51. Louis D. Rubin Jr., *An Honorable Estate: My Time in the Working Press* (Baton Rouge: Louisiana State University Press, 2001), 5–12.

52. Tom Sancton Jr., *Song for My Fathers: A New Orleans Story in Black and White* (New York: Other Press, 2006); Thomas Sancton Sr., "Slowly Crumbling Levees," *New Republic,* March 8, 1948, 18–21.

53. Christopher Dickey, *Summer of Deliverance: A Memoir of Father and Son* (New York: Simon and Schuster, 1998).

54. Bronwen Dickey, "The Truth as a 'Lie': James Dickey and the Spirit of Poetic Revelation," *South Carolina Review* 37, no. 2, Spring 2005, 19–23.

55. Bronwen Dickey, "My Turn: He Caught the Dream," *Newsweek,* March 24, 1997, 19.

SELECTED BIBLIOGRAPHY

BOOKS

Alderman, Edwin A., and Joel Chandler Harris, eds. *The Library of Southern Literature.* 17 vols. Atlanta: Martin and Hoyt Co., 1909–23.

Allen, Michael. *Poe and the British Magazine Tradition.* New York: Oxford University Press, 1969.

Andrews, J. Cutler. *The South Reports the Civil War.* Pittsburgh, Pa.: University of Pittsburgh Press, 1970.

Applebome, Peter. *Dixie Rising: How the South Is Shaping American Values, Politics, and Culture.* New York: Times Books, 1996.

Ashmore, Harry. *Epitaph for Dixie.* New York: W. W. Norton and Co., 1958.

———. *Hearts and Minds.* Cabin John, Md.: Seven Locks Press, 1988.

Bagby, George W. *The Old Virginia Gentleman and Other Sketches,* edited by Ellen M. Bagby. Richmond, Va.: Dietz Press, 1943.

Barry, John M. *Rising Tide: The Great Mississippi Flood of 1927 and How It Changed America.* New York: Simon and Schuster, 1997.

Bartley, Numan V. *The New South, 1945–1980.* Baton Rouge: Louisiana State University Press, 1995.

Bass, Jack. *Unlikely Heroes: The Dramatic Story of the Southern Judges of the Fifth Circuit.* New York: Simon and Schuster, 1981.

Bode, Carl. *Mencken.* Carbondale: Southern Illinois University Press, 1969.

Braden, Waldo W. *The Oral Tradition in the South.* Baton Rouge: Louisiana State University Press, 1983.

Bragg, Rick. *All Over but the Shoutin'.* New York: Vintage Books, 1998.

Branch, Taylor. *Parting the Waters.* New York: Simon and Schuster, 1988.

———. *Pillar of Fire: America in the King Years, 1963–65.* New York: Touchstone, 1998.

Brasch, Walter M. *Brer Rabbit, Uncle Remus, and the "Cornfield Journalist."* Macon, Ga.: Mercer University Press, 2000.

Bronner, Simon J., ed., *Lafcadio Hearn's America: Ethnographic Sketches and Editorials.* Lexington: University Press of Kentucky, 2002.

Bryan, Ferald J. *Henry Grady or Tom Watson? The Rhetorical Struggle for the New South, 1880–1890.* Macon, Ga.: Mercer University Press, 1994.

Cable, George W. *The Negro Question: A Selection of Writings on Civil Rights in the South by George W. Cable,* edited by Arlin Turner. Garden City, N.Y.: Doubleday and Co., 1958.

———. *Old Creole Days: A Story of Creole Life.* Gretna, La.: Pelican Publishing Co., 2001.

Calridge, Henry. "Edgar Allan Poe." In *Companion to the Literature and Culture of the American South,* edited by Richard J. Gray and Owen Robinson, 355–69. Malden, Mass.: Blackwell Publishers, 2004.

Carey, James. *Communication as Culture: Essays on Media and Society.* Boston: Unwin Hyman, 1989.

Carson, Clayborne, David Garrow, Bill Kovach, and Carol Polsgrove, comps. *Reporting Civil Rights.* 2 vols. New York: Library of America, 2003.

Cash, W. J. *The Mind of the South.* 1941. Reprint, New York: Alfred A. Knopf, 1975.

Claiborne, Jack. *The* Charlotte Observer: *Its Times and Place, 1869–1986.* Chapel Hill: University of North Carolina Press, 1986.

Clark, E. Culpepper. *Francis Warrington Dawson and the Politics of Restoration: South Carolina, 1874–1889.* Tuscaloosa: University of Alabama Press, 1980.

Clark, Emily. *Innocence Abroad.* New York: Alfred A. Knopf, 1931.

Classen, Steven D. *Watching Jim Crow: The Struggles over Mississippi TV, 1955–1969.* Durham, N.C.: Duke University Press, 2004.

Clayton, Bruce. *The Savage Ideal: Intolerance and Intellectual Leadership in the South, 1890–1914.* Baltimore: Johns Hopkins University Press, 1972.

———. *W. J. Cash: A Life.* Baton Rouge: Louisiana State University Press, 1991.

Clowse, Barbara Barksdale. *Ralph McGill: A Biography.* Macon, Ga.: Mercer University Press, 1998.

Cooper, John Milton. *Walter Hines Page: The Southerner as American, 1855–1918.* Chapel Hill: University of North Carolina Press, 1977.

Couch, W. T., ed. *Culture in the South.* Chapel Hill: University of North Carolina Press, 1935.

Cousins, Paul M. *Joel Chandler Harris: A Biography.* Baton Rouge: Louisiana State University Press, 1968.

Dabbs, James McBride. *Civil Rights in Recent Southern Fiction.* Atlanta: Southern Regional Council, 1969.

———. *The Southern Heritage.* New York: Alfred A. Knopf, 1958.

———. *Who Speaks for the South?* New York: Funk and Wagnalls, 1964.

Dabney, Virginius. *The Jefferson Scandals: A Rebuttal.* New York: Dodd, Mead and Co., 1981.

———. *Liberalism in the South.* Chapel Hill: University of North Carolina Press, 1932.

———. *Pistols and Pointed Pens: The Dueling Editors of Old Virginia.* Chapel Hill: University of North Carolina Press, 1987.

Davidson, Donald. *Southern Writers in the Modern World.* Athens: University of Georgia Press, 1958.

Davidson, Edward. *Poe: A Critical Study.* Cambridge, Mass.: Harvard University Press, 1957.

Davies, David R., ed. *The Press and Race: Mississippi Journalists Confront the Movement.* Jackson: University Press of Mississippi, 2001.

Davis, Townsend. *Weary Feet, Rested Souls: A Guided History of the Civil Rights Movement.* New York: W. W. Norton and Co., 1998.

Dawson, Francis W. *Reminiscences of Confederate Service: 1861–1865.* Baton Rouge: Louisiana State University Press, 1980.

Dickey, James, and Herbert Shuptrine, *Jericho: The South Beheld.* Birmingham, Ala.: Oxmoor House, 1974.

DuBois, W. E. B. *The Souls of Black Folk.* New York: Dover Publications, 1994.

Dunford, Earle. Richmond Times-Dispatch: *The Story of a Newspaper.* Richmond, Va.: Cadmus Publishing, 1995.

Eaton, Clement. *Freedom of Thought in the Old South.* Durham, N.C.: Duke University Press, 1940.

Edgerton, John. *The Americanization of Dixie.* New York: Harper's Magazine Press, 1974.

———. *Speak Now Against the Day.* New York: Alfred A. Knopf, 1994.

Edwards, Anne. *The Road to Tara.* New York: Tichnor and Fields, 1983.

Escott, Paul D., ed. *W. J. Cash and the Minds of the South.* Baton Rouge: Louisiana State University Press, 1992.

Fleming, Karl. *Son of the Rough South: An Uncivil Memoir.* New York: Public Affairs, 2005.

Frady, Marshall. *Billy Graham: A Parable of American Righteousness.* Boston: Little, Brown, 1979.

———. *Southerners: A Journalist's Odyssey.* New York: New American Library, 1980.

Friedrich, Otto. *Decline and Fall.* New York: Ballantine Books, 1970.

Gaines, Francis P. *Southern Oratory: A Study in Idealism.* Tuscaloosa: University of Alabama Press, 1945.

———. *The Southern Plantation: A Study in the Development and the Accuracy of a Tradition.* New York: Columbia University Press, 1925.

Genovese, Eugene D. *The Southern Tradition: The Achievement and Limitations of an American Conservatism.* Cambridge, Mass.: Harvard University Press, 1994.

Glasser, Theodore L., ed. *The Idea of Public Journalism.* New York: Guilford Press, 1999.

Gray, Richard. *Writing the South: Ideas of an American Region.* Cambridge, U.K.: Cambridge University Press, 1986.

Harlan, Louis. *Booker T. Washington: The Making of a Black Leader, 1856–1901.* New York: Oxford University Press, 1972.

Harris, Joel Chandler. *Life of Henry W. Grady, Including His Writings and Speeches.* New York: Cassell Publishing Co., 1890.

Hayes, Harold. Introduction to *Smiling Through the Apocalypse: Esquire's History of the Sixties.* New York: McCall Publishing Co., 1969.

Hellmann, John. *Fables of Fact: The New Journalism as New Fiction.* Champaign: University of Illinois Press, 1980.

Helper, Hinton Rowan. *The Impending Crisis of the South: How to Meet It.* New York: Burdick Brothers, 1857.

Hemphill, Paul. *Leaving Birmingham.* New York: Viking, 1993.

Hobson, Fred. *But Now I See: The White Southern Racial Conversion Narrative.* Baton Rouge: Louisiana State University Press, 1999.

———. *Mencken: A Life.* New York: Random House, 1994.

———. *Serpent in Eden: H. L. Mencken and the South.* Chapel Hill: University of North Carolina Press, 1974.

———. *The Silencing of Emily Mullen and Other Essays.* Baton Rouge: Louisiana State University Press, 2005.

Hollis, Daniel Webster. *An Alabama Newspaper Tradition: Grover C. Hall and the Hall Family.* Tuscaloosa: University of Alabama Press, 1983.

Hudson, Frederick. *Journalism in the United States from 1690 to 1872.* 1873. Reprint, New York: Haskell House Publishers, 1968.

Jackson, David K. *Poe and the* Southern Literary Messenger. Richmond, Va.: Dietze Printing Co., 1934.

Jacobs, Robert D. *Poe: Journalist and Critic.* Baton Rouge: Louisiana State University Press, 1969.

Jarding, Steve, and Dave Saunders. *Foxes in the Henhouse: How the Republicans Stole the South and the Heartland, and What Democrats Must Do to Run 'Em Out.* New York: Touchstone, 2006.

Jefferson, Thomas. *Notes on the State of Virginia,* edited by William Peden. Chapel Hill: University of North Carolina Press, 1982.

Jenkins, McKay. *The South in Black and White: Race, Sex, and Literature in the 1940s.* Chapel Hill: University of North Carolina Press, 1999.

Johnson, Gerald W. *An Honorable Titan: A Biographical Sketch of Adolph S. Ochs.* New York: Harper and Row, 1946.

———. *South-Watching: Selected Essays by Gerald W. Johnson,* edited by Fred Hobson. Chapel Hill: University of North Carolina Press, 1983.

Johnson, Walter C., and Arthur T. Robb, *The South and Its Newspapers: The Story of the Southern Newspaper Publishers Association and Its Part in the South's Economic Revival, 1903–1953.* Chattanooga, Tenn.: Southern Newspaper Publishers Association, 1954.

Kennedy, Richard S., ed., *Literary New Orleans: Essays and Meditations.* Baton Rouge: Louisiana State University Press, 1992.

Key, V. O., and Alexander Heard, *Southern Politics in State and Nation.* New York: Alfred A. Knopf, 1949.

Kilpatrick, James J. *The Foxes' Union: And Other Stretchers, Tall Tales, and*

Discursive Reminiscences of Happy Years in Scrabble, Virginia. McLean, Va.: EPM Publications, 1977.

———. *The Southern Case for School Segregation.* New York: Crowell-Collier Press, 1962.

———. *The Sovereign States: Notes of a Citizen of Virginia.* Chicago: H. Regnery Co., 1957.

———. *The Writer's Art.* Kansas City, Mo.: Andrews, McMeel and Parker, 1984.

King, Larry L. *In Search of Willie Morris: The Mercurial Life of a Legendary Writer and Editor.* New York: Public Affairs, 2006.

King, Martin Luther, Jr. *Stride Toward Freedom: The Montgomery Story.* New York: Harper and Brothers, 1959.

Kirby, Jack Temple. *Media-Made Dixie: The South in the American Imagination.* Baton Rouge: Louisiana State University Press, 1978.

Kneebone, John T. *Southern Liberal Journalists and the Issue of Race, 1920–1944.* Chapel Hill: University of North Carolina Press, 1985.

Leonard, George. *Walking on the Edge of the World.* New York: Houghton Mifflin, 1988.

Levine, Stuart, and Linda Levine, eds. *The Short Fiction of Edgar Allan Poe.* Indianapolis: Bobbs-Merrill, 1976.

Lewis, Anthony. *Make No Law: The Sullivan Case and the First Amendment.* New York: Random House, 1991.

Leyburn, James. *The Scotch-Irish: A Social History.* Chapel Hill: University of North Carolina Press, 1962.

Logue, John, and Gary McCalla. *Life at Southern Living: A Sort of Memoir.* Baton Rouge: Louisiana State University Press, 2000.

Loveland, Anne C. *Lillian Smith: A Southerner Confronting the South.* Baton Rouge: Louisiana State University Press, 1986.

Manchester, William. *Disturber of the Peace: The Life of H. L. Mencken.* Amherst: University of Massachusetts Press, 1966.

McGill, Ralph. *The South and the Southerner.* Boston: Little, Brown, 1963.

Meacham, Jon, ed. *Voices in Our Blood: America's Best on the Civil Rights Movement.* New York: Random House, 2001.

Mencken, H. L. *Prejudices—Second Series.* New York: Alfred A. Knopf, 1920.

———. *Prejudices—Sixth Series.* New York: Alfred A. Knopf, 1927.

————. *The Vintage Mencken,* introduction by Alistair Cooke. New York: Vintage Books, 1956.

Meyers, Jeffrey. *Edgar Allan Poe: His Life and Legacy.* New York: Charles Scribner's Sons, 1992.

Mims, Edwin. *The Advancing South: Stories of Progress and Reaction.* New York: Doubleday, Page and Co., 1926.

Mitchell, Betty L. *Edmund Ruffin: A Biography.* Bloomington: Indiana University Press, 1981.

Morris, Willie. *New York Days.* Boston: Little, Brown, 1993.

————. *North Toward Home.* New York: Houghton, Mifflin, 1967.

————. *Terrains of the Heart and Other Essays on Home.* Oxford, Miss.: Yoknapatawpha Press, 1981.

————. *Yazoo: Integration in a Deep-Southern Town.* New York: Harper, 1971.

Morrison, Joseph L. *W. J. Cash: Southern Prophet.* New York: Alfred A. Knopf, 1967.

Moss, Sidney P. *Poe's Literary Battles: The Critic in the Context of His Literary Milieu.* Durham, N.C.: Duke University Press, 1963.

Mott, Frank Luther. *American Journalism, A History: 1690–1960,* 3rd. ed. New York: Macmillan Co., 1962.

————. *A History of American Magazines: 1885–1905.* Cambridge, Mass.: Harvard University Press, 1957.

————. *Jefferson and the Press.* Baton Rouge: Louisiana State University Press, 1943.

Myrdal, Gunnar. *An American Dilemma: The Negro Problem and Modern Democracy.* With Richard Sterner and Arnold Rose. New York: Harper and Brothers, 1944.

Nelson, John Herbert. *The Negro Character in American Literature.* Lawrence, Kans.: Department of Journalism Press, 1926.

Nixon, Raymond B. *Henry W. Grady: Spokesman for the New South.* New York: Alfred A. Knopf, 1943.

O'Brien, Michael. *Conjectures of Order: Intellectual Life and the American South, 1810–1860.* 2 vols. Chapel Hill: University of North Carolina Press, 2004.

————. *Rethinking the South: Essays in Intellectual History.* Baltimore: Johns Hopkins University Press, 1988.

Olmsted, Frederick Law. *The Cotton Kingdom: A Traveller's Observations on Cotton and Slavery in the American Slave States,* edited by Arthur M. Schlesinger. New York: Alfred A. Knopf, 1953.

Osthaus, Carl R. *Partisans of the Southern Press: Editorial Spokesmen of the Nineteenth Century.* Lexington: University Press of Kentucky, 1994.

Page, Walter Hines. *The Southerner: A Novel.* New York: Doubleday, Page and Co., 1909.

Pascoe, Craig S., Karen Trahan Leathem, and Andy Ambrose, eds. *The American South in the Twentieth Century.* Athens: University of Georgia Press, 2005.

Patterson, James T. *Brown v. Board of Education: A Civil Rights Milestone and Its Troubled Legacy.* Oxford, U.K.: Oxford University Press, 2001.

Penn Warren, Robert, ed. *Faulkner: A Collection of Critical Essays.* Englewood Cliffs, N.J.: Prentice-Hall, 1966.

Percy, Walker. *Signposts in a Strange Land.* New York: Farrar, Straus and Giroux, 1991.

Peterson, Merrill D. *Thomas Jefferson and the New Nation.* London: Oxford, 1970.

Phillips, Kevin. *Cousins' War: Religion, Politics, and the Triumph of Anglo-America.* New York: Basic Books, 1999.

Pierce, Robert N. *A Sacred Trust: Nelson Poynter and the* St. Petersburg Times. Gainesville: University of Florida Press, 1993.

Poe, Edgar Allan. *Collected Works of Edgar Allan Poe.* New York: Gordian Press, 1986.

———. *The Letters of Edgar Allan Poe.* Vol. 1, edited by John Ward Ostrom. Cambridge, Mass.: Harvard University Press, 1948.

———. *The Poems and Three Essays on Poetry, Narrative of Arthur Gordon Pym, Miscellanies.* London: Oxford University Press, 1938.

Powledge, Fred. *Free at Last? The Civil Rights Movement and the People Who Made It.* Boston: Little, Brown, 1991.

Rachels, David, ed. *Augustus Baldwin Longstreet's Georgia Scenes Completed.* Athens: University of Georgia Press, 1998.

Raines, Howell. *My Soul Is Rested: Movement Days in the Deep South Remembered.* New York: G. P. Putnam's Sons, 1977.

Reddick, Lawrence D. *Crusader Without Violence: A Biography of Martin Luther King Jr.* New York: Harper and Brothers, 1959.

Reed, John Shelton. *Minding the South*. Columbia: University of Missouri Press, 2003.

———. *Whistling Dixie: Dispatches from the South*. Columbia: University of Missouri Press, 1990.

Riley, Sam G. *Magazines of the American South*. New York: Greenwood Press, 1986.

Roberts, Gene, and Hank Klibanoff. *The Race Beat: The Press, the Civil Rights Struggle, and the Awakening of a Nation*. New York: Alfred A. Knopf, 2006.

Rodgers, Marion Elizabeth. *Mencken: The American Iconoclast*. Oxford, U.K.: Oxford University Press, 2005.

Rubin, Louis D., Jr., *George W. Cable: The Life and Times of a Southern Heretic*. New York: Pegasus, 1969.

———. *An Honorable Estate: My Time in the Working Press*. Baton Rouge: Louisiana State University Press, 2001.

———, ed. *I'll Take My Stand: The South and the Agrarian Tradition, by Twelve Southerners*. Baton Rouge: Louisiana State University Press, 1977.

———, ed. *The Literary South*. New York: John Wiley and Sons, 1979.

Salisbury, Harrison E. *Without Fear or Favor: The* New York Times *and Its Times*. New York: Times Books, 1980.

Sancton, Tom. *Song for My Fathers: A New Orleans Story in Black and White*. New York: Other Press, 2006.

Sarratt, Reed. *The Ordeal of Desegregation*. New York: Harper and Row, 1966.

Schudson, Michael. *Discovering the News: A Social History of American Newspapers*. New York: Basic Books, 1978.

Scura, Dorothy M., ed. *Conversations with Tom Wolfe*. Jackson: University of Mississippi Press, 1990.

Shafer, Byron E., and Richard Johnston. *The End of Southern Exceptionalism: Class, Race, and Partisan Change in the Postwar South*. Cambridge, Mass.: Harvard University Press, 2006.

Silver, James W. *Mississippi: The Closed Society*. New York: Harcourt, Brace and World, 1964.

Silverman, Kenneth. *Edgar A. Poe: Mournful and Never-Ending Remembrance*. New York: HarperCollins, 1991.

Simms Oliphant, Mary C., Alfred Taylor Odell, and T.C. Duncan Eaves, eds. *Simms, Letters of William Gilmore.* 6 vols. 1952. Reprint, Columbia: University of South Carolina Press, 1982.

Singal, Daniel Joseph. *The War Within: From Victorian to Modernist Thought in the South, 1919–1945.* Chapel Hill: University of North Carolina Press, 1982.

Smith, Lillian. *Killers of the Dream.* New York: W. W. Norton, 1949.

Smith, Stephen. *Myth, Media, and the Southern Mind.* Fayetteville: University of Arkansas Press, 1985.

Sosna, Morton. *In Search of the Silent South.* New York: Columbia University Press, 1977.

Southern Publication Society. *The South in the Building of the Nation: A History of the Southern States Designed to Record the South's Part in the Making of the American Nation; to Portray the Character and Genius, to Chronicle the Achievements and Progress and to Illustrate the Life and Traditions of the Southern People.* 8 vols. Richmond, Va.: Southern Publication Society, 1909.

Starr, S. Frederick, ed. *Inventing New Orleans: Writings of Lafcadio Hearn.* Jackson: University of Mississippi Press, 2001.

Talese, Gay. *A Writer's Life.* New York: Alfred A. Knopf, 2006.

Terrell, Russell Franklin. *A Study of the Early Journalistic Writings of Henry W. Grady.* Nashville, Tenn.: Peabody College, 1927.

Thompson, G. R., ed. *Edgar Allan Poe: Essays and Reviews.* New York: Library of America, 1984.

Tifft, Susan E., and Alex S. Jones. *The Trust: The Private and Powerful Family Behind the* New York Times. Boston: Little, Brown, 1999.

Trent, William P. *William Gilmore Simms.* Boston: Houghton, Mifflin and Co., 1892.

Turner, Arlin, ed. *Critical Essays on George W. Cable.* Boston: G. K. Hall and Co., 1980.

———. *Mark Twain and George W. Cable: The Record of a Literary Friendship.* East Lansing: Michigan State University Press, 1960.

Twain, Mark. *The Writings of Mark Twain.* Vol. 19. 1875. Reprint, New York: Harper and Brothers, 1903.

van Tuyll, Debra Reddin, and Amy Reynolds. *The Greenwood Library of*

American War Reporting, edited by David Copeland. Vol. 3. West-port, Conn.: Greenwood Press, 2005.

Wade, John Donald. *Augustus Baldwin Longstreet: A Study in the Development of Culture in the South.* New York: Macmillan Co., 1924.

Watters, Pat. *Down to Now: Reflections on the Southern Civil Rights Movement.* New York: Pantheon Books, 1971.

Weaver, Richard M. "The South and the American Union," in *The Lasting South: Fourteen Southerners Look at Their Home.* Chicago: Henry Regnery Co., 1957.

———. *The Southern Tradition at Bay: A History of Postbellum Thought,* edited by George Core and M. E. Bradford. New Rochelle, N.Y.: Arlington House, 1968.

Webb, James. *Born Fighting: How the Scots-Irish Shaped America.* New York: Broadway Books, 2004.

Whalen, Terence. *Edgar Allan Poe and the Masses.* Princeton, N.J.: Princeton University Press, 1999.

Williams, Jack K. *Dueling in the Old South.* College Station: Texas A&M Press, 1980.

Williamson, Joel. *The Crucible of Race: Black-White Relations in the American South Since Emancipation.* New York: Oxford University Press, 1984.

Wilmer, Lambert A. *Our Press Gang; or, A Complete Exposition of the Corruptions and Crimes of the American Newspapers.* 1859. Reprint, New York: Arno Press, 1970.

Wilson, Charles R., and William Ferris, eds. *Encyclopedia of Southern Culture.* Chapel Hill: University of North Carolina Press, 1989.

Wilson, Edmund. *Patriotic Gore: Studies in the Literature of the American Civil War.* New York: Oxford University Press, 1962.

———. *The Shock of Recognition.* New York: Doubleday, Doran and Co., 1943.

Wise, John S. *End of an Era.* Boston: Houghton, Mifflin and Co., 1899.

Wolfe, Tom. *The New Journalism.* New York: HarperCollins, 1973.

———. *The Purple Decades: A Reader.* New York: Farrar, Straus and Giroux, 1982.

Woodward, C. Vann. *The Burden of Southern History.* Baton Rouge: Louisiana State University Press, 1960.

————. Introduction to *A Southern Prophecy* (1889) by Lewis H. Blair. Boston: Little, Brown, 1964.

————. *The Origins of the New South, 1877–1913.* Baton Rouge: Louisiana State University Press, 1951.

Wright, Gavin. "Persisting Dixie: The South as an Economic Region." In *The American South in the Twentieth Century,* 77–90. Athens: University of Georgia Press, 2005.

————. *The Political Economy of the Cotton South: Households, Markets and Wealth in the Nineteenth Century.* New York: W. W. Norton, 1978.

ARTICLES

Bean, W. G. "Anti-Jeffersonianism in the Ante-Bellum South," *North Carolina Historical Review* 12, no. 2 (April 1935): 103–25.

Boney, F. N. "Rivers of Ink, A Stream of Blood: The Tragic Career of John Hampden Pleasants," *Virginia Cavalcade* (Summer 1968): 33–39.

Boyer, Peter J. "Miracle Man," *New Yorker,* April 12, 1999, 64–82.

Carroll, J. Speed. "Bright Boy from Yazoo," *New Republic,* November 18, 1967, 32–34.

Carter, Hodding, III, "The Difficult Isolation Courage Can Bring," *Nieman Reports,* Summer 2006, 90–91.

Cash, W. J., "Genesis of the Southern Cracker," *American Mercury* 55 (May 1935): 105–8.

Coleman, Charles W. "The Recent Movement in Southern Literature," *Harper's New Monthly Magazine* 74, no. 444 May 1887, 837–55.

Collum, Danny Duncan. "The Tupelo Miracle: How Faith and a Newspaper Transformed a Mississippi Community," *Sojourner's,* October 2004: 32–37.

Dickey, Bronwen. "The Truth as a 'Lie': James Dickey and the Spirit of Poetic Revelation," *South Carolina Review* 37, no. 2 (Spring 2005): 19–23.

Digiacomo, Frank. "The Esquire Decade," *Vanity Fair* 557 (January 2007): 124–41.

"Dilemma in Dixie," *Time,* February 20, 1956, 76–81.

Emerson, William A., Jr. "Atlanta, Georgia: As Pretty as a Fable out of Camelot," *Georgia,* November 1972, 26–28, 58.

Fitzgerald, Bishop Oscar Penn. "John M. Daniel and Some of His Contemporaries," *South Atlantic Quarterly* 4, no. 1 (1905): 13–17.

Flournoy, Craig, and Tracy Everback. "Damage Report," *Columbia Journalism Review* (July/August 2007): 33–37.

Gates, Sharon Joyce, and Catherine C. Mitchell. "Adolph Ochs: Learning What's Fit to Print," *American Journalism* 8, no. 4 (Fall 1991): 228–29.

Griffin, Barbara. "Thomas Ritchie and the Code Duello," *The Virginia Magazine of History and Biography* 92 (January 1984): 71–95.

Henrick, Hertzberg. "Journals of Opinion: An Historical Sketch," *Gannett Center Journal* (Spring 1989): 61–80.

Johnson, G. W. "The South Faces Itself," *Virginia Quarterly Review* 7, no. 1 (January 1931): 152–57.

Krauth, Leland. "Mark Twain Fights Sam Clemens' Duel," *Mississippi Quarterly* 33, no. 2 (1980): 141–53.

Levenson, Jacob. "Divining Dixie," *Columbia Journalism Review* (March/April 2004): 20–27.

McCollum, Douglas. "Uncharted Waters," *Columbia Journalism Review* (November/December 2005): 28–34.

McKnight, C. A. "Troubled South: Search for a Middle Ground," *Collier's,* June 22, 1956, 25–31.

Moncure, John. "John M. Daniel: The Editor of *The Examiner.*" *Sewanee Review* 15, no. 3 (July 1907): 258–70.

Post, Robert C. "The Social Foundations of Defamation Law: Reputation and the Constitution." *California Law Review* 74, no. 3 (May 1986): 693–717.

Risen, Clay. "Washington Diarist: Endangered Species." *New Republic* (December 27, 2004–January 10, 2005): 42.

Sawyer, Nathania K. "Harry S. Ashmore: On the Way to Everywhere," paper presented in the History Division, AEJMC, Washington, D.C., August 5, 2001.

Scott, Elizabeth S. "'In Fame, Not Specie.'" *Virginia Cavalcade* (Winter 1978): 128–43.

Stepp, Carl Sessions. "Transforming the Architecture." *American Journalism Review* (October/November 2007): 15–21.

Thompson, Tracy. "A Newsroom Hero—Journalist Bill Kovach." *Washington Monthly,* May 2000, 17–23.

Williams, Roger. "Newspapers in the South." *Columbia Journalism Review* 6 (Summer 1967): 26–35.

THESES

Cumming, Doug. "Facing Facts, Facing South: The SERS and the Effort to Inform the South After *Brown v. Board,* 1954–1960," Ph.D. diss., University of North Carolina at Chapel Hill, 2002.

Gilpin, Patrick J. "Charles S. Johnson: An Intellectual Biography." Ph.D. diss., Vanderbilt University, 1973.

Miller, Allison Mae. "George Washington Cable and Walter Hines Page: The Southerner as Self-Critic," master's thesis in English, University of North Carolina at Chapel Hill, 1990.

Nitschke, Marie M. "Virginius Dabney of Virginia: Portrait of a Southern Journalist in the Twentieth Century," Ph.D. diss., Emory University, 1987.

Wagnon, Judy Means. "Grover C. Hall Jr.: Profile of a Writing Editor," master's thesis in Journalism, University of Alabama, 1975.

INDEX

Doug Cumming is an associate professor of journalism at Washington and Lee University, a former Nieman Fellow, and a George Polk Award–winning journalist. He lives in Lexington, Virginia.

Hodding Carter III is a professor of public policy at the Center for the Study of the American South at the University of North Carolina, a former assistant secretary of state for public affairs, and the author of *The Reagan Years* and *The South Strikes Back*. He lives in Chapel Hill, North Carolina.